America's Top 100 Jobs for People Without a Four-Year Degree

By Ron and Caryl Krannich

CAREER AND BUSINESS BOOKS AND SOFTWARE

101 Dynamite Answers to Interview Questions
101 Secrets of Highly Effective Speakers
201 Dynamite Job Search Letters
America's Top 100 Jobs for People Without a Four-Year Degree
America's Top Jobs for People Re-Entering the Workforce
America's Top Internet Job Sites
Best Jobs for the 21st Century
Change Your Job, Change Your Life
The Complete Guide to Public Employment
The Directory of Federal Jobs and Employers
Discover the Best Jobs for You!
Dynamite Cover Letters
Dynamite Resumes
Dynamite Salary Negotiations
Dynamite Tele-Search
The Educator's Guide to Alternative Jobs and Careers
Find a Federal Job Fast!
From Air Force Blue to Corporate Gray
From Army Green to Corporate Gray
From Navy Blue to Corporate Gray
Get a Raise in 7 Days
High Impact Resumes and Letters
I Want to Do Something Else, But I'm Not Sure What It Is
Interview for Success
The Job Hunting Guide: Transitioning From College to Career
Job Hunting Tips for People With Not-So-Hot Backgrounds
Job Interview Tips for People With Not-So-Hot Backgrounds
Job-Power Source and *Ultimate Job Source* (software)
Jobs and Careers With Nonprofit Organizations
Military Resumes and Cover Letters
Moving Out of Education
Moving Out of Government
Nail the Job Interview!
No One Will Hire Me!
Re-Careering in Turbulent Times
Savvy Interviewing
Savvy Networker
Savvy Resume Writer

TRAVEL AND INTERNATIONAL BOOKS

Best Resumes and CVs for International Jobs
The Complete Guide to International Jobs and Careers
The Directory of Websites for International Jobs
International Jobs Directory
Jobs for Travel Lovers
Mayors and Managers in Thailand
Politics of Family Planning Policy in Thailand
Shopping and Traveling in Exotic Asia
Shopping in Exotic Places
Shopping the Exotic South Pacific
Travel Planning On the Internet
Treasures and Pleasures of Australia
Treasures and Pleasures of Bermuda
Treasures and Pleasures of China
Treasures and Pleasures of Egypt
Treasures and Pleasures of Hong Kong
Treasures and Pleasures of India
Treasures and Pleasures of Indonesia
Treasures and Pleasures of Italy
Treasures and Pleasures of Mexico
Treasures and Pleasures of Paris and the French Riviera
Treasures and Pleasures of Rio and São Paulo
Treasures and Pleasures of Santa Fe, Taos, and Albuquerque
Treasures and Pleasures of Singapore and Bali
Treasures and Pleasures of Singapore and Malaysia
Treasures and Pleasures of South America
Treasures and Pleasures of Southern Africa
Treasures and Pleasures of Thailand and Myanmar
Treasures and Pleasures of Turkey
Treasures and Pleasures of Vietnam and Cambodia

America's Top 100 Jobs
— *for People Without a* —
Four-Year Degree

GREAT JOBS WITH A PROMISING FUTURE

Ronald L. Krannich, Ph.D
Caryl Rae Krannich, Ph.D

IMPACT PUBLICATIONS
Manassas Park, Virginia

America's Top 100 Jobs for People Without a Four-Year Degree

ISBN: 1-57023-214-8

Library of Congress: 2004100409

Publisher: For information on Impact Publications, including current and forthcoming publications, authors, press kits, online bookstore, and submission requirements, visit the left navigation bar on the front page of our main company website: www.impactpublications.com.

Publicity/Rights: For information on publicity, author interviews, and subsidiary rights, contact the Media Relations Department: Tel. 703-361-7300, Fax 703-335-9486, or e-mail: info@impactpublications.com.

Sales/Distribution: All bookstore sales are handled through Impact's trade distributor: National Book Network, 15200 NBN Way, Blue Ridge Summit, PA 17214, Tel. 1-800-462-6420. All special sales and distribution inquiries should be directed to the publisher: Sales Department, IMPACT PUBLICATIONS, 9104 Manassas Drive, Suite N, Manassas Park, VA 20111-5211, Tel. 703-361-7300, Fax 703-335-9486, or e-mail: info@impactpublications.com.

Contents

6 Science, Math, Engineering, and Technology Jobs 105

7 Government, Legal, and Public Safety Jobs 120

8 Building and Construction Jobs 136

9 Sports, Entertainment, and Media Jobs 162

America's Top 100 Jobs for People Without a Four-Year Degree

1

The Best Jobs in the New Economy

WHAT ARE THE BEST JOBS for someone without a four-year degree? Which jobs are most likely to be the fastest growing and highest paying jobs in the decade ahead? Are certain jobs likely to be outsourced to cheap labor markets abroad or made obsolete by automation and technology? Which jobs are the safest and most secure ones that can lead to long-term career success? How can I quickly prepare for the best jobs in the decade ahead?

The New Boom/Bust/Offshored Economy

The past decade has been a turbulent one for jobs and careers in America. A recurring boom/bust and cowboy/casino economy (described in *Change Your Job, Change Your Life*, 9th edition, Impact Publications, 2005) created millions of new jobs as well as witnessed the disappearance of millions of other jobs. Some jobs and their occupants became victims of **structural unemployment** (permanent displacement of old-economy jobs due to technological advances that make industries and skills obsolete, such as slide-rule, VCR, and film camera makers) while others experienced **cyclical unemployment** (temporary business downturns that rebound with improved economic conditions, such as real estate and automobile manufacturing). And still others have became unemployed due to the **outsourcing and offshoring** of jobs to cheaper labor markets at home and abroad. One result of these changes is what many observers optimistically refer to as the New Economy – an unpredictable high-tech driven economy that is constantly evolving within a rapidly changing global economy.

One of the major implications of today's uncertain New Economy is clearly expressed in a key question millions of individuals ask themselves each year:

> *How should I prepare for the future when I don't know what the good jobs will look like in the future? After all, someone working in a so-called "hot job" today could well become another victim of structural, cyclical, or outsourced unemployment within the next decade!*

This question becomes increasingly important in what was termed a "jobless recovery" in the highly charged political environment of 2003-2004 – economic growth accelerated due to increased productivity, but this growth was not part of the traditional pattern of cyclical unemployment. Jobs that normally would return to the American economy were, instead, outsourced to other countries. According to Goldman Sachs (*Forbes*, April 12, 2004: 98), between 2001 and 2003 nearly 400,000 service jobs and 1 million manufacturing jobs in the U.S. were lost to offshoring. Between 2004 and 2013, another 3.3 million white-collar jobs ($136 billion in wages) are expected to be offshored. Many of these jobs used to be considered hot growth jobs within the U.S. that required various levels of higher education – engineer, radiologist, software designer, and accountant. Now many of these jobs can be offshored to Bangalore, Shanghai, Hong Kong, Manila, Singapore, Kuala Lumpur, and Penang.

Offshoring of white-collar jobs, many of which require a college degree, appears to be a new and perhaps permanent pattern of employment change in America. This new phenomenon has developed in response to structural changes in the global economy brought about by the convergence of seven important developments:

- improved Internet connections
- increased bandwidth
- powerful fiber optic cable
- cheap international telecom prices
- large pool of well-educated and trained English-speaking workers in several developing countries
- efficient international transportation links and delivery services
- enhanced global organization and management systems

White-collar jobs that were once part of cyclical unemployment were increasingly absorbed into a new form of structural unemployment – the geographic shift of jobs to cheaper labor markets. Creation of new jobs to replace what were once attractive value-added jobs supporting the middle- and upper-middle classes in the American economy perplexed many politicians, economists,

You are well advised to avoid jobs that may soon disappear because of global outsourcing and automation.

and employment specialists who seemed to be at a loss to identify new and better paying jobs that normally replaced the ones lost to outsourcing and offshoring. Instead, many of tomorrow's **safe jobs** are low-wage face-to-face jobs in the food, entertainment, health care, hospitality, transportation, and personal services industries or minimum-wage part-time and temporary jobs. Requiring only a high school education, many of these jobs offer limited benefits and little career advancement.

The College Track to Career Success

During the past few decades, individuals have been well advised to get a college education in order to succeed in the increasingly degree-oriented white-collar world of work. In fact, most studies have shown that individuals with a four-year college degree earn more than those without a college degree. According to the U.S. Department of Labor in 2002, education definitely pays off in terms of employment security and earnings:

Unemployment rate in 2002 (percent)	Education attained	Median earnings in 2001 (dollars)
2.8	Master's degree	$56,600
3.1	Bachelor's degree	$47,000
4.0	Associate degree	$36,400
4.8	Some college, no degree	$34,300
5.3	High school graduate	$29,200
9.2	Some high school, no diploma	$22,400

However, this pattern may be changing because of a global economy that places highly educated and skilled workers from low-wage countries in direct competition with similarly skilled high-wage earners in America. In other words, your education level in the future will most likely give you a distinct employment and economic advantage in safe jobs – face-to-face jobs that are difficult to offshore. Consequently, you are well advised to avoid becoming educated for jobs that are likely to disappear in the future due to global outsourcing and automation.

In the past most structural employment affected industries and blue-collar jobs that did not require college degrees. Until recently, most outsourcing of jobs to Mexico, Guatemala, China, Indonesia, Thailand, and India related to lower-level manufacturing jobs that required limited education and training. Many of these were low-wage jobs in the textile, clothing, footwear, electronics, furniture, and home furnishings industries. However, within the past few years, outsourcing has increasingly affected white-collar jobs, especially in the service industries and once hot field of information technology, that traditionally required a college degree.

As a result, an old rule of the employment game, which your mother and teachers articulated – *"get a college education and you'll have a safe and secure employment future,"* seems to have eroded in the new high-tech and service-oriented global economy. Today many jobs requiring a college degree are no longer safe and secure jobs. These jobs are becoming increasingly susceptible to productivity gains and offshoring to low-wage countries that have highly educated and skilled English-speaking populations, such as India, China, Malaysia, and the Philippines. For example, a $70,000 a year software developer in the United States can be replaced with a talented $20,000 a year software developer in Bangalore,

India. A $50,000 a year Web designer in the United States can be replaced with a $15,000 a year Web designer in the Philippines, Egypt, or the Ukraine. Many hot high-tech jobs of the 1990s can now be offshored to other countries at a fraction of the labor costs incurred in the United States. Despite political controversies surrounding this phenomenon (calls for protectionism and trade barriers), such outsourcing and job losses are likely to accelerate in the foreseeable future as the global economy develops into a competitive and global job market where many white-collar jobs will go to the lowest bidder.

Many students pursuing a four-year degree today may find themselves studying in occupational fields that are especially susceptible to offshoring. They are well advised to pursue some of the jobs outlined in this book for people without four-year degrees. These jobs have a safe and secure future that may soon challenge the standard college-to-career "best jobs" assumption of the past few decades. Indeed, many of the best jobs (high paying and secure) in the future do not require a four-year degree. Accordingly, many individuals with four-year degrees are starting to get re-trained for these increasingly desirable jobs that appear safe and secure for building a long-term career.

The New World of Safe Jobs

Downsizing and outsourcing have been going on in America for years as companies attempt to cut high labor and overhead costs as well as improve productivity through the use of new technology. Indeed, many companies have moved their operations from high-cost urban centers to low-cost towns and rural areas. For example, in 1989, Philadelphia-based Rosenbluth International, once the nation's largest travel management company (acquired by American Express in 2004), moved many of its back office operations to Fargo, North Dakota. It recently decided to offshore its Fargo, North Dakota operations to an even lower-cost labor market in India. Some of the largest telemarketing and customer service operations in the United States are centered in military base communities such as Norfolk, Virginia and San Diego, California, which disproportionately employ low-wage military spouses. However, many of these jobs are no longer safe jobs since they can be easily offshored to English-speaking countries in Asia. In addition, many of these same jobs, especially customer service and scheduling jobs, can be automated through the use of "rules-based" digitized voice software (see Frank Levy's and Richard Murnane's *The New Division of Labor: How Computers Are Creating the Next Job Market*, Princeton University Press, 2004).

Given the increased capacity of employers to offshore all types of jobs, you may want to carefully consider whether or not your chosen career path is likely to be susceptible to outsourcing at home or abroad. In fact, many of today's safe jobs do not require a college degree and some only require short- or moderate-term training. Most of these jobs require a physical presence in a community. For example, safety and security, health care, transportation, hospitality, delivery, repair services, building construction, and lawn care are relatively safe jobs. Unsafe jobs include any that can be performed abroad, via the Internet or telephone, and/or use efficient shipping and delivery services – many manufacturing, back office (accounting, insurance, billing, collections), health care (radiology), engineering, software development, and design functions.

Sailing Into an Uncertain Future

> *The best jobs go to those who get a good education, work hard, and demonstrate entrepreneurship and drive.*

The past decade has been both a rocky and exhilarating road for many individuals who have experienced a combination of job loss, downsizing, and advancement. It has almost become a cliche that you should expect to have several jobs and careers throughout your worklife; that the job you have today may disappear tomorrow; that you must constantly acquire new skills in order to survive and prosper in today's volatile job market; that you must think like an entrepreneur; and that you must take charge of your own career future. In other words, education and hard work, along with a keen sense of new opportunities, entrepreneurship, and drive, should serve you well in the coming decade.

Yes, it's true what your mother and teachers told you long ago – the best jobs go to those who get a good education and work hard! That's the basic message we've learned in our examination of the best jobs for today and in the decade ahead. Indeed, underlying the many lists of the 10, 25, 50, or 100 "best" or "top" jobs for the future are two common themes – education and hard work. While serendipity and luck play roles in getting ahead, education and hard work tend to predominate.

However, underlying these individual-level success factors is the single most important element determining whether or not education and hard work will result in rewarding jobs – an expanding economy that continues to generate quality jobs in one's community. Without such a dynamic community-based economy, all the talk about a continuing job or work revolution is nonsense. As we have witnessed in the past decade, a rapidly expanding service economy driven by high-tech, managerial, and communication revolutions resulted in generating millions of new jobs. Whether or not this economy will continue to transform the job market in the foreseeable future is uncertain.

The cyclical boom-bust American economy of the past 30 years often resulted in periods of high employment followed by recessions and high unemployment. This pattern appears to be well and alive, but the job recovery period on the upside of this cycle appears to have slowed considerably because of productivity gains and the offshoring of jobs. Employment gains attendant with local economic growth now take place within a larger global job market rather than confined to a specific geographic area. This new pattern was especially evident in what was termed the "jobless recovery" in 2004 – an expanding economy outpacing job growth.

Key Success Factors

Whether you define the "best" as the top paying, fastest growing, safest, or most satisfying, two themes remain the same. Over and over we find **education and hard work** at the center of the best jobs for the future. We also see two additional "success factors" that appear again and again when examining the best jobs for the coming decade:

1. **You must be fast on your feet and entrepreneurial** in today's and tomorrow's job markets by frequently acquiring new skills, keeping yourself marketable, being flexible, and changing jobs and careers when necessary.

2. **You should do what you really love** rather than chase after dreams not of your own making. In the end, the best job for you is one you really love doing rather than one that temporarily ranks at the top of someone's list or one purported to be "the best" based on some so-called objective criteria and analyses.

If you only get one message from this book, let it be this: The best jobs of the future will go to those who empower themselves with a capacity to shape their future. Understanding the dynamics of both the economy and job market, they take responsibility for their own employability. They dream possible dreams, because they are smart, work hard, and know they must be prepared for handling constant change in the economy, the job market, and their worklife. They prepare for uncertainty with more of the same – education, hard work, and realistic dreams. They are positive thinkers, but they do more than periodically get "pumped up" on positive thinking. They focus on the nuts and bolts of success in a talent-driven economy – they acquire skills through training and retraining and know when and where to apply those skills in the rapidly changing world of work.

Welcome to the Talent-Driven Economy

America's post-industrial economy has essentially become a talent-driven economy. Highly entrepreneurial and competitive, this economy's leading industries require more and more individuals skilled in today's latest technologies as well as capable of learning new technologies. In such a talent-driven economy, employers:

- face intense competition for their products and services
- need to constantly innovate and out-position their competition
- carefully watch their bottom line
- focus on increasing productivity and profits
- recruit or partner with top talent
- pay top dollar and extend the most generous benefits to those who demonstrate talent

It's a booming economy for individuals who are well educated and work hard at their jobs. It's a bust economy for those who lack appropriate education, workplace skills, and job search savvy.

At least for the next decade, the talent-driven economy will be the predominant model that defines the job market. The real winners in this job market will be highly talented and entrepreneurial individuals who know how to market their skills to receptive employers.

What We Know and Don't Know

Let's talk truth about the future. No one really knows what the future will bring. Nor do we have a crystal ball or some magical formula that will reveal the best jobs of the future. Too many unexpected and unique events can derail the best forecasts and predictions.

What we do know is very interesting and well worth your attention, consideration, and possible action. We do know about **job trends** based upon employment and census data compiled, analyzed, and disseminated by the U.S. Department of Labor. Economists, employment specialists, and career experts also tell us what they foresee as the future for jobs and careers based upon their familiarity with present trends, their interpretations of employment and labor market data, and, perhaps best of all, their intuition. Based on this information, we're willing to make some educated guesses, in the pages that follow, about the best jobs for people without a four-year degree.

> *The U.S. economy and job market tend to go through a recurring boom/bust cycle every 10 years.*

What we do know is this: the future is very uncertain and thus unpredictable. The economy and job market tend to go through a recurring boom/bust cycle every 10 years. Several **unique events**, such as earthquakes, floods, epidemics, droughts, terrorist activities, wars, and financial irregularities can quickly negate popular economic trends and predictions for forecasting employment, including some we outline in this book. In the world of work, we're probably in the midst of a profound revolution, the implications of which are still difficult to foresee.

The volatile economy, with its technological, managerial, and out-sourcing revolutions, simultaneously destroys and creates jobs. Companies downsize, jobs disappear or move offshore, and skills become obsolete at a breath-taking pace – so fast that it is difficult to prepare for the jobs of tomorrow when we don't know what they really look like today! It's a revolution that is transforming the way we both find and do work. Jobs we perform today may be radically transformed or disappear altogether within just a few years. One thing is certain – we're riding a revolution whose end is nowhere in sight.

Let's start by looking at the present, factor in uncertainty, project ourselves into the future, and make some realistic predictions based upon our intuition and best educated guesses.

Good Guesses and Feeling Good

Many individuals and institutions periodically attempt to predict the best jobs for the future. It's a popular topic for magazine and newspaper articles as well as for radio and television talk shows. Indeed, everyone seems to be interested in predicting the future, especially if it looks like tomorrow will be better than today! Some of these predictions are good guesses; others may miss the mark altogether.

> *Most of these trends and predictions are at best 50 to 60 percent accurate.*

Let's start by summarizing the research findings and "best guesses" of the U.S. Department of Labor on future jobs and employment trends. However, we caution you in making career decisions based on these trends since such predictions are at best 50 to 60 percent accurate. Nonetheless, this is a good starting point since almost all examinations of this subject begin with the U.S. Department of Labor data and projections.

According to the latest government predictions, the U.S. workforce is projected to expand from 144 million in 2002 to 165 million in 2012 – representing an increase of 14.8 percent. According to the most recent analysis (May 2004), these increases are disproportionately related to the following fastest growing occupations ("hot jobs") and industries as well as the largest job growth by occupations for the period 2002-2012:

Fastest Growing Occupations, 2002-2012
(Numbers in thousands of jobs)

Occupational Title	Employment 2002	2012	Percent Change	Postsecondary Education or Training
▪ Medical assistants [3]	365	579	59	Moderate-term on-the-job training
▪ Network systems and data communications analysts [1]	186	292	57	Bachelor's degree
▪ Physician assistants [3]	63	94	49	Bachelor's degree
▪ Social and human service assistants [3]	305	454	49	Moderate-term on-the-job training
▪ Home health aides [4]	580	859	48	Short-term on-the-job training
▪ Medical records and health information technicians [3]	147	216	47	Associate degree
▪ Physical therapist aides [3]	37	54	46	Short-term on-the-job training
▪ Computer software engineers, applications [1]	394	573	46	Bachelor's degree
▪ Computer software engineers [1]	281	409	45	Bachelor's degree
▪ Physical therapist assistants [2]	50	73	45	Associate degree
▪ Fitness trainers and aerobics instructors [3]	183	264	44	Postsecondary vocational award
▪ Database administrators [1]	110	159	44	Bachelor's degree
▪ Veterinary technologists and technicians [3]	53	76	44	Associate degree
▪ Hazardous materials removal workers [2]	38	54	43	Moderate-term on-the-job training
▪ Dental hygienists [1]	148	212	43	Associate degree
▪ Occupational therapist aides [3]	8	12	43	Short-term on-the-job training
▪ Dental assistants [3]	266	379	42	Moderate-term on-the-job training
▪ Personal and home care aides [4]	608	854	40	Short-term on-the-job training
▪ Self-enrichment education teachers [2]	200	281	40	Work experience in a related occupation
▪ Computer systems analysts [1]	468	653	39	Bachelor's degree

▪ Occupational therapist assistants [2]	18	26	39	Associate degree
▪ Environmental engineers [1]	47	65	38	Bachelor's degree
▪ Postsecondary teachers [1]	1,581	1,284	38	Doctoral degree
▪ Network and computer systems administrators [1]	251	345	37	Bachelor's degree
▪ Environmental science and protection technicians, including health [2]	28	38	37	Associate degree
▪ Preschool teachers, except special education [4]	424	577	36	Postsecondary vocational award
▪ Computer and information systems managers [1]	284	387	36	Bachelor's or higher degree, plus work experience
▪ Physical therapists [1]	137	185	35	Master's degree
▪ Occupational therapists [1]	82	110	35	Bachelor's degree
▪ Respiratory therapists [2]	86	116	35	Associate degree

[1] Very high average annual earnings ($42,820 and over)
[2] High average annual earnings ($27,500 to $41,780)
[3] Low average annual earnings ($19,710 to $27,380)
[4] Very low average annual earnings (up to $19,600)

Occupations With the Largest Job Growth, 2002-2012
(Numbers in thousands of jobs)

Occupational Title	Employment 2002	Employment 2012	Percent Change	Postsecondary Education or Training
▪ Registered nurses [1]	2,284	2,908	27	Associate degree
▪ Postsecondary teachers [1]	1,581	2,184	38	Doctoral degree
▪ Retail salespersons [4]	4,076	4,672	15	Short-term on-the-job training
▪ Customer service representatives [3]	1,894	2,354	24	Moderate-term on-the-job training
▪ Combined food preparation and service workers, including fast food [3]	1,990	2,444	23	Short-term on-the-job training
▪ Cashiers, except gaming [4]	3,432	2,886	13	Short-term on-the-job training

Janitors and cleaners, except maids and housekeeping cleaners [4]	2,267	2,681	18	Short-term on-the-job training
General and operations managers [1]	2,049	2,425	18	Bachelor's or higher degree + experience
Waiters and waitresses [4]	2,097	2,464	18	Short-term on-the-job training
Nursing aides, orderlies, and attendants [3]	1,375	1,718	25	Short-term on-the-job training
Truck drivers, heavy and tractor-trailer [2]	1,767	2,104	19	Moderate-term on-the-job training
Receptionists and information clerks [3]	1,100	1,425	29	Short-term on-the-job training
Security guards [4]	995	1,313	32	Short-term on-the-job training
Office clerks, general [3]	2,991	3,301	10	Short-term on-the-job training
Teacher assistants [4]	1,277	1,571	23	Short-term on-the-job training
Sales representative, wholesale and manufacturing, except technical and scientific products [1]	1,459	1,738	19	Moderate-term on-the-job training
Home health aides [4]	580	859	48	Short-term on-the-job training
Personal and home care aides [4]	608	854	40	Short-term on-the-job training
Truck drivers, light or delivery services [3]	1,022	1,259	23	Short-term on-the-job training
Landscaping and groundskeeping workers [3]	1,074	1,311	22	Short-term on-the-job training
Elementary school teachers, except special education [2]	1,467	1,690	15	Bachelor's degree
Medical assistants [3]	365	579	59	Moderate-term on-the-job training
Maintenance and repair workers, general [2]	1,266	1,472	16	Moderate-term on-the-job training
Accountants and auditors [1]	1,055	1,261	19	Bachelor's degree
Computer systems analysts [1]	468	653	39	Bachelor's degree
Secondary school teachers, except special and vocational education [1]	988	1,167	18	Bachelor's degree
Computer software engineers [1]	394	573	46	Bachelor's degree

▪ Management analysis [1]	577	753	30	Bachelor's or higher degree, plus work experience
▪ Food preparation workers [4]	850	1,022	20	Short-term on-the-job training
▪ First-line supervisors/ manager of retail sales workers [2]	1,798	1,962	9	Work experience in a related occupation

[1] Very high average annual earnings ($42,820 and over)
[2] High average annual earnings ($27,500 to $41,780)
[3] Low average annual earnings ($19,710 to $27,380)
[4] Very low average annual earnings (up to $19,600)

Fastest Growing Industries, 2002-2012
(Numbers in thousands of jobs)

Industry Description	Jobs 2002	Jobs 2012	Percent Change	Average annual rate of change
▪ Software publishers	256.0	429.7	173.7	5.3
▪ Management, scientific, and technical consulting services	731.8	1,137.4	405.6	4.5
▪ Community care facilities for the elderly and residential care facilities	695.3	1,077.6	382.3	4.5
▪ Computer systems design and related services	1,162.7	1,797.7	635.0	4.5
▪ Employment services	3,248.8	5,012.3	1,763.5	4.4
▪ Individual, family, community, and vocational rehabilitation services	1,238.8	1,866.6	597.3	3.9
▪ Ambulatory health care services except offices of health practitioners	1,443.6	2,113.4	669.8	3.9
▪ Water, sewage, and other systems	48.5	71.0	22.5	3.9
▪ Internet services, data processing, and other information services	528.8	773.1	244.3	3.9
▪ Child day care services	734.2	1,050.3	316.1	3.6

20 Jobs With High Median Earnings and a
Significant Number of Job Openings, 2002-2012

Occupation	Average Annual Projected Job Openings, 2002-2012	Median Earnings 2002
▪ Registered nurses	110,119	$48,090
▪ Postsecondary teachers	95,980	$49,090
▪ General and operations managers	76,245	$68,210
▪ Sales representatives, wholesale and manufacturing, except technical and scientific products	66,239	$42,730
▪ Truck drivers, heavy and tractor-trailer	62,517	$33,210
▪ Elementary school teachers, except special education	54,701	$41,780
▪ First-line supervisors or managers of retail sales workers	48,645	$29,700
▪ Secondary school teachers, except special education	45,761	$43,950
▪ General maintenance and repair workers	44,978	$29,370
▪ Executive secretaries and administrative assistants	42,444	$33,410
▪ First-line supervisors or managers of office and administrative support workers	40,909	$38,820
▪ Accountants and auditors	40,465	$47,000
▪ Carpenters	31,917	$34,190
▪ Automotive service technicians and mechanics	41,887	$30,590
▪ Police and sheriff's patrol officers	31,290	$42,270
▪ Licenses practical and licensed vocational nurses	29,480	$31,440
▪ Electricians	28,485	$41,390
▪ Management analysts	25,470	$60,340
▪ Computer systems analysts	23,735	$62,890
▪ Special education teachers	23,297	$43,450

Patterns, Trends, and Your Future

Certain patterns are clearly evident from the U.S. Department of Labor's employment projections for the coming decade:

1. The hot occupational fields are in health care and computers and involve increased technical education and training on an on-going basis.

2. Education is closely associated with earnings – the higher the education, the higher the average annual earnings.

3. Many of the fastest growing jobs require short- or moderate-term education.

4. Two-year associate degrees in several medical-related fields offer some of the best paying jobs.

5. Nearly 50 percent of the fastest growing jobs that generate relatively high median earnings, such as carpenters, truck drivers, repair workers, and auto mechanics, do not require a four-year degree.

Only future realities will tell us whether or not these and other jobs were really the best ones. But for now, if you are already in one of these jobs, such a list will probably make you feel good, and especially good if you are near the top. As we will see later, these rankings are very similar to our own in the following chapters. But what do they suggest to you, the curious reader or job seeker? Are these the types of jobs you want to pursue? Do they offer a bright career future in terms of earnings, security, job satisfaction, and location? Will many of these jobs undergo dramatic transformations in the decade ahead? What new skills, education, and training will you need to acquire in order to gain entry into and advance within these fields? Do you have the proper mix of interests, skills, and motivations to continue long-term in these jobs?

Always remember that such labor market statistics are for industries and occupations **as a whole**. They tell you little about the shift in employment emphasis **within the industry**, and nothing about the outlook of particular jobs for you, **the individual.** For example, employment in agriculture was projected to decline by 14 percent between 1985 and 2000, but the decline consisted of an important shift in employment emphasis within the industry: there would be 500,000 fewer self-employed workers but 150,000 more wage and salary earners in the service-end of agriculture. The employment statistics also assume a steady state of economic growth with consumers having more and more disposable income to stimulate a wide variety of service and trade industries.

Therefore, be careful in how you interpret and use this information in making your own job and career decisions. If, for example, you want to become a railroad conductor, and the data tells you there will be a 18.9 percent decline in this occupation during the next 10 years, which means only 4,000 job openings available each year, this does not mean you could not find employment, as well as advance, in this field. It merely means that, on the whole, competition may be keen for these jobs, and that future advancement and mobility in this occupation may not be very good – on the whole. At the same time, there may be numerous job opportunities available in a declining occupational field as many individuals abandon the field for more attractive occupations. In fact, you may do much better in this declining occupation than in a growing field, depending on your interests, motivations, abilities, job search savvy, and level of competition. And if the decade ahead experiences another boom-and- bust cycle, expect most of these U.S. Department of Labor statistics and projections to be invalid in the face of new and unexpected economic realities.

> *Be careful in how you interpret and use this information in making your own job and career decisions.*

We recommend using this industrial and occupational data to expand your awareness of various job and career options. By no means should you make critical education, training, and occupational choices based upon this information alone. Such choices require additional types of information – subjects of the following chapters – about you, the individual. If identified and used properly, this information will help clarify exactly which jobs are best for you.

2

Prepare for the Future

REVOLUTION IS TAKING place in the world of work. It's more than just the latest management jargon; new and transformed jobs; "reinvented" and "empowered" workplaces; downsizing, outsourcing, and offshoring; telecommuting, entrepreneurship, and project teams; the role of the Internet; the impact of technology on jobs and the workplace; transparency; and behavioral and situational interviewing. The revolution affects how you find jobs, plan careers, move on to other jobs throughout your worklife, and even retire and re-enter the job market. It's a revolution that is reshaping our notions of work. For some, it's a scary revolution that potentially threatens job security and requires constant training and retraining. For others, it's an exciting revolution of new opportunities. It's a revolution you should know more about as well as be prepared to participate in during the years ahead.

Make no mistake about it. The future is **now** in the world of work. A powerful combination of demographic, technological, economic, and political changes are fundamentally altering the way we both find and do work. These changes have important implications for you today and in the decade ahead. They will affect what you will be doing and whom you will be working with throughout your work life.

Take Charge of Your Future

While we would all like to better know and control our future, many people still believe they have little influence over their future. Living from day to day, they seldom dream about tomorrow. Going from job to job, few people think about planning and taking control of their career.

> *Without dreams you will probably wander aimlessly through life.*

But those who fail to seriously think about their futures are likely to experience very disappointing futures. Without dreams you will probably wander aimlessly through life. You'll wonder why others are so lucky in finding interesting jobs and careers that seem to pay well and have a bright future.

It's time to stop thinking about others' "good luck" and begin dreaming about and shaping your own career future. Think about and plan your future now before today becomes tomorrow!

You should take charge of your future rather than let others, or the whims of economic change, decide what you will be doing in the decade ahead. Begin by considering and planning for the kind of work you want to do over the next decade. Learn what skills are likely to be in demand for tomorrow's growing occupations. Most important, make sure you have the necessary skills and abilities to function in tomorrow's job markets.

Test Your Future Careering Capabilities

Let's begin by examining how well prepared you are for shaping your future in the world of work. You can easily identify your present level of capabilities to acquire the best jobs in the decade ahead by completing the following exercise:

Your Careering Capabilities

INSTRUCTIONS: Respond to each statement by circling which number at the right best represents your situation:

SCALE: 1 = strongly agree   4 = disagree
              2 = agree   5 = strongly disagree
              3 = maybe, not certain

1. I can identify the 20 fastest growing jobs in the
    decade ahead.   1 2 3 4 5

2. I can identify the 20 fastest declining jobs
    in the decade ahead.   1 2 3 4 5

3. I know which jobs will offer the best salaries
    in the decade ahead.   1 2 3 4 5

4. I can identify the jobs that offer the most
    security in the decade ahead.   1 2 3 4 5

5. I know the education and skill requirements
    for the best jobs in the decade ahead.   1 2 3 4 5

6. I have a clear set of career goals I hope to
    achieve in the decade ahead.   1 2 3 4 5

7. I know which jobs are right for my interests,
    skills, and abilities.   1 2 3 4 5

8. I know where to find information on the jobs
    that interest me.   1 2 3 4 5

9. I know where I will be going in my current
    job during the next decade.   1 2 3 4 5

10. I know how to acquire the necessary skills
    for the jobs I want.   1 2 3 4 5

11. I have a five-year career plan that will put me
    into one of the best jobs for the decade ahead.   1 2 3 4 5

12. I can write my ideal job description for one of
    the best jobs in the decade ahead.   1 2 3 4 5

13. I usually keep focused on my goals.   1 2 3 4 5

14. I often dream of my ideal job.   1 2 3 4 5

15. I set high goals and am tenacious in achieving
     those goals.   1 2 3 4 5

16. I am highly motivated to acquire the necessary
     skills for getting a good job.   1 2 3 4 5

17. I can find both the time and money to achieve
     my career goals.   1 2 3 4 5

18. I've assessed my interests, skills, and abilities
     and can clearly communicate these to employers.   1 2 3 4 5

19. I know what I do well and enjoy doing in the
     world of work.   1 2 3 4 5

20. I can write a one- to two-page resume that
     grabs the attention of employers and results
     in invitations to job interviews.   1 2 3 4 5

21. I know how to write at least five types of job
     search letters.   1 2 3 4 5

22. I'm good at small talk and networking both in
     face-to-face situations and on the telephone
     and Internet for developing job leads.   1 2 3 4 5

23. I know how to conduct informational
     interviews.   1 2 3 4 5

24. I know how to use the Internet for finding a job.   1 2 3 4 5

25. I know how to use online career services
     available on the Internet.   1 2 3 4 5

26. I can conduct an effective job interview.   1 2 3 4 5

27. I can negotiate a salary at least 10% higher
     than what an employer offers.   1 2 3 4 5

TOTAL   [   ]

You can calculate your overall careering capabilities for the future by adding the numbers you circled to get a composite score. If your total is more than 75 points, this book should help you substantially increase your careering capabilities. If your score is under 50 points, you are well on your way to handling your career future. In either case, this book should help you better focus your career hopes and dreams on opportunities in the decade ahead.

Prepare for Uncertainty

This book is all about preparing for uncertainty in the world of work. It will help you create a vision of the future for making smart job and career choices. If you think and plan accordingly, you will shape your future in the direction of the best jobs for the future for people without a four-year degree.

For the job or career you are involved in today most likely will not be the same one you find yourself in a decade from now. Many skills you routinely use today will be obsolete ten years from now.

Twenty years from now you may look back at the early 2000s with fond memories and conclude that this was a major watershed period in your worklife. Hopefully, you and many others will remember this as a time in which you decided to prepare yourself for job and career uncertainty. You took charge of your career. You read the signs, acquired the necessary skills, and made strategic career choices that prepared you well for the best jobs of the future.

If you plan and prepare today for the jobs of tomorrow, you will discover you put yourself on the right road to job and career success in the years ahead. But the choices are by no means obvious, especially given the turbulent nature of the economy as well as the demographic and technological changes taking place in the workplace. Like the fortune teller, you must first read the future before you can chart a path for securing your own future. And like the sailor, the exact course to your destination may vary depending on several variables; you may tack back and forth through turbulent waters.

Let's take a look into the future to see what lies ahead for you and millions of others who are concerned about the shape of their worklife in the years ahead. It's a fascinating picture of a work world that is coming faster than many people ever predicted.

Forecast the Future

The future is something we would all like to better understand, predict, and control. However, our best understanding of the future is based on analyzing past patterns and recent trends and then projecting them into the future. Such an approach assumes the future will largely be a replay of past trends. Forecasts based on this approach are often inaccurate, because they cannot foresee **unique events** that may significantly alter past patterns and trends. Consequently, important career decisions made on the basis of future forecasts may be subject to unexpected changes. For example, many engineers who pursued careers in the growing aerospace and defense industries of the 1960s, 1970s, and 1980s experienced career shock in the 1980s and 1990s; aerospace industries cut back in response to economic downturns, and defense industries began reeling from major downsizing attendant with the ending of the Cold War. Many talented workers experienced unemployment; they saw little likelihood of returning to their previous jobs or careers. The same unexpected shocks were experienced by thousands of students who pursued the highly touted MBA and law degrees of the 1980s. Many of these graduates experienced the "disappearing job phenomenon" when they entered a shrinking job market, due to economic changes, at the time when thousands of other new graduates were doing the same thing.

> *Forecasts are often inaccurate, because they cannot foresee **unique events** that may significantly alter past patterns and trends.*

The latest casualties may be nurses. As nursing become a "hot" and increasingly well paid field in the early 1990s, enrollments in nursing schools increased accordingly and thousands of retired nurses reentered the job market. At the same time, the health care industry increasingly came under cost containment pressure by government and the insurance industry. More and more hospitals treated patients on an out-patient basis, thus freeing up more and more hospital beds normally serviced by nurses. By 1995 nursing appeared to have become another glutted field as fewer and fewer nurses were being hired. New nursing graduates who had entered this popular field just two or three years earlier were having difficulty finding jobs in the new and highly volatile health care economy. However, in 1998 nursing was beginning to turn around again. By 2004, nursing had become one of the hottest career fields – large job growth and attractive salaries – for the coming decade. Nonetheless, the long-term future of nursing remained uncertain because of the uncertainty of America's highly unpredictable health care economy.

Tomorrow's Economy

Any discussion of jobs in the future must be based on some assumptions about the future economy and its ability to generate jobs for specific industries. After all, regardless of your interests, skills, educational attainment, specialized training, and entrepreneurial talents, it is the larger domestic and international economies that generate jobs which, in turn, create career opportunities for individuals. For example, much of tomorrow's job growth will be dependent upon increased U.S. exports, rather than domestic consumption, which are projected to increase by 4.5 percent each year for the coming decade. Significant changes in U.S. economic performance abroad – in part dependent upon negotiating favorable trade agreements and in part due to a cheap U.S. dollar in relation to foreign currencies – will affect the overall domestic employment picture. Economic downturns in Asia during 1997-2000 had an impact on the U.S. economy, especially on the states of California and Washington which in recent years have done a disproportionate amount of trade with the booming Asian economies.

Most realistic predictions of tomorrow's job-generating economy are based upon analyses of past trends coupled with the realities of recent economic performance. It is these predictions that form the basis for identifying the fastest growing, hottest, or best jobs for the decade ahead. For example, most forecasters agree that the rate of economic growth for the coming decade will be slower than during the 1970s, mid-1980s, and latter half of the 1990s – the era of the baby-boom generation entering the workforce. This slower job growth rate is largely attributed to changing demographics – slow population growth rate. For the period 2002 to 2012, the labor force is expected to grow by nearly 1.5 percent each year as compared to nearly 2 percent annual increase during the previous two decades.

By the year 2012 the total labor force is projected to be 165 million, representing an increase of 21 million jobs since 2002 or a total labor force growth of 14.8 percent. Most of this job growth is expected to take place in the service-producing industries. Unfortunately, a large percentage of these jobs will be low paying, entry-level jobs which offer few opportunities for career advancement.

In predicting the future, the U.S. Department of Labor's Bureau of Labor Statistics forecasts three levels of economic performance in the decade ahead – low, medium, and high. In other words, their projections should be considered pessimistic, realistic, and optimistic. Each level of economic performance generates different rates of job growth. A lower than expected rate of economic growth, for example, could significantly alter the employment picture in the decade ahead. A recession, or even a depression, could result in turning these slow growth rates into new rates of employment decline.

The Coming Job Transformation

Growth in the labor force and jobs is only part of the employment picture in the decade ahead. Most important for individuals is that job opportunities will grow and decline at different rates for different occupations and industries, and the quality of jobs will change significantly. Job opportunities in several goods-producing industries will continue to decline while those in service-producing industries will continue to increase.

At the same time, the nature of many jobs will change within organizations. As more and more industries acquire advanced technology, automate operations, improve their managerial systems, and downsize, fewer high-paying jobs will be available in the decade ahead. Indeed, a disproportionate number of jobs in tomorrow's economy will be low-paying service jobs. Dubbed by some as the "coming job drought," this will be an important change for individuals who expect to advance far beyond basic entry-level positions and steadily increase their incomes in their later years. If current patterns are any indication of things to come, we can expect a high rate of employment accompanied by declining wages. Indeed, in 2004 unemployment stood at a 5.8 percent, but real wages had fallen considerably during the past 15 years. Wage erosion in a seemingly robust economy is directly attributable to the shedding of middle- to high-paying jobs which continues throughout the workplace. Employers, from large Fortune 500 to small businesses, continue to downsize and offshore their workforces in order to compete more effectively.

You in Tomorrow's New World of Work

The pages that follow outline what we and others see as the best jobs for people without a four-year degree in the decade ahead. Given changing demographics, technological changes, slow economic growth, a projected job drought, wage erosion, declining benefits, offshoring of jobs, and the continuing decline of jobs in the goods-producing industries, we believe you should be knowledgeable about your career future in this period of rapid and turbulent change. You should know what skills you will need for the jobs of tomorrow. You should be aware that if you are just entering the workforce, you will probably have four careers and more than 15 jobs in your worklife. And you should be prepared to experience some wage erosion in the years ahead.

> *If you are just entering the workforce, you will probably have four careers and more than 15 jobs in your worklife.*

If you are to do well in the job markets of tomorrow, you must be prepared to make job and career changes, acquire appropriate job performance skills, and relocate to where the jobs are most plentiful. This means knowing how to contact employers for jobs, taking advantage of education and training opportunities, and being willing and able to move to new job sites when necessary.

Choose the Right Resources

We wish you well as you take this journey into the future world of work. We are primarily concerned with relating key job and career issues to your situations – from understanding the nature of the job market to developing job search skills, acquiring work-content skills, relocating to other communities, and translating this book into action. Many of these issues, which are also job search steps, are outlined in our other books: *Change Your Job Change Your Life, No One Will Hire Me!, Discover the Best Jobs for You, High Impact Resumes and Letters,*

Dynamite Resumes, Dynamite Cover Letters, 201 Dynamite Job Search Letters, Interview for Success, Nail the Job Interview, Job Interview Tips for People With Not-So-Hot Backgrounds, The Savvy Networker, America's Top Internet Job Sites, and *Dynamite Salary Negotiations.* We also address particular jobs and career fields in the following books: *The Complete Guide to Public Employment, The Directory of Federal Jobs and Employers, Find a Federal Job Fast, The Directory of Websites for International Jobs,* and *Jobs for Travel Lovers.* Many of these books are available in your local library and bookstore, or they can be ordered directly from Impact Publications (see the "Career Resources" sections at the end of this book). Most of these resources, along with hundreds of others, are available through Impact's comprehensive online bookstore:

www.impactpublications.com

Impact's site also includes new titles, specials, downloadable catalogs and flyers, and an online newsletter for keeping in touch with the latest in career information and resources.

The U.S. Department of Labor provides a wealth of information on jobs and careers. Much of the data relating to the jobs identified in this book as well as hundreds of additional jobs are available through two government publications: *Occupational Outlook Handbook* and the *O*NET Dictionary of Occupational Titles* (see the order form at the end of this book). This and other related data can be accessed online by visiting these two key U.S. Department of Labor websites:

- *Occupational Outlook Handbook*   www.bls.gov

- *The O*NET Dictionary of Occupational Titles*   http://onlineonetcenter.org

Empower Yourself

The chapters that follow are all about empowerment – you have within you the power to shape your own destiny. You can begin this process by creating a vision of your future worklife. If you clearly see your future and act upon your vision, you can shape your future in the direction of your interests, values, skills, and abilities. For seeing and believing in your future are the most important steps for shaping your future.

We wish you the very best as you plan for the future. May you see it, believe it, and shape it in the form of exciting jobs and careers for the decade ahead. For if you grasp the importance of education and hard work in the talent-driven economy, you will have within you the ability to turn uncertainty and turbulence into new and exciting opportunities in the world of work.

3

The Top 100 Jobs

W E SELECTED 100 JOBS for people without a four-year degree from thousands of possible jobs. Working closely with the job forecast data of the U.S. Department of Labor and its latest edition of the *Occupational Outlook Handbook*, our criteria for selecting the 100 best jobs is seven-fold:

- Jobs that are likely to experience continuing growth in the decade ahead.

- Jobs that pay reasonably well or potentially lead to well paying jobs.

- Jobs that report high levels of satisfaction.

- Entry-level jobs that serve as important stepping stones to other jobs and/or jobs that lead to long-term career development.

- Face-to-face jobs that are difficult to outsource or offshore.

- Jobs that are least likely to disappear because of automation and technology.

- Jobs than may initially require minimal levels of formal education, including a few that don't require a high school diploma.

The Hottest Jobs

Not surprisingly, many of our 100 jobs are disproportionately found in the health care and computer industries. These jobs are expected to grow faster and pay better than most other jobs. These jobs also require specialized education and training, often a two-year associate degree, and constant training and retraining because of significant technology components to these jobs. But many jobs in business, finance, government, entertainment, travel, hospitality, and transportation also pay reasonably well and report very high levels of job satisfaction.

Taken together, our 100 jobs represent some of today's best job and career opportunities for enterprising individuals who do not plan to complete a four-year college degree.

The 100 Best

We've classified our 100 top jobs by major industry and career fields. In so doing, you will see the rich array of job options available in each field. In addition, each field has its own hiring culture and job search resources. Wherever possible, we've identified resources appropriate for finding jobs in each of these fields, including many useful Internet sites of professional associations.

In the following chapters we profile these 100 jobs associated with nine major classifications of industries and careers:

Medical and Health Care Careers

- Biomedical equipment technicians
- Cardiovascular technologists
- Clinical laboratory technologists and technicians
- Dental assistants
- Dental hygienists

- Diagnostic medical sonographers
- Dialysis technicians
- Dietetic technicians
- Dispensing opticians
- Electroneurodiagnostic technologists
- Emergency medical technicians and paramedics
- Licensed practical nurses
- Massage therapists
- Medical assistants
- Medical laboratory technicians
- Medical records and health information technicians
- Medical secretaries
- Medical transcriptionists
- Nuclear medicine technologists
- Nursing, psychiatric, and home health aides
- Orthotic and prosthetic technicians
- Pedorthists
- Pharmacy technicians
- Phlebotomy technicians
- Physical therapy assistants and aides
- Occupational therapists assistants and aides
- Radiologic technologists and technicians
- Recreational therapists
- Registered nurses (R.N.)
- Respiratory therapists
- Surgical technologists
- Veterinary technicians and technicians

Computer and Internet Jobs

- Computer and office machine service technicians
- Computer programmers
- Computer software engineer
- Computer support service owners
- Web developer
- Webmaster

Science, Math, Engineering, and Technology Jobs

- Drafters
- Engineering technicians
- Electronic and electronics installers and repairers

- Electricians
- Laser technicians
- Marine service technicians
- Science technicians
- Semiconductor technicians

Government, Legal, and Public Safety Jobs

- Court reporters
- Correctional officers
- Firefighters
- Paralegals and legal assistants
- Private detectives and investigators

Building and Construction Jobs

- Brickmasons, blockmasons, and stonemasons
- Carpenters
- Construction and building inspectors
- Drywall installers, ceiling tile installers, and taper
- Glaziers
- Hazardous materials removal workers
- Insulation workers
- Painters and paperhangers
- Pipelayers, plumbers, pipefitters, and steamfitters
- Sheet metal workers
- Structural and reinforcing iron and metal workers

Sports, Entertainment and Media Jobs

- Actors
- Athletes, Coaches, umpires, and related workers
- Artists and related workers
- Broadcasters and sound engineering technicians and radio operators
- Designers
- Desktop publishers
- Gaming services
- Musicians, singers, and related workers
- Photographers
- Public relations specialists
- Recreation and fitness workers

- Television, video, and motion picture camera operators and editors

Travel and Hospitality Careers

- Air traffic controllers
- Aircraft and avionics equipment mechanics and service technicians
- Airlines pilots and flight engineers
- Chefs, cooks, and food preparation workers
- Cruise line jobs
- Flight attendants
- Food and beverage service workers
- Hotel managers and assistants
- Hotel, motel, and resort desk clerks
- Restaurant and food service managers
- Tour operators and guides

Business, Sales, and Financial Jobs

- Advertising sales agent
- Claims examiners: property and casualty insurance
- Insurance adjusters and investigators
- Real estate brokers and sales agents
- Retail salespersons
- Sales representatives: wholesale and manufacturing
- Travel agents

Transportation, Maintenance, Service, and Office Jobs

- Automotive service technicians and mechanics
- Cargo and freight agents
- Customer service representatives
- Executive secretaries and administrative assistants
- Financial clerks
- General maintenance and repair workers
- Truck drivers

Key Resources

For more information on these and other jobs appropriate for people without a four-year degree, please consult two publications produced by the U.S. Department of Labor, which are available through Impact Publications (see page 272):

> *Occupational Outlook Handbook*
> *O*NET Dictionary of Occupational Titles*

For a rich collection of resume examples relevant to many of these jobs, please see our list of resume guides on pages 271-272, which includes such titles as:

> *Best Resumes for People Without a Four-Year Degree*
> *Blue Collar Resumes*
> *Expert Resumes for Computer and Web Jobs*
> *Expert Resumes for Manufacturing Careers*
> *Gallery of Best Resumes for People Without a Four-Year Degree*
> *Real Resumes for Administrative Support, Office, and*
>   *Secretarial Jobs*
> *Real Resumes for Auto Industry Jobs*
> *Real Resumes for Aviation and Travel Jobs*
> *Real Resumes for Computer Jobs*
> *Real Resumes for Construction Jobs*
> *Real Resumes for Firefighting Jobs*
> *Real Resumes for Legal and Paralegal Jobs*
> *Real Resumes for Manufacturing*
> *Real Resumes for Media, Newspapers, Broadcasting, and*
>   *Public Affairs Jobs*
> *Real Resumes for Medical Industry Jobs*
> *Real Resumes for Nursing Jobs*
> *Real Resumes for Police, Law Enforcement and Security Jobs*
> *Real Resumes for Restaurant Food Service and Hotel Jobs*
> *Real Resumes for Sales Jobs*
> *Real Resumes for Sports Industry Jobs*
> *Resumes for Health Care Professionals*
> *Resumes for High School Graduates*

These resources, along with a special *Resumes for People Without a Four-Year Degree* kit with 46 resume guides, are available through Impact Publications's career resource center: www.impactpublications.com.

4

Medical and
Health Care Jobs

MEDICAL AND HEALTH CARE jobs represent some of the
fastest growing and best paying opportunities for people
without a four-year degree. All of these jobs require some
form of post-secondary education, training, or certification.
Many of the jobs require two-year associate degrees provided by community or junior colleges while other jobs only require on-the-job training
or a 9- to 24-month training program offered by hospitals, vocational
schools, or community colleges.

Great Opportunities

Five of the 10 fastest growing jobs in the decade ahead will be found in
health care. Altogether, nearly 15 million people work in the health care
industry. While major restructuring of health care financing and services
may negatively affect some jobs in this fields, especially nurses in
hospitals and physicians in private practice, despite such restructuring,

medicine and health care are hot career fields for the decade ahead. Entry into the medical field will most likely result in a long-term career.

Increased job opportunities are largely due to seven major changes which translate into a boom for the health care industry:

1. Increased public and private financing of health care services.

2. New medical breakthroughs for the prevention, detection, and treatment of diseases.

3. An increasingly aging population requiring and demanding more health care services.

4. The increasing acceptance of alternative medical approaches.

5. Shortage of key medical professionals, such as nurses and dental hygienists.

6. Increased delegation of traditional roles of medical professionals to para-medical professionals or assistants, who are given such titles as technologists, technicians, aides, or assistants.

7. The development of numerous specialized certification and training programs, with placement services, promoted by professional associations and sponsored by hospitals, vocational schools, and community colleges.

Good Pay and Promising Growth

In general, jobs in the medical and health care industries pay better than in most other industries. They also offer good advancement opportunities for those who seek additional training and certification within or between related medical fields. The best paying jobs will go to those with high levels of education and specialized training, such as surgeons, radiologists, gynecologists, and anesthesiologists. These industries also will generate hundreds of thousands of lower paying entry-level support positions, especially for medical assistants, technicians, technologists, nursing aides, and home health aides, which require the least amounts of medical education and training.

We expect job opportunities in medicine and health care to continue to expand throughout the coming decade. New medical breakthroughs relating to genetic engineering and biochemistry will create new occupational specialties. However, don't expect this to be a constantly expanding and rosy occupational field. The organization and management of medical and health care services will continue to undergo major changes in the next decade. The field faces some difficult and challenging years ahead with hospitals and HMOs being at the center of a major upheaval in managed care health services. Key service delivery centers, such as hospitals and HMOs, are experiencing numerous difficulties relating to financing and the delivery of quality services. Indeed, the health care field is undergoing a fundamental revolution in how it finances, delivers, and gets paid for its services.

> *Changes in health care financing should place increased demands on health care services.*

Many of the changes are a result of insurance companies and government legislation that largely determine how health care services will be financed and thus delivered.

Coming Changes

The revolution in medicine and health care will have a significant impact on traditional medical roles and medical providers, such as physicians, nurses, hospitals, and an army of technologists, technicians, assistants, and aides. The major factors affecting the job outlook will be the financing of health care and the restructuring of health care roles. Changes in health care financing are the key to understanding the increased demand for health care services. As health care financing undergoes major changes, expect the demand for health care services to change accordingly. The current system of health care financing, as well as proposals to increase the scope of financing, could result in an even greater demand for medical and health care services in the decade ahead. Be prepared for new approaches to health care financing as well as new

roles for nurses and medical aides in delivering health care services –
changes which could significantly alter future job opportunities within the
health care field.

Top Jobs

Eleven of the jobs appearing in this chapter are usually included on most
lists of the "50 best jobs":

- Dental hygienists
- Electroneurodiagnostic technologists
- Emergency medical technicians and paramedics
- Licensed practical nurses
- Medical assistants
- Medical records and health information technicians
- Nursing, psychiatric, and home health aides
- Physical therapy assistants and aides
- Radiologic technologists ad technicians
- Registered nurses
- Respiratory therapists

While not necessarily the best paying jobs, they are in high demand and
offer excellent entry into the expanding health care industry. Landing a
job in one of these fields should result in expanding career opportunities.

Biomedical Equipment Technicians

- ⇨ **Annual Earnings:** $36,400
- ⇨ **Education/Training:** Certificate or associate degree
- ⇨ **Outlook:** Excellent

Employment Outlook: Employment growth is expected to be above
average for biomedical equipment technicians due to the overall growth of
the health care industry and elderly population demanding the use of more
sophisticated medical equipment.

Nature of Work: Biomedical equipment technicians are responsible for inspecting, maintaining, repairing, installing, and testing various types of medical diagnostic treatment equipment, such as patient monitors, defibrillators, heart monitors, medical imaging equipment (x-rays, CAT scanners, and ultrasound equipment), electric wheelchairs, artificial kidney machines, chemical analyzers, heart-lung machines, and other electronic, mechanical, and pneumatic devices. Individuals in this position often find themselves in troubleshooting situations where they work with hand and power tools and instructional books. While most work a 40-hour week, many are on call 24 hours a day. Biomedical equipment technicians must keep detailed records of all maintenance and repair conducted on each piece of equipment.

Working Conditions: Biomedical equipment technicians are employed in a variety of work settings, from hospitals and clinics to physicians' offices. They are required to take special safety precautions given the fact that they work with electrical equipment.

Education, Training, Qualifications: Biomedical equipment technicians need to complete specialized training programs or serve as apprentices or assistants in the use and repair of medical equipment. Many of these workers complete associate degree programs in electronics or medical technology. Individuals qualified to repair such sophisticated equipment as CAT scanners and defibrillators are required to complete specialized training and certification exams.

Earnings: The median hourly wage for biomedical equipment technicians in 2002 was $17.49, which translates into yearly earnings of nearly $36,400. Salaries can range from a low of $22,000 a year to over $45,000 a year, depending on experience, specialty skills, and employers.

Key Contacts: Information on education and careers for biomedical equipment technicians is available through:

- Association for the Advancement of Medical Instrumentation: 1110 North Glebe Road, Suite 220, Arlington, VA 22201-4795. Website: www.aami.org.

Cardiovascular Technologists and Technicians

⇨ **Annual Earnings:** $36,430
⇨ **Education/Training:** 2- to 4-year training programs
⇨ **Outlook:** Good – faster than average growth

Employment Outlook: Employment of cardiovascular technologists and technicians is expected to grow faster than average in the coming decade. This growth is in response to an aging population with a higher incidence of heart problems. Employment of vascular technologists and echocardiographers will grow as advances in vascular technology and sonography reduce the need for more costly and invasive procedures. However, fewer EKG technicians will be needed, as hospitals train nursing aides and others to perform basic EKG procedures.

Nature of Work: Cardiovascular technologists and technicians held nearly 45,000 jobs in the United States in 2002. Three out of four jobs were in hospitals (primarily in cardiology departments). The remaining jobs were with offices of physicians, including cardiologists; or in medical and diagnostic laboratories, including diagnostic imaging centers.

Cardiovascular technologists and technicians assist physicians in diagnosing and treating cardiac (heart) and peripheral vascular (blood vessel) ailments. Cardiovascular technologists specialize in three areas – invasive cardiology, echocardiography, and vascular technology. Technologists prepare patients for cardiac catheterization and balloon angioplasty by first positioning them on an examining table and then shaving, cleaning, and administering anesthesia to the top of their leg near the groin. During the procedures, they monitor patients' blood pressure and heart rate with EKG equipment and notify the physician if something appears wrong. Cardiovascular technologists who specialize in echocardiography or vascular technology often run noninvasive tests using ultrasound instrumentation, such as Doppler ultrasound. Those who assist physicians in the diagnosis of disorders affecting the circulation are known as vascular technologists or vascular sonographers. They perform a medical history and evaluate pulses by listening to the sound of the arteries for abnormalities. Technologists who use ultrasound to examine the heart chambers, valves, and vessels are referred to as cardiac sonographers, or echocardiographers. Cardiovascular technicians who obtain EKGs are known as electrocardiograph (or EKG) technicians. They administer a basic EKG, which traces electrical impulses transmitted by the heart; technicians attach electrodes to the patient's chest, arms, and legs, and then manipulate switches on an EKG machine to obtain a reading. EKG technicians also administer treadmill stress tests. Some cardiovascular technologists and technicians schedule appointments, type doctors' interpretations, maintain patient files, and perform equipment checks and maintenance.

Working Conditions: Technologists and technicians generally work a five-day, 40-hour week that may include weekends. Those in catheterization labs tend to work longer hours, may work evenings, and are often on call during the night and on weekends. Cardiovascular technologists and technicians spend a lot of time walking and standing. Those working in catheterization labs may face stressful working conditions because they are in close contact with patients with serious heart ailments.

Education, Training, Qualifications: While a few cardiovascular technologists, vascular technologists, and cardiac sonographers are trained on the job, most receive training in two- to four-year programs. These individuals normally complete a two-year junior or community college program. For basic EKGs, Holter monitoring, and stress testing, one-year certification programs exist, but most EKG technicians are still trained on the job, which lasts 6-16 weeks, by an EKG supervisor or a cardiologist. Most employers prefer to train people already in the health care field, such as nursing aides.

Earnings: Median annual earnings of cardiovascular technologists and technicians were $36,430 in 2002. The middle 50 percent earned between $26,730 and $46,570.

Key Contacts: For general information about a career in cardiovascular technology as well as information on accredited programs, contact:

- **Alliance of Cardiovascular Professionals:** 4456 Thalia Landing Offices, Building 2, 4356 Bonney Road, Suite 103, Virginia Beach, VA 23452-1200. Website: www.acp-online.org.

- **Committee on Accreditation of Allied Health Education Programs:** 39 East Wacker Drive, Suite 1970, Chicago, IL 60601. Website: www. caahep.org.

- **Society of Vascular Ultrasound:** 4601 Presidents Drive, Suite 260, Lanham, MD 20706-4831. Website: www.svunet.org.

- **American Society of Echocardiography:** 1500 Sunday Drive, Suite 102, Raleigh, NC 27607. Website: www.asecho.org.

- **Cardiovascular Credentialing International:** 1500 Sunday Drive, Suite 102, Raleigh, NC 27607. Website: www.cci-online.org.

- **American Registry of Diagnostic Medical Sonographers:** 51 Monroe Street, Plaza East One, Rockville, MD 20850-2400. Website: www.ardms.org.

Clinical Laboratory Technologists and Technicians

⇨ **Annual Earnings:** $29,000 to $43,000
⇨ **Education/Training:** Certificate, associate degree, or BA
⇨ **Outlook:** Excellent

Employment Outlook: Nearly 300,000 jobs in the U.S. were occupied by clinical laboratory technologists and technicians in 2002. While over 50 percent of the jobs were in hospitals, nearly 40 percent were in medical and diagnostic laboratories, physicians' offices, ambulatory health care services, outpatient care centers, educational services, and scientific research and development services. Jobs for clinical laboratory technicians are expected to experience steady growth due to the increased volume of laboratory tests in the decade ahead, with most of the growth taking place with employers outside hospitals.

Nature of Work: Also known as medical technologists and technicians, individuals in these jobs play a key role in the detection, diagnosis, and treatment of diseases. They examine and analyze body fluids, tissues, and cells to determine bacteria, parasites, and other micro-organisms; match blood for transfusions; test for drug levels; prepare specimens; and conduct numerous medical tests using a variety of sophisticated laboratory equipment. **Clinical laboratory technologists** normally have a bachelor's degree in medical technology or one of the life sciences or a combination of formal training and work experience. They perform complex chemical, biological, hematological, immunologic, microscopic, and bacteriological tests. They also evaluate test results, develop and modify procedures, and establish and monitor programs. Some will supervise clinical laboratory technicians. **Clinical laboratory technicians** perform less complex tests and laboratory procedures. Working under the supervision of medical and clinical laboratory technologists or laboratory managers, they may prepare specimens and operate automated analyzers or perform manual tests according to detailed instructions.

Working Conditions: Work settings and conditions vary, from large hospitals to small commercial laboratories. While half work in hospitals, the trend is to employ more and more medical technologists and technicians in independent laboratories. Hours also vary, from day, evening, night shift, and weekend and holiday work. Given the use of proper precautions with handling infectious specimens, clinical laboratory work is relatively safe.

Education, Training, Qualifications: Most entry-level medical technology positions require a bachelor's degree in one of the life sciences or in medical technology. However, it is possible be qualified through a combination of education, on-the-job, and specialized training. Course work usually includes chemistry, biological sciences, microbiology, mathematics, and computer technology. Medical laboratory technicians receive training in two-year community college programs, hospitals, vocational and technical schools, or in the Armed Forces. Medical and clinical laboratory technicians usually have either an associate degree from a community or junior college or a certificate from a hospital, a vocational or technical school, or one of the U.S. Armed Forces. Some states require laboratory personnel to be licensed or registered.

Earnings: Median annual earnings of full time, salaried medical and clinical laboratory technologists were $42,910 in 2002. Half earned between $36,400 and $50,820. The lowest 10 percent earned less than $30,530, and the top 10 percent earned more than $58,000. The median annual salary of medical and clinical laboratory technicians was $29,040 in 2002. Half earned between $23,310 and $35,840. The lowest 10 percent earned less than $19,070. For medical laboratory technicians, the median was $31,928; for histotechnicians, the median was $34,549; for cytotechnologists, the median was $49,920; and for phlebotomists, the median was $21,168.

Key Contacts: Career and certification information is available through:

- **American Association of Blood Banks:** 8101 Glenbrook Road, Bethesda, MD 20814-2749. Website: www.aabb.org.

- **American Medical Technologists:** 710 Higgins Road, Park Ridge, IL 60068. Website: www.amt1.com.

- **American Society for Clinical Laboratory Science:** 6701 Democracy Boulevard, Suite 300, Bethesda, MD 20817. Website: www. ascls.org.

- **American Society of Clinical Pathologists:** 2100 West Harrison Street, Chicago, IL 60612. Website: www.ascp.org.

- **American Society of Cytopathology:** 400 West 9th St., Suite 201, Wilmington, DE 19801. Website: www.cytopathology.org.

- **National Credentialing Agency for Laboratory Personnel:** P.O. Box 15945-289, Lenexa, KS 66285. Website: www.nca-info.org.

Dental Assistants

- ⇨ **Annual Earnings:** $27,250
- ⇨ **Education/Training:** 9-12 month training programs
- ⇨ **Outlook:** Excellent. 16,000 annual job openings

Employment Outlook: The employment outlook for dental assistants should be excellent in the decade ahead as more individuals use dental services. More and more dentists hire dental assistants to perform routine dental tasks so they can concentrate on performing more profitable procedures. Dentists currently employ nearly 270,000 dental assistants. This number should increase by 16,000 a year.

Nature of Work: Dental assistants serve as a second pair of hands for dentists. They perform a wide range of office, patient care, and laboratory tasks. They usually work next to dentists as they examine and treat patients. Office duties include scheduling appointments, receiving patients, keeping records, sending bills, receiving payments, and ordering dental supplies. Patient care involves preparing patients for treatment, assisting dentists with instruments and materials, and keeping patients comfortable. Some dental assistants may perform the roles of dental hygienists, such as process dental x-ray film, remove sutures, and apply anesthetics. Laboratory duties include making casts of teeth and temporary crowns as well as maintaining cleanliness and quality control of appliances. They should not be confused with dental hygienists who are licensed to perform other clinical tasks and who are required to have different levels of education and training.

Working Conditions: Dental assistants work in well-lighted, clean environments where infectious diseases and dangers posed by x-ray machines are minimized by proper safety equipment and procedures – gloves, masks, eyewear, and protective clothing. Most work in private dental offices, but some also work in dental schools, hospitals, physicians' offices, and public health clinics. Nearly half of all dental assistants work part time.

Education, Training, Qualifications: While many dental assistants attend 9- to 12-month dental assisting programs sponsored by community colleges, trade schools, technical institutes, or the Armed Forces, most dental assistants pick up their skills through on-the-job experience. Many dental assistants with chairside experience go back to school to become dental hygienists. Others go on to become office managers. In 2002 the American Dental Association's Commission on Dental Accreditation approved 259 dental-assisting training programs. Most states regulate the duties of dental assistants through licensure or registration, which may require a written or practical examination.

Earnings: Median hourly earnings of dental assistants in 2002 were $13.10. The middle 50 percent earned between $10.35 and $16.20 an hour. The lowest 10 percent earned less than $8.45, and the highest 10 percent earned more than $19.41 an hour. Full-time dental assistants can expect to earn between $19,000 and $33,000 a year.

Key Contacts: Information on education and careers for dental assistants is available through:

- **American Dental Assistants Association:** 35 East Wacker Drive, Suite 1730, Chicago, IL 60601. Website: www. dentalassistant.org/prof/ ed/accred/commission/index.asp .

- **Commission on Dental Accreditation:** American Dental Association, 211 East Chicago Avenue, Suite 1814, Chicago, IL 60611. Website: www.ada.org.

- **Dental Assisting National Board:** 676 North Saint Clair, Suite 1880, Chicago, IL 60611. Website: www.danb.org.

- **National Association of Dental Assistants:** 900 South Washington Street, Suite G-13, Falls Church, VA 22046.

Dental Hygienists

⬧ **Annual Earnings:** $55,000
⬧ **Education/Training:** Associate degree
⬧ **Outlook:** Outstanding. 5,000 annual job openings

Employment Outlook: This continues to be one of the hottest career fields for individuals without a four-year degree. Indeed, this is a well paid growth field with excellent working conditions. Jobs in this field should be plentiful as the population continues to grow and age and requires more dental services, as incomes rise, and as dentists increasingly delegate routine procedures to dental hygienists. Over the next decade employment for dental hygienists is expected to grow much faster than other occupations – by 37.1 percent. An estimated 148,000 dental hygienists were employed in 2002. More than half of all dental hygienists work part time (less than 35 hours a week), and many hold multiple jobs.

Nature of Work: Dental hygienists provide preventive dental care and teach patients about good oral hygiene. Depending on state regulations, dental hygienists may provide any or all of these services: remove calculus, stain, and plaque; apply cavity preventive agents such as fluorides and pit and fissure sealants; and take and develop dental x-rays. In some states they also may administer anesthetics; place and carve filling materials, temporary fillings, and periodontal dressings; remove sutures; and smooth and polish metal restorations.

Working Conditions: This is a terrific career field for someone who prefers a flexible work schedule. Most dental hygienists work in dental offices where they may have a wide range of flexible work schedules – full-time, part-time, evening, and weekend. Many work two or three days a week in one office and two or three days in other offices. They normally work in clean, well-lighted rooms. Working conditions are relatively safe since they adhere to proper radiological procedures and wear safety glasses, surgical masks, and gloves to protect themselves and patients from infectious diseases.

Education, Training Qualifications: Each state licenses dental hygienists who are required to graduate from an accredited dental hygiene school as well as pass both a written and a clinical examination. Over 265 dental hygiene programs are accredited by the Commission on Dental Accreditation. Most programs grant an associate degree, but some also offer a certificate as well as bachelor's and master's degrees. Many of these programs require applicants to have completed one year of undergraduate education with course work in biology, health, chemistry, physiology, pharmacology, and nutrition. An associate degree or certificate is required for working in private dental offices. A bachelor's or master's degree is required for research, teaching, or clinical practice in public or school health programs. High school students interested in this field are well advised to study biology, chemistry, and mathematics in preparation for such programs.

Earnings: This is a relatively well paying field for individuals with one or two years of college education. The median hourly earnings of dental hygienists in 1998 were $26.59. The middle 50 percent earned between $21.96 and $32.48 an hour. The lowest 10 percent earned less than $17.34, and the highest 10 percent earned more than $39.24 an hour.

Key Contacts: Information on careers in dental hygiene and educational requirements is available through:

- **American Dental Association:** 211 East Chicago Avenue, Suite 1814, Chicago, IL 60611. Website: www.ada.org.

- **American Dental Education Association:** 1625 Massachusetts Avenue, NW, Suite 600, Washington, DC 20036-2212. Website: www.adca.org.

- **American Dental Hygienists' Association:** Division of Education, 444 N. Michigan Avenue, Suite 3400, Chicago, IL 60611. Website: www.adha.org.

- **Commission on Dental Accreditation:** American Dental Association, 211 East Chicago Avenue, Suite 1814, Chicago, IL 60611. Website: www.ada.org/prof/ed/accrd/commission/index.asp .

Dental hygienists' associations operate at the local level in most states. To locate these associations, search for "dental hygienists association" by using such search engines as google.com or yahoo.com

Diagnostic Medical Sonographers

➪ **Annual Earnings:** $48,660
➪ **Education/Training:** Associate to bachelor's degree
➪ **Outlook:** Excellent – faster than average job growth

Employment Outlook: Employment of diagnostic medical sonographers should grown faster than average for all occupations during the next decade as the population grows and ages, increasing the demand for diagnostic imaging and therapeutic technology. Sonography is becoming an increasingly attractive alternative to radiologic procedures as patients seek safer treatment methods. Sonographic technology is expected to evolve rapidly with many new sonography procedures, such as 3D-sonography for use in obstetric and ophthalmologic diagnosis.

Nature of Work: Sonography, or ultrasonography, uses sound waves to generate an image for the assessment and diagnosis of various medical conditions. While long associated with obstetrics – viewing the fetus in the womb – this technology also has many other applications in the diagnosis and treatment of medical conditions. Diagnostic medical sonographers, also known as ultrasonographers, use special equipment to direct nonionizing, high frequency sound waves into areas of the patient's body. Sonographers operate the equipment, which collects reflected echoes and forms an image that may be videotaped, transmitted, or photographed for interpretation and diagnosis by a physician. Diagnostic medical sonographers may specialize in obstetric and gynecologic sonography (the female reproductive system), abdominal sonography (the liver, kidneys, gallbladder, spleen, and pancreas), neurosonography (the brain), or ophthalmologic sonography (the eyes). Some may also specialize in vascular technology or echocardiography. Diagnostic medical sonographers held about 37,000 jobs in 2002. More than half work in hospitals.

Working Conditions: Most full-time sonographers work a 40-hour week. Most sonographers work in health care facilities that are clean and well lighted. Some travel to patients in large vans equipped with sophisticated diagnostic equipment. Sonographers are on their feet for long periods and may have to lift or turn disabled patients.

Education, Training, Qualifications: Sonographers may be trained through hospitals, vocational-technical institutions, colleges and universities, and the Armed Forces. Colleges and universities offer formal training in both two- and four-year programs, culminating in an associate or a bachelor's degree. Some health workers, such as obstetric nurses and radiologic technologists, may complete a one-year training program to become certified in this field. Sonographers should have a background in mathematics and science.

Earnings: Overall median annual earnings of diagnostic medical sonographers were $48,660 in 2002. The middle 50 percent earned between $41,420 and $56,020 a year. Median annual earnings of diagnostic medical sonographers in 2002 were $50,390 in offices of physicians and $47,530 in hospitals.

Key Contacts: For information on a career as a diagnostic medical sonographer, including educational programs, contact:

- **Society of Diagnostic Medical Sonography:** 2745 Dallas Parkway, Suite 350, Plano, TX 75093-8730. Website: www.sdms.org.

- **American Registry of Diagnostic Medical Sonographers:** 51 Monroe Street, Plaza East 1, Rockville, MD 20850-2400. Website: www.ardms.org.

- **Joint Review Committee on Education in Diagnostic Medical Sonography:** 2025 Woodlane Drive, St. Paul, MN 55125-2998. Website: www.jrcdms.org.

- **Commission on Accreditation for Allied Health Education Programs:** 39 East Wacker Drive, Suite 1970, Chicago, IL 60601. Website: www. caahep.org.

Dialysis Technicians

- ➪ **Annual Earnings:** $32,700
- ➪ **Education/Training:** Certificate to associate degree
- ➪ **Outlook:** Good

Employment Outlook: According to the National Kidney Foundation, more than 20 million Americans have chronic kidney disease, and most do not know it. The main cause for this disease is diabetes, which affects over 16 million Americans and is expected to continue to increase in the next two decades (projected at 22 million for 2025). Accordingly, the need for dialysis technicians to treat people experiencing kidney failure should increase.

Nature of Work: Dialysis technicians, also known as nephrology technicians or renal dialysis technicians, treat people with chronic renal failure (CRF). They administer kidney dialysis with the use of hemodialysis artificial kidney machines, which filters a patient's blood through a dialysis machine to remove impurities. Dialysis technicians include patient-care technicians, biomedical equipment technicians, and dialyzer reprocessing (reuse) technicians.

Working Conditions: Most dialysis technicians work in dialysis facilities found in hospitals, out patient facilities, or home dialysis programs.

Education, Training, Qualifications: Dialysis technicians receive on-the-job training or attend employer-sponsored training programs or programs conducted by vocational schools or junior colleges. Most training programs run from six to 12 weeks. While most states do not require registration, certification, or licenses in this field, California, New Mexico, and a few other states do require certification.

Earnings: Dialysis technicians earn from $8 to $18 an hour ($16,640 to $37,400 a year). Certified dialysis technicians receive higher salaries than those without certification. The average salary of dialysis technicians in private dialysis centers was $34,200 in 2002.

Key Contacts: For information on education programs and careers relating to dialysis technicians, contact:

- **Board of Nephrology Examiners, Nursing and Technology:** P.O. Box 15945-282, Lenexa, KS 66285. Website: www.goamp.com/bonent

- **National Association of Nephrology Technicians/Technologists:** P.O. Box 2307, Dayton, OH 45401. Website: www.dialysistech.org.

- **National Kidney Foundation:** 30 East 33rd Street, New York, NY 10016. Website: www.kidney.org.

Dietetic Technicians

⇨ **Annual Earnings:** $24,300
⇨ **Education/Training:** On-the-job training to associate degree
⇨ **Outlook:** Good

Employment Outlook: The employment outlook for dietetic technicians should be good in the decade ahead as the population becomes more nutrition and health conscious and as a growing elderly population requires more institutional-based food and nutrition services.

Nature of Work: Dietetic technicians provide food management and nutritional care services under the supervision of a registered dietitian. If they work in food service management, they usually supervise food service employees and the production process, plan menus, and scrutinize recipes to conform to nutritional guidelines. A dietetic technician also may assist a clinical or community dietitian in screening patients, recording diet histories, choosing menus, providing dietary counseling, and educating patients on best nutritional practices.

Working Conditions: Most dietetic technicians work independently or in teams with registered dietitians. They work in several different types of settings – health care, business, industry, day-care programs, food service, research, and government agencies. Most full-time dietetic technicians work a 40-hour week. They usually work in clean, well-lighted, and well-ventilated areas. However, some work in warm, congested kitchens. Many dietetic technicians are on their feet for much of the workday.

Education, Training, Qualifications: Dietetic technicians are encouraged to complete an educational training program for certification through the American Dietetic Association, even though states do not require dietetic technicians to be licensed or certified. Several junior colleges offer two-year associate degrees for dietetic technicians.

Earnings: Median annual earnings for dietetic technicians were $24,300 in 2002. The starting salary for a dietetic technician is around $19,000 a year.

Key Contacts: For information on education programs and careers relating to dietetic technicians, contact:

- **American Dietetic Association:** 120 S. Riverside Plaza, Suite 2000, Chicago, IL 60606-6995. Website: www.eatright.org.

- **Center for Nutrition Policy and Promotion:** U.S. Department of Agriculture. Website: www.usda.gov/cnpp.

Dispensing Opticians

▷ **Annual Earnings:** $25,600
▷ **Education/Training:** On-the-job training and apprenticeships
▷ **Outlook:** Good

Employment Outlook: Employment of dispensing opticians is expected to increase about as fast as the average for all occupations in the decade ahead as the number of middle-aged and elderly persons needing corrective lenses increases. Demand also will increase for dispensing opticians due to changing styles and colors of frames and improvements in bifocal, extended-wear, and disposable contact lenses.

Nature of Work: Dispensing opticians fit eyeglasses and contact lenses, following prescriptions written by ophthalmologists or optometrists. They recommend eyeglass frames, lenses, and lens coatings after considering the prescription and the customer's occupation, habits, and facial features. They measure the eyes and adjust the frames to fit the customer's face. Some dispensing opticians also specialize in fitting contacts, artificial eyes, or cosmetic shells to cover blemished eyes. They keep records on customers' prescriptions, work orders, and payments; track inventory and sales; and perform other administrative duties. Dispensing opticians held about 63,000 jobs in 2002. About two out of five worked in health and personal care stores, including optical goods stores.

Working Conditions: Dispensing opticians work indoors in attractive, well-lighted, and well-ventilated surroundings. They may work in medical offices or small stores where customers are served one at a time. Opticians spend a great deal of time on their feet. Most dispensing opticians work a 40-hour week, although some work longer hours. Those in retail stores may work evenings and weekends.

Education, Training, Qualifications: Employers usually hire individuals with no background as a dispensing optician or those who have worked as ophthalmic laboratory technicians. The employers then provide the required training. Most dispensing opticians receive training on the job or through apprenticeships lasting two or more years. Some employers, however, seek people with postsecondary training in the field. Over 20 states require dispensing opticians to be licensed. Several community colleges and a few colleges and universities provide formal training for dispensing opticians.

Earnings: Median annual earnings of dispensing opticians were $25,600 in 2002. The middle 50 percent earned between $19,960 and $33,530. Median annual earnings in industries employing the largest numbers of dispensing opticians in 2002 were $28,250 for offices of physicians; $25,860 for health and personal care stores; and $24,900 for other offices.

Key Contacts: For information on educational programs and careers related to dispensing opticians, contact:

- **National Academy of Opticianry:** 8401 Corporate Drive, Suite 605, Landover, MD 20785. Website: www.nao.org.

- **Commission on Opticianry Accreditation:** P.O. Box 3073, Merrifield, VA 22116-3073. **Website: www.coaccreditation.com.**

- **American Board of Opticianry:** 6506 Loisdale Road, Suite 209, Springfield, VA 22150. Website: www.abo.org.

- **National Contact Lens Examiners:** 6506 Loisdale Road, Suite 209, Springfield, VA 22150. Website: www.abo.org.

Electroneurodiagnostic Technologists

- ⇨ **Annual Earnings:** $40,498
- ⇨ **Education/Training:** Associate degree or certificate
- ⇨ **Outlook:** Slower than average.

Employment Outlook: Employment of electroneurodiagnostic technologists (also known as EEG technologists) is expected to be slower than average and replacement needs will be low in the decade ahead. In 2004 approximately 7,000 electroneurodiagnostic technologists held positions in neurology laboratories of hospitals, offices and clients of neurologists and neurosurgeons, sleep centers, and psychiatric facilities.

Nature of Work: EEG technologists, which include electroneurodiagnostic or neurophysiologic technologists (electric brain scan operators), operate electroencephalograph (EEG) machines that help neurologists diagnose brain tumors, strokes, toxic-metabolic disorders, and epilepsy as well as detect infectious diseases and organic impairments affecting the brain.

Working Conditions: Most EEG technologists work a standard 40-hour week in hospitals or clinics and are often on call for evening, weekend, and holiday work. Their work involves a great deal of bending and lifting; half of their time is spent on their feet.

Education, Training, Qualifications: Most EEG technologists acquire on-the-job training, although some complete formal training. Employers increasingly prefer one- to two-year formal postsecondary training offered by hospitals and community colleges. Most hospital trainee positions require a high school diploma.

Earnings: The median annual base salary of full-time EEG technologists in 2004 was $40,598. The middle 50 percent earned between $30,449 and $50,748.

Key Contacts: For additional information on these jobs, contact the following organizations:

- **American Society of Electroneurodiagnostic Technologists, Inc.** 426 W. 42nd Street, Kansas City, MO 64111. Website: www.aset.org.

- **Joint Review Committee on Electroneurodiagnostic Technology:** Route 1, Box 63A, Genoa, WI 54632.

- **American Board of Registration of Electroencephalographic Technologists and Evoked Potential Technologists:** 1904 Croydon Drive, Springfield, IL 62703. Website: www.abret.org.

- **American Association of Electrodiagnostic Technologists:** 28 Sabins Lane, North Chatham, MA 02650. Website: www.aaet.info.

- **Association of Polysomnographic Technologists:** One Westbrook Corporate Center, Suite 920, Westchester, IL 60154 (focuses on sleep studies.) Website: www.aptweb.org.

Emergency Medical Technicians and Paramedics

➪ **Annual Earnings:** $24,030
➪ **Education/Training:** Certificate
➪ **Outlook:** Excellent

Employment Outlook: Job growth for emergency medical technicians and paramedics is expected to be faster than average for all occupations in the decade ahead. In 2004 over 185,000 EMTs and paramedics held jobs. Most were in metropolitan areas. Smaller communities tend to have a large number of volunteer EMTs and paramedics. Continuing population growth and urbanization will increase the demand for full-time paid EMTs and paramedics, as will continuing replacement needs due to the stressful nature, modest pay, and limited advancement opportunities in this occupational specialty. The largest number of opportunities will be with private ambulance services. Competition will be greatest for jobs in local government, especially fire, police, and independent third-service rescue squad departments where salaries and benefits tend to be better than with private ambulance services. Individuals with advanced certifications, such as EMT-Intermediate and EMT-Paramedic, will have the best opportunities.

Nature of Work: Yes, you've seen them on television and in the movies as emergency lifesavers. Responding to automobile accident injuries, heart attacks, near drownings, unscheduled childbirths, poisonings, and gunshot wounds, emergency medical technicians (EMTs) – also known as paramedics – provide immediate medical care and transport the sick or injured to medical facilities. Two-fifths of EMTs work with private ambulance services; one-third work with municipal fire, police, or rescue squad departments; one-fourth work with hospitals.

Working Conditions: The work of EMTs is both physically strenuous and stressful, involving indoor and outdoor work and in all kinds of weather. Much of their work involves standing, kneeling, bending, and lifting. EMTs may be exposed to hepatitus B and AIDS as well as violent drug victims.

Education, Training, Qualifications: EMTs must receive formal classroom and internship training. EMT-Basic training involves 110-120 hours of classroom work plus 10 hours of internship experience in a hospital or emergency room. EMT-Intermediate training includes 35-55 hours of additional instruction. The basic entry requirement for training programs is a high school diploma. Training programs for EMT-Paramedics lasts between 750 and 2,000 hours.

Earnings: The median annual earnings of EMTs and paramedics were $24,030 in 2002. The middle 50 percent earned between $19,040 and $31,600. The highest paid EMTs work in fire departments.

Key Contacts: For information on EMT careers and training programs, contact your State Emergency Medical Service Director. For general information on EMT's and paramedics, contact:

- National Association of Emergency Medical Technicians: P.O. Box 1400, Clinton, MS 39060-1400. Website: www.naemt.org.

- National Registry of Emergency Medical Technicians: P.O. Box 29233, Columbus, OH 43229. Website: www.nremt.org.

- National Highway Transportation Safety Administration, EMS Division: 400 7th Street, NW, NTS-14, Washington, DC 20590. Website: www.nhtsa.dot.gov/people/injury/ems.

Licensed Practical Nurses

- ⮞ **Annual Earnings:** $31,440
- ⮞ **Education/Training:** One-year training program
- ⮞ **Outlook:** Good – average growth

Employment Outlook: Employment for licensed practical nurses (LPNs) is expected to experience average growth due to long-term health care needs of an aging population, the overall growth in health care needs and services, and the large number of openings due to replacement needs. Licensed practical nurses held 702,000 jobs in 2002, with 28 percent working in hospitals, 26 percent in nursing care facilities, and 12 percent in physicians' offices. Others work in home health care services, employment services, community care facilities for the elderly, public and private educational services, outpatient care centers, and federal, state, and local government agencies. One in five LPNs work part time.

Nature of Work: Licensed practical nurses care for the sick, injured, convalescing, and disabled under the direction of physicians and registered nurses. Most provide basic bedside care – take temperature, blood pressure, pulse, and respiration; treat bedsores; prepare and give injections and enemas; apply dressings; give alcohol rubs and massages; apply ice packs and hot water bottles; insert catheters; feed patients and help them with bathing, dressing, and personal hygiene. Some states allow LPNs to administer prescribed medicines, start intravenous fluids, and help deliver, care for, and feed infants.

Working Conditions: Most LPNs work a 40-hour week, but some work nights, weekends, and holidays. They spend a great deal of time on their feet, helping move patients and equipment. Many LPNs are exposed to caustic chemicals, radiation, and infectious diseases such as AIDS and hepatitis. LPNs in nursing homes and private homes often have heavy workloads and long hours.

Education, Training, Qualifications: Most LPNs complete a one-year state-approved practical nursing program. They must also pass a state licensing examination. Approximately 1,100 state-approved programs are operated by trade, technical and vocational schools; community and junior colleges; and high schools, hospitals, and colleges and universities.

Earnings: In 2002 the median annual earnings of full-time, salaried LPNs were $31,440. The middle 50 percent earned between $26,430 and $37,050. LPNs working in chain nursing homes averaged an annual salary of $23,900. Those working in hospitals and medical centers earned a median annual salary of $30,310.

Key Contacts: For information on practical nursing careers, contact:

- National Association for Practical Nurse Education and Service, Inc.: 8607 2nd Avenue, #404A, Silver Spring, MD 20910. Website: www.napnes.org.

- National League for Nursing: 61 Broadway, New York, NY 10006. Website: www.nln.org.

- National Federation of Licensed Practical Nurses, Inc.: 605 Poole Drive, Garner, NC 27529. Website: www.nflpn.org.

Massage Therapists

◇ **Annual Earnings:** Vary greatly
◇ **Education/Training:** Certificate and on-the-job training
◇ **Outlook:** Excellent

Employment Outlook: Employment of massage therapists, who used to be called masseur and masseuse, is expected to grow faster than average in the coming decade as more and more people recognize the health benefits of massage therapy as well as its role in rehabilitation. Also, registered massage therapists are now covered in most health insurance plans (the massage therapists usually must be referred from another health care provider in order to qualify).

Nature of Work: Message therapists specialize in "bodywork." They use a variety of techniques – from deep manipulation of tissue to the use of heated stones – to relax the body, reduce stress, and improve the physical well-being of patients suffering muscular difficulties. They may offer everything from Swedish massage and Rolfing to acupressure and reflexology to affect all systems of the body, especially muscular, circulatory, lymphatic (immune), and nervous systems. They hand manipulate the soft tissue and joints of the body. Soft tissues include muscle, skin, tendons, and associated facia, ligaments, and joint capsules. The work is often physically challenging and requires a great deal of physical stamina and standing. However, few work 40 hours a week since they work on an hourly basis with clients. Over 92,000 massage therapists were employed in 2002.

Working Conditions: Many massage therapists operate their own businesses or work closely with chiropractors, physical therapists, and physicians in acquiring clients. Since their work tends to be organized into one-hour sessions with individual clients, full-time massage therapists may only work 20 hours a week with clients. They also must spend time on administrative work, which may take another 20 hours a week.

Education, Training, Qualifications: Many massage therapists acquire their skills through on-the-job training or they attend training programs where they learn various massage techniques. Over 25 states currently require licensure, certification, or registration of massage therapists.

Earnings: Annual earnings and hours of massage therapists vary greatly depending on the nature of the practice. Many well-established massage therapists earn in excess of $50,000 a year. Charging clients by the hour, which can range from $20 to $100 an hour, experienced massage therapists may only work with 20 clients a week in one-hour sessions each.

Key Contacts: For information on massage therapists, contact:

- **American Massage Therapy Association:** 820 Davis Street, Suite 100, Evanston, IL 60201-4444. Website: www.amtamassage.org.

- **Commission on Massage Therapy Accreditation:** 1007 Church Street, Suite 302, Evanston, IL 60201. Website: www.comta.org.

- **National Certification Board for Therapeutic Massage and Body-work:** 8201 Greensboro Drive, Suite 300, McLean, VA 22102. Website: www.ncbtmb.com.

Medical Assistants

⇨ **Annual Earnings:** $23,940
⇨ **Education/Training:** 1-2 year training program
⇨ **Outlook:** Excellent – faster than average growth

Employment Outlook: This will be one of the fastest growing occupations in the decade ahead. Growth in job opportunities reflects the overall expansion of the health care industry in response to an aging population as well as major advances in medical technology. Employment growth will be driven by the increase in the number of group practices, clinics, and other health care facilities that need a high proportion of support personnel, particularly the flexible medical assistant who can handle both administrative and clinical duties. Medical assistants work primarily in outpatient settings, which are expected to exhibit much faster than average growth.

Nature of Work: Medical assistants help physicians examine and treat patients and conduct routine office tasks. They perform numerous clerical duties, from answering telephones and greeting patients to completing insurance forms and scheduling appointments. Many arrange examining room instruments and equipment, handle supplies, and maintain waiting and examining rooms. Medical assistants held nearly 365,000 jobs in 2002. Sixty percent worked in physicians' offices; nearly 14 percent worked in public and private hospitals, including inpatient and outpatient facilities; and almost 10 percent worked in offices of other health practitioners, such as chiropractors and podiatrists. The remainder worked in outpatient care centers, public and private educational services, other ambulatory health care services, state and local government agencies, medical and diagnostic laboratories, nursing care facilities, and employment services.

Working Conditions: Medical assistants work a regular 40-hour week in medical offices. They constantly interact with patients and perform multiple responsibilities. Some work part time, evenings, or weekends.

Education, Training, Qualifications: Until recently, this was one of the few health occupations open to individuals with little formal training. Applicants normally needed a high school diploma or equivalent and were given on-the-job training. High school courses in mathematics, health, biology, typing, bookkeeping, computers, and office skills were helpful. However, most employers are now hiring graduates of formal programs in medical assisting, which are offered in vocational-technical high schools, postsecondary vocational schools, and community and junior colleges. Most of these programs last one to two years and result in a certificate, diploma, or associate degree.

Earnings: Earnings vary widely depending on experience, skill level, and location. Median annual earnings of medical assistants were $23,940 in 2002. The middle 50 percent earned between $20,260 and $28,410. The median annual earnings for medical assistants working in general medical and surgical hospitals were $24,460; offices of physicians, $24,260; outpatient care centers, $23,980; other ambulatory health care services, $23,440; and offices of other health practitioners, $21,620.

Key Contacts: For information on educational programs and careers related to medical assistant, contact:

- **American Association of Medical Assistants:** 20 N. Wacker Drive, Suite 1575, Chicago, IL 60606-2903. Website: www.aama-ntl.org.

- **American Society of Podiatric Medical Assistants:** 2124 S. Austin Blvd., Cicero, IL 60804. Website: www.aspma.org.

- **Registered Medical Assistants of American Medical Technologists:** 710 Higgins Road, Park Ridge, IL 60068-5765.

- **Accrediting Bureau of Health Education Schools:** 7777 Leesburg Pike, Suite 314 North, Falls Church, VA 22043. Website: www.abhes.org.

- Joint Commission on Allied Health Personnel in Ophthalmology: 2025 Woodlane Drive, St. Paul, MN 55125-2998. Website: www. jcahpo.org.

Medical Laboratory Technicians

- ➪ **Annual Earnings:** $29,040
- ➪ **Education/Training:** Associate degree
- ➪ **Outlook:** Excellent

Employment Outlook: Employment opportunities for medical laboratory technicians is expected to be excellent in the decade ahead as the number of laboratory tests increases with both population growth and the development of new types of tests. While hospitals continue to be the major employer of medical laboratory technicians, employment is expected to grow faster in medical and diagnostic laboratories, offices of physicians, and other ambulatory health care services, including blood and organ banks.

Nature of Work: Medical laboratory technicians may prepare specimens and operate automated analyzers, or they may perform manual tests in accordance with detailed instructions of clinical laboratory technologists. Like technologists, they may work in several areas of the clinical laboratory or specialize in just one. Histotechnicians cut and stain tissue specimens for microscopic examination by pathologists, and phlebotomists collect blood samples. They usually work under the supervision of medical and clinical laboratory technologists or laboratory managers.

Working Conditions: Hours and working conditions vary depending on the size and type of employment setting. In large hospitals or in independent laboratories that operate continuously, personnel usually work the day, evening, or night shift and may work weekends and holidays. In many facilities, laboratory personnel are on call several nights a week or on weekends, in case of an emergency.

Education, Training, Qualifications: Medical laboratory technicians usually have either an associate degree from a community or junior college or a certificate from a hospital, a vocational or technical school, or one of the U.S. Armed Forces. A few technicians learn their skills on the job.

Earnings: Median annual earnings of medical and clinical laboratory technicians were $29,040 in 2002. The middle 50 percent earned between

$23,310 and $35,840. Median annual earnings in the industries employing the largest numbers of medical and clinical laboratory technicians in 2002 were $30,500 for general medical and surgical hospitals; $30,350 for colleges, universities, and professional schools; $27,820 for offices of physicians; $27,550 for medical and diagnostic laboratories; and $26,710 for other ambulatory health care services.

Key Contacts: For information on educational programs and careers related to medical laboratory technicians, contact:

- **American Association of Bioanalysts, Board of Registry:** 917 Locust Street, Suite 1100, St. Louis, MO 63101. Website: www.aab. org.

- **American Society for Clinical Pathology, Board of Registry:** 2100 West Harrison Street, Chicago, IL 60612. Website: www.ascp.org/bor.

- **National Credentialing Agency for Laboratory Personnel:** P.O. Box 15945-289, Lenexa, KS 66285. Website: www.nca-info.org.

- **American Association of Blood Banks:** 8101 Glenbrook Road, Bethesda, MD 20814-2749. Website: www.aabb.org.

- **American Society for Clinical Laboratory Science:** 6701 Democracy Blvd., Suite 300, Bethesda, MD 20817. Website: www.ascls.org.

- **American Society for Clinical Pathology:** 2100 West Harrison Street, Chicago, IL 60612. Website: www.ascp.org.

- **American Society for Cytopathology:** 400 West 9th Street, Suite 201, Wilmington, DE 19801. Website: www.cytopathology.org.

- **Clinical Laboratory Management Association:** 989 Old Eagle School Road, Wayne, PA 19087. Website: www.clma.org.

Medical Records and Health Information Technicians

ᗌ **Annual Earnings:** $23,890
ᗌ **Education/Training:** Associate degree
ᗌ **Outlook:** Excellent

Employment Outlook: This occupational field should experience excellent job growth due to the rapid growth in the number of medical tests, treatments, and procedures that will be increasingly scrutinized by third-party payers, regulators, courts, and consumers.

Nature of Work: Medical records and health information technicians organize and evaluate medical records for completeness and accuracy. They ensure that medical charts are complete and all forms are properly identified, coded properly, signed, and on file. Much of this work is computerized and involves learning information management programs and regularly communicating with physicians and other health care professionals to clarify diagnoses or to obtain additional information. Technicians also use computer programs to tabulate and analyze data to help improve patient care, to control costs, for use in legal actions, in response to surveys, or for use in research studies.

Working Conditions: Most medical record technicians work a 40-hour week in pleasant and comfortable office settings. In hospitals, where many health information departments operate 24 hours a day, seven days a week, technicians may work day, evening, and night shifts. Their jobs require accuracy, attention to detail, and concentration. Technicians who work at computer monitors for prolonged periods must guard against eyestrain and muscle pain.

Education, Training, Qualifications: Medical records and health information technicians normally complete a two-year associate degree program at a community or junior college. Some receive training through an Independent Study Program in Medical Record Technology offered by the American Medical Record Association. Hospitals occasionally adva nce promising health information clerks with two to four years work experience to jobs as medical records and health information technicians. Most employers prefer hiring Accredited Record Technicians (ART), who are accredited by passing a written examination offered by the American Medical Record Association.

Earnings: The median annual earnings of medical records and health information technicians were $23,890 in 2002. The middle 50 percent earned between $19,550 and $30,600. The median annual earnings in industries employing the largest numbers of medical records and health information technicians in 2002 were $25,160 in nursing care facilities; $24,910 in general medical and surgical hospitals; $22,380 in outpatient care centers; and $21,320 in offices of physicians.

Key Contacts: For more information on careers in medical records and health information technology, including the Independent Study Program, contact:

- **American Medical Association:** Commission on Allied Health Education & Accreditation, 515 N. State St., Chicago, IL 60610. Website: www.ama-assn.org.

- **American Health Information Management Association:** 233 N. Michigan Avenue, Suite 2150, Chicago, IL 60601-5800. Website: www.ahima.org.

Medical Secretaries

⮩ **Annual Earnings:** $26,690
⮩ **Education/Training:** Certificate or short-term training
⮩ **Outlook:** Good

Employment Outlook: The growth in opportunities for medical secretaries is expected to slow in the coming decade as more and more traditional secretarial functions are dispersed to support personnel and as typing and filing duties are replaced with more computer and technical work. Nonetheless, the growth in medical secretary jobs will be average for most jobs.

Nature of Work: Medical secretaries perform administrative and clerical work in medical offices, hospitals, and physicians' offices. They are responsible for a wide variety of functions, from answering phone calls, handling correspondence, and scheduling appointments to billing patients, completing insurance forms, arranging hospital admissions, and maintaining paper and electronic files. Medical secretaries need to be proficient in the use of office equipment (fax machines, photocopiers, telephone systems, computers) and a variety of software programs (word processing, spreadsheet, database management).

Working Conditions: Medical secretaries work in a variety of modern office settings which are often very busy, stressful, and require a great deal of multitasking. The job involves sitting for long periods. Much of the time is spent typing in front of a computer terminal, which may result in problems relating to eyestrain, stress, and repetitive motion, such as carpal tunnel syndrome. Approximately 340,000 individuals are employed as medical secretaries in the United States.

Education, Training, Qualifications: While certification and licences are not required for medical secretaries, individuals who become a Certified Professional Secretary (CPS) have a distinct advantage in the medical job market. Many medical secretaries have some postsecondary education and technical training.

Earnings: Median annual earnings for medical secretaries in 2002 were $26,690. The middle 50 percent earned from $21,090 to $31,070.

Key Contacts: For information on training programs, certification, and opportunities for medical secretaries, contact:

- **International Association of Administrative Professionals:** P.O. Box 20404, 10502 NW Ambassador Drive, Kansas City, MO 64195-0404. Website: www.iaap-hq.org.

- **All Allied Health Schools:** All Star Directories, Inc., 123 NW 36th Street, Suite 220, Seattle, WA 98107. Website: www.allalliedhealth schools.com/faqs/medical_secretary.php.

Medical Transcriptionists

- ➪ **Annual Earnings:** $27,200
- ➪ **Education/Training:** Certificate or associate degree
- ➪ **Outlook:** Good

Employment Outlook: Employment of medical transcriptionists is expected to grow faster than the average for all occupations in the decade ahead. Demand for medical transcription service will be in response to a growing and aging population requiring more and more medical tests, treatments, and procedures that require documentation. Demand also will increase for electronic documentation that can be easily shared among providers, third-party payers, regulators, and consumers. While some of these jobs can be offshored to countries such as India, demand for domestic medical transcriptionists should continue to be strong, especially in offices of physicians or other health practitioners in large group practices. Voice recognition technology is not expected to have much impact on the overall employment of medical transcriptionists.

Nature of Work: Medical transcriptionists held approximately 101,000 jobs in 2002. They listen to dictated recordings made by physicians and other health care professionals and transcribe them into medical reports, correspondence, and other administrative material. The usually listen to recordings on a headset, using a foot pedal to pause the recording when necessary, and key the text into a personal computer or word processor, editing as necessary for grammar and clarity. The documents they produce include discharge summaries, history and physical examination reports, operative reports, consultation reports, autopsy reports, diagnostic imaging studies, process notes, and referral letters. Medical transcriptionists return transcribed documents of the physicians or other health care professionals who dictated them for review and signature, or correction. These documents eventually become part of patients' permanent files.

Working Conditions: The majority of medical transcriptionists work in comfortable settings, such as hospitals, physicians' offices, transcription service offices, clinics, laboratories, medical libraries, government medical facilities, or at home. Work in this occupation presents hazards from sitting in the same position for long periods, and workers can suffer wrist, back, neck, or eye problems due to strain and risk repetitive motion injuries such as carpal tunnel syndrome. The pressure to be accurate and productive also can be stressful. Many medical transcriptionists work a standard 40-hour week.

Education, Training, Qualifications: Employers prefer to hire transcriptionists who have completed postsecondary training in medical transcription, which is offered by many vocational schools, community colleges, and distance-learning programs. Completion of a two-year associate degree or one-year certificate programs is highly recommended but not always required. The American Association for Medical Transcription (AAMT) awards the voluntary designation of Certified Medical Transcriptionist (CMT) to those who earn passing scores on written and practical examinations. However, many medical transcriptionists are given on-the-job training or have other medical-related experience.

Earnings: Medical transcriptionists had median hourly earnings of $13.05, or $27,200 median annual earnings in 2002. The middle 50 percent earned between $10.87 and $15.63 per hour. Median hourly earnings in the industries employing the largest numbers of medical transcriptionists in 2002 were $13.20 in general medical and surgical hospitals; $13.00 in offices of physicians; and $12.42 in business support services.

Key Contacts: For more information on careers for medical transcriptionists, send a self-addressed, stamped envelope to:

- **American Association for Medical Transcription:** 100 Sycamore Avenue, Modesto, CA 95354-0550. Website: www.aamt.org.

Nuclear Medicine Technologists

⇨ **Annual Earnings:** $47,750
⇨ **Education/Training:** Certificate, associate degree, or BS
⇨ **Outlook:** Excellent

Employment Outlook: Employment of nuclear medicine technologists is expected to grow faster than the average for all occupations in the coming decade. This growth is in respond to an increase in the number of middle-aged and older persons, who are the primary users of diagnostic procedures, including nuclear medicine tests. However, the number of openings each year will be relatively low because the occupation is small.

Nature of Work: Nuclear medicine technologists operate cameras that detect and map the radioactive drug in a patient's body to create diagnostic images. After explaining test procedures to patients, technologists prepare a dosage of the radiopharmaceutical and administer it by mouth, injection, or other means. They position patients and start a gamma scintillation camera, or "scan," which creates images of the distribution of a radiopharmaceutical as it localizes in, and emits signals from, the patient's body. The images are produced on a computer screen or on film for a physician to interpret. Technologists keep patient records and record the amount and type of radionuclides received, used, and discarded. Nuclear medicine technologists also perform radioimmunoassay studies that assess the behavior of a radioactive substance inside the body.

Working Conditions: Nuclear medicine technologists generally work a 40-hour week. Some work evening or weekend hours in departments that operate on an extended schedule as well as have opportunities for part-time and shift work. Most people working in this field are on their feet much of the day and may lift or turn disabled patients. Although the potential for radiation exposure exists in this field, it is kept to a minimum by the use of shielded syringes, gloves, and other protective devices.

Education, Training, Qualifications: Many employers and an increasing number of states require certification or licensure of nuclear medicine technologists. Training programs range in length from one to four years and lead to a certificate, associate degree, or bachelor's degree. Certificate programs are offered in hospitals. One-year certificate programs are for health professionals – especially radiologic technologists and diagnostic medical sonographers – who wish to specialize in nuclear medicine. The Joint Review Committee on Education Programs in Nuclear Medicine Technology accredits most formal training programs in nuclear medicine technology. In 2002, there were 92 accredited programs in the continental United States and Puerto Rico.

Earnings: Compared to many other medicine fields for people without a four-year degree, this one is relatively well compensated. Median annual earnings of nuclear medicine technologists were $48,750 in 2002. The middle 50 percent earned between $41,460 and $57,200. Median annual earnings of nuclear medicine technologists in 2002 were $48,210 in general medical and surgical hospitals.

Key Contacts: For information on a career as a nuclear medicine technologists, contact:

- **Society of Nuclear Medicine:** 1850 Samuel Morse Drive, Reston, VA 20190-5316. Website: www.snm.org.

- **American Society of Radiologic Technologists:** 15000 Central Avenue, SE, Albuquerque, NM 87123-3917. Website: www.asrt.org.

For information on accredited programs and certification in nuclear medicine technology, contact:

- **Joint Review Committee on Educational Programs in Nuclear Medicine Technology:** PMB #418, #1 2nd Avenue East, Suite C, Polson, MT 59860-2107. Website: www.jrcnmt.org.

- **American Registry of Radiologic Technologists:** 1255 Northland Drive, St. Paul, MN 55120-1155. Website: www.arrt.org.

■ **Nuclear Medicine Technology Certification Board:** 2970 Clairmont Road, Suite 935, Atlanta, GA 30329. Website: www.nmtch.org.

Nursing, Psychiatric, and Home Health Aides

⇨ **Earnings:** $20,000
⇨ **Education/Training:** Very minimal
⇨ **Outlook:** Excellent – faster than average growth

Employment Outlook: Numerous job openings for nursing, psychiatric, and home health aides are expected in the decade ahead due to a combination of fast employment growth and high replacement needs. These increases reflect greater emphasis on rehabilitation and long-term care for a rapidly growing population aged 75 years old and older. Many also will require mental health services. High replacement needs reflect modest entry requirements, low pay, high physical and emotional demands, and lack of advancement opportunities. In 2002 nearly 1.7 million people held jobs in these positions.

Nature of Work: Nursing, psychiatric, and home health aides help care for physically or mentally ill, injured, disabled, or infirm individuals confined to hospitals, nursing or residential care facilities, and mental health settings. Nursing aides, also known as nursing assistants or hospital attendants, answer patients' call bells, deliver messages, serve meals, make beds, and feed, dress, and bathe patients. Psychiatric aides – also known as mental health assistants, psychiatric nursing assistants, or ward attendants – help patients dress, bathe, groom, eat, socialize, and engage in educational and recreational activities.

Working Conditions: Aides normally work a five-day, 40-hour week, although many work evenings, nights, weekends, and holidays, and part-time. Much of their work involves standing and helping patients move, stand, and walk. Nursing aides often have unpleasant duties – empty bed pans, change soiled bed linens, and care for disoriented and irritable patients. Psychiatric aides are often confronted with violent patients.

Education, Training, and Qualifications: While these are relatively low paying, very demanding, and high turnover positions, they do offer young people and those without a high school diploma or previous work experience entry into the work world. Only a few employers require some training or experience. Hospitals may require experience as a nursing aide or home health aide. Nursing care facilities often hire inexperienced workers who must complete a minimum of 75 hours of mandatory training and pass a competency evaluation program within four months of their employment. Aides who complete the program are certified and placed on the state registry of nursing aides. Most health facilities provide on-the-job training.

Earnings: These are generally low paying jobs with little or no advancement opportunities. Median annual earnings of full-time nursing aides, orderlies, and attendants were $20,000 in 2002. The middle 50 percent earned between $16,800 and $23,700. The median earnings of home health aides were $18,100. The middle 50 percent earned between $15,700 and $21,600. The median earnings of psychiatric aides were $23,000. The middle 50 percent earned between $18,700 and $28,600.

Key Contacts: For information on home health aides, contact:

- **National Association for Home Care and Hospice:** 228 7th Street, SE, Washington, DC 20003. Website: www.nahc.org.

Orthotic and Prosthetic Technicians

- ⇨ **Annual Earnings:** $36,400
- ⇨ **Education/Training:** Certificate, associate degree, or BS
- ⇨ **Outlook:** Excellent

Employment Outlook: Opportunities for orthotic and prosthetic technicians are expected to grow faster than average in the coming decade. This increase is due to a growing health care industry, new and improved technologies, and an aging population which is expected to experience most amputations. Indeed, a study by the National Commission on Prosthetic Education expects the number of people requiring prosthetic devices will increase by nearly 50 percent by the year 2020. Technological improvements in orthotic and prosthetic devices also will enable more people with difficult disabilities to be fitted for these devices who may not been candidates for such devices in the past.

Nature of Work: Orthotic and prosthetic technicians work closely with orthotists and prosthetists in building, fitting, repairing, and maintaining orthotic and prosthetic devises. They assist in rehabilitating patients with disabling conditions of limbs and spine or with partial or total absence of limbs by fitting and preparing orthopedic braces and prostheses. Orthotic devises consist of braces, callipers, and related appliances for supporting weak joints or muscles or for correcting physical defects, such as spinal deformities and injuries. Prosthetic devices consist of artificial limbs and plastic cosmetic devices that are designed and fitted to best meet the mobility needs of patients. In addition to making models of limbs, technicians spend a great deal of time building these devices.

Working Conditions: Most full-time orthotic and prosthetic technicians with work a 40-hour week. They work in laboratories under the guidance of professional prosthetists and orthotists. They use a variety of tools and machinery as well as work with plastic, wood, and metal to make and repair devises. The jobs require a great deal of hand work, good eyesight, and strong hand-eye coordination.

Education, Training, Qualifications: While no licensing is required for orthotic and prosthetic technicians, the American Board for Certification in Orthotics and Prosthetics (ABC) offers a program for voluntary certification. Individuals with certification are offered better opportunities and pay in these fields. Many individuals complete one- to two-year certification programs or acquire a two-year associate degree.

Earnings: Annual earnings in these fields vary considerably depending on the type of certification and experience. ABC certified practitioners with less than two years experience earn nearly $50,000 a year. BOC certified practitioners with similar experience average less than $40,000 a year.

Key Contacts: For more information on career opportunities and certification for orthotic and prosthetic technicians, contact:

- **American Board for Certification in Orthotics and Prosthetics:** 330 John Carlyle Street, Suite 210, Alexandria, VA 22314. Website: www.abcop.org.

- **American Orthotic and Prosthetic Association:** 330 John Carlyle Street, Suite 210, Alexandria, VA 22314. Website: www.abcop.org.

- **American Academy of Orthotists and Prosthetists:** 526 King Street, Suite 201, Alexandria, VA 22314. Website: www.oandp.org.

- International Association of Orthotics and Prosthetics: 5613 Powell Grove Drive, Midlothian, VA 23112. Website: www.iaop.org.

Pedorthists

⇨ **Annual Earnings:** $30,700
⇨ **Education/Training:** Certificate or associate degree
⇨ **Outlook:** Excellent

Employment Outlook: Pedorthists should find ample job opportunities in the decade ahead given the increased emphasis on foot care in sports and fitness and an aging population with chronic foot problems related to arthritis and bone diseases.

Nature of Work: Pedorthists are board-certified foot care professionals and therapists who design, fabricate, fit, construct, and modify shoes and foot orthotic devices prescribed by physicians, who diagnose conditions. They examine patients' feet, make adjustments to footwear, or design new footwear appropriate for solving a variety of foot-related problems of patients. They specialize in good footwear and the need to modify footwear to improve the comfort of patients without resorting to surgical procedures. They often treat patients experiencing a variety of foot-related problems – plantar fasciitis (pain in heal or arch), metatarsalgia (pain in the ball of the foot), diabetes, arthritis, pes planus (flat feet), and pes cavus (high arches). Many pedorthists specialize in a particular area, such as amputations, arthritis, geriatrics, pediatrics, sports-related injuries, foot deformities, or congenital deformities.

Working Conditions: Full-time pedorthists work a 40-hour week in a variety of settings – shoe stores, clinics, and hospitals. Many work in offices of physicians who specialize in foot-related problems and injuries. They have extensive patient contact and work closely with physicians and other health care professionals. The job requires a great deal of kneeling and standing and the use of the hands.

Education, Training, Qualifications: While some people enter this field with little or no training and experience, more and more pedorthists are certified through one- to two-year training programs. Several states require pedorthists to be licensed. The Board for Certification in Pedorthics provides voluntary certification.

Earnings: Entry-level workers in this field make between $22,000 and $30,000 a year. Certified and experienced pedorthists earn between $32,000 and $37,000 a year. Some make up to $60,000 a year.

Key Contacts: For information on careers and certification for pedorthists, contact:

- **Board for Certification in Pedorthics:** 2517 Eastlake Avenue E, Suite 200, Seattle, WA 98102. Website: www.cpeds.org.

- **Pedorthic Footwear Association:** 7150 Columbia Gateway Drive, Suite G, Columbia, MD 21046. Website: www.pedorthics.org.

Pharmacy Technicians

- ➭ **Annual Earnings:** $22,300
- ➭ **Education/Training:** On-the-job training
- ➭ **Outlook:** Good

Employment Outlook: Good job opportunities are expected for full-time and part-time work, especially for technicians with formal training or previous experience. Job openings for pharmacy technicians will result from the expansion of retail pharmacies and other employment settings, and from the need to replace workers who transfer to other occupations or leave the labor force.

Nature of Work: Pharmacy technicians help licensed pharmacists provide medication and other health care products to patients. Technicians usually perform routine tasks to help prepare prescribed medication for patients, such as counting tablets and labeling bottles. They refer any questions regarding prescriptions, drug information, or health matters to a pharmacist. In hospitals, nursing homes, and assisted-living facilities, technicians have added responsibilities. They read patient charts and prepare and deliver the medicine to the patient. Technicians may also assemble a 24-hour supply of medicine for every patient.

Pharmacy technicians held about 211,000 jobs in 2002. Two-thirds of all jobs were in retail pharmacies, either independently owned or part of a drugstore chain, grocery store, department store, or mass retailer. About 22 percent were in hospitals and a small portion was in mail order and Internet pharmacies, clinics, pharmaceutical wholesalers, and the federal government.

Working Conditions: Pharmacy technicians work in clean, organized, well-lighted, and well-ventilated areas. Most of their workday is spent on their feet. Technicians work the same hours that pharmacists work. These may include evenings, nights, weekends, and holidays. Because some hospital and retail pharmacies are open 24 hours a day, technicians may work varying shifts.

Education, Training, Qualifications: Although most pharmacy technicians receive informal on-the-job training, employers favor those who have completed formal training and certification. However, there are few state and no federal requirements for formal training or certification of pharmacy technicians. In addition to the military, some hospitals, proprietary schools, vocational or technical colleges, and community colleges offer formal education programs. Certified technicians must be recertified every two years. Technicians must complete 20 contact hours of pharmacy-related topics within the two-year certification period to become eligible for recertification. Teamwork is very important because technicians are often required to work with pharmacists, aides, and other technicians.

Earnings: Median hourly earnings of pharmacy technicians in 2002 were $10.70. The middle 50 percent earned between $8.74 and $13.19. The highest paid technicians worked for general medical and surgical hospitals, earning a median hourly rate of $12.32. Technicians in grocery stores earned $11.34 per hour. Technicians with drugs and druggists' sundries merchant wholesalers earned $10.60 per hour. Those with health and personal care stores earned $9.70 per hour, and those with department stores earned $9.69 per hour.

Key Contacts: For information on certification and training programs, contact:

- **Pharmacy Technician Certification Board:** 2215 Constitution Avenue, NW, Washington, DC 20037-2985. Website: www.ptcb.org.

- **American Society of Health-System Pharmacists:** 7272 Wisconsin Avenue, Bethesda, MD 20814. Website: www.ashp.org.

Phlebotomy Technicians

○ **Annual Earnings:** $22,000
○ **Education/Training:** Certificate
○ **Outlook:** Good

Employment Outlook: Employment for phlebotomy technicians should steadily increase in the decade ahead as the growing number of elderly require more and more health care services requiring blood testing. An above average demand for such professionals should increase in hospitals.

Nature of Work: Phlebotomy technicians specialize in drawing blood from patients or donors. They primarily work in hospitals, clinics, testing labs, blood banks, and physicians' offices. Their work involves screening patients or donors, verifying identification, preparing them for the procedure, drawing blood, and then labeling, storing, and/or shipping blood for analysis. Technicians also are prepared to deal with any adverse reactions to these procedures, such as nausea or fainting.

Working Conditions: Phlebotomy technicians work in offices, hospitals, and laboratory settings. Most full-time phlebotomy technicians work a 40-hour week. Since they work with blood that occasionally may be contaminated, especially from HIV-positive patients, they are trained to take special precautions in avoiding direct contact with patients' blood and in handling and testing blood samples.

Education, Training, Qualifications: Several states require the certification and licensing of phlebotomy technicians. Certification programs lasting less than one year are sponsored by hospitals and community colleges.

Earnings: These are relatively low paying jobs where the average phlebotomy technician earns around $22,000 a year. Most are paid on an hourly basis, earning from $9.00 to $12.00 per hour.

Key Contacts: For information on careers and certification for phlebotomy technicians, contact:

■ **American Association of Blood Banks:** 8101 Glenbrook Road, Bethesda, MD 20814-2749. Website: www.aabb.org.

- **American Medical Technologists:** 710 Higgins Road, Park Ridge, IL 60068-5765. Website: www.amt1.com.

- **American Society of Phlebotomy Technicians:** P.O. Box 1831, Hickory, NC 28603. Website: www.aspt.org.

- **National Accrediting Agency for Clinical Laboratory Sciences:** 8410 West Bryn Mawr Avenue, Suite 670, Chicago, IL 60631. Website: www. naacls.org.

Physical Therapy Assistants and Aides

↪ **Annual Earnings:** $36,080
↪ **Education/Training:** On-the-job training to associate degree
↪ **Outlook:** Excellent

Employment Outlook: Employment of physical therapy assistants is expected to grow much faster than average in the coming decade. This is due in part to the growing number of elderly patients experiencing chronic and debilitating conditions who require therapeutic services as well as the growing number of heart attack and stroke victims who require cardiac and physical rehabilitation. Physical therapists are expected to increasingly use assistants to reduce the cost of physical therapy services.

Nature of Work: Physical therapist assistants and aides perform components of physical therapy procedures and related tasks selected by a supervising physical therapist. They assist physical therapists in providing services that help improve mobility, relieve pain, and prevent or limit permanent physical disabilities of patients suffering from injuries or disease. Patients include accident victims and individuals with disabling conditions, such as low-back pain, arthritis, heart disease, fractures, head injuries, and cerebral palsy. Physical therapist assistants perform a variety of services that may include exercises, massages, electrical stimulation, paraffin baths, hot and cold packs, traction, and ultrasound. Physical therapist assistants record the patient's responses to treatment and report the outcome of each treatment to the physical therapist. Physical therapist aides help make therapy sessions productive, under the direct supervision of a physical therapist or physical therapist assistant. They usually are responsible for keeping the treatment area clean and organized and for preparing for each patient's therapy. Because they are not licensed, aides do not preform the clinical tasks of a physical therapist assistant.

Working Conditions: The hours and days that physical therapist assistants and aides work vary with the facility and whether they are full- or part-time employees. Many outpatient physical therapy offices and clinics have evening and weekend hours that coincide with patients' personal schedules. Since these professionals often provide physical assistance to patients, they may need to lift patients. Constant kneeling, stooping, and standing for long periods also are part of the job.

Education, Training, Qualifications: Physical therapist aides are trained on the job, but physical therapist assistants typically earn an associate degree from an accredited physical therapist assistant program. Over 40 states require licensure or registration of physical therapist assistants. Nearly 250 accredited physical therapist assistant programs operate in the United States. Most physical therapist aides receive on-the-job training.

Earnings: Median annual earnings of physical therapist assistants were $36,080 in 2002. The middle 50 percent earned between $30,260 and $42,780. Median annual earnings of physical therapist aides were $20,670 in 2002. The middle 50 percent earned between $17,430 and $24,560. Physical therapist assistants and aides working in medical and surgical hospitals tend to earn slightly more than those working elsewhere.

Key Contacts: For career information on physical therapist assistants and a list of schools offering accredited programs, contact:

- **American Physical Therapy Association:** 1111 North Fairfax Street, Alexandria, VA 22314-1488. Website: www.apta.org.

Occupational Therapist Assistants and Aides

⇨ **Earnings:** $36,660
⇨ **Education/Training:** Associate degree or certificate
⇨ **Outlook:** Excellent – much faster than average

Employment Outlook: Occupational therapy is one of the fastest growing occupations that also offers excellent compensation. The demand for such services is largely driven by an increasing number of middle-aged and elderly individuals requiring therapeutic services. In 2002 occupational therapists and aides occupied 27,000 jobs (18,000 occupational therapist assistants and 8,300 occupational therapist aides).

Nature of Work: Occupational therapists work under the direction of occupational therapists. They provide rehabilitative services to persons with mental, physical, emotional, or developmental impairments. They help these individuals lead more independent, productive, and satisfying lives. They assist clients with all types of activities, from using a computer to taking care of daily needs such as dressing, cooking, and eating. Occupational therapist aides usually prepare materials and assemble equipment used during treatment. They are responsible for several clerical tasks, including scheduling appointments, answering the telephone, restocking or ordering depleted supplies, and filling out insurance forms or other paperwork. Aides are not licensed. Occupational therapists and aides often work with individuals in a particular age group or those with a specific type of disability.

Working Conditions: Occupational therapists and aides working in hospitals and other health care and community settings usually put in a 40-hour workweek. About one-third of occupational therapists work part-time. The work can be very tiring since therapists are on their feet much of the time and are often lifting and moving clients and equipment. Occupational therapists need patience and strong interpersonal skills in working with clients.

Education, Training, Qualifications: Occupational therapist assistants normally need an associate degree or a certificate from an accredited community college or technical school. Occupational therapist aides usually receive most of their training on the job.

Earnings: The mediam annual earnings for full-time salaried occupational therapist assistants in 2002 were $36,660. The middle 50 percent earned between $31,090 and $43,030. The median annual earnings of occupational therapist aides were $22,040 in 2002. The middle 50 percent earned between $18,040 and $29,130.

Key Contacts: For information on opportunities as an occupational therapist assistant or aide, contact:

- **American Occupational Therapy Association:** 4720 Montgomery Lane, Bethesda, MD 20824-1220. Website: www.aota.org.

Radiologic Technologists and Technicians

⇨ **Annual Earnings:** $38,970
⇨ **Education/Training:** Associate degree
⇨ **Outlook:** Excellent

Employment Outlook: Employment opportunities for radiologic technologists and technicians should be excellent in the decade ahead as demand for these positions increases. Increased demand should occur as the population grows and ages and places increased demand on diagnostic imaging and therapeutic technology. Radiologic technologists who also are experienced in more complex diagnostic imaging procedures, such as CT or MRI, will have better employment opportunities, as employers seek to control costs by using multi-skilled employees. Radiologic technologists and technicians held nearly 174,000 jobs in 2002.

Nature of Work: Radiologic technologists perform a variety of jobs related to the use of x-ray equipment. Radiographers produce x-ray films (radiographs) of parts of the human body for use in diagnosing medical problems. Radiation therapy technologists prepare cancer patients for treatment and administer prescribed doses of ionizing radiation to specific body parts. Radiographers position radiographic equipment at the correct angle and height over the appropriate area of a patient's body. Experienced radiographers may perform more complex imaging procedures. Sonographers, also known as ultrasound technologists, use non-ionizing, ultrasound equipment to transmit high frequency sound waves into patients' bodies to form images for diagnostic purposes.

Working Conditions: Most radiologic technologists work a 40-hour week. They spend a great deal of time on their feet and may lift or turn disabled patients. Although radiation hazards exist in this occupation, they are minimized by the use of lead aprons, gloves, and other shielding devices, as well as by instruments monitoring radiation exposure.

Education, Training, Qualifications: Most radiological technologists attend one- to four- year training programs offered in hospitals, colleges and universities, vocational-technical institutes, and the Armed Forces. One-year certificate programs are available for experienced radiographers or individuals from other health occupations, such as medical technologists and registered nurses, who want to change fields or specialize in CT or MRI. Nearly 40 states require radiographers and radiation therapy technologists to be licensed.

Earnings: The median annual earnings for full-time radiologic technologists in 2002 were $38,970. The middle 50 percent earned between $32,370 and $46,510. Radiological technologists and technicians in medical and diagnostic laboratories earned on average $42,470; those in general and medical and surgical hospitals earned $39,580; and those in offices of physicians averaged $36,490.

Key Contacts: For information on opportunities for radiologic technologists, contact:

- **American Healthcare Radiology Administrators**: 490B Boston Post Road #101, Sudbury, MA 01776. Tel, 978-443-7591. Website: www. ahraonline.org.

- **American Society of Radiologic Technologists**: 15000 Central Ave. SE, Albuquerque, NM 87123-3917. Tel. 800-444-2778. Website: www.asrt.org.

- **American Registry of Radiologic Technologists**: 1255 Northland Drive, St. Paul, MN 55120-1155. Website: www.arrt.org.

- **Society of Diagnostic Medical Sonography**: 2745 Dallas Parkway, Suite 350, Plano, TX 75093-8730. Website: www.sdms.org.

Recreational Therapists

- ⇨ **Annual Earnings:** $30,540
- ⇨ **Education/Training:** Associate to bachelor's degree
- ⇨ **Outlook:** Slower than average growth but promising

Employment Outlook: Employment opportunities for recreational therapists are projected to be slower than average for the decade ahead. Employment will grow slightly faster than the occupation as a whole in nursing care facilities, which employ the largest number of recreational therapists. Employment is expected to decline in hospitals as services shift to outpatient settings and employers emphasize cost containment. Fast employment growth is expected in the residential and outpatient settings that serve disabled persons, the elderly, or those diagnosed with mental retardation, mental illness, or substance abuse problems. Recreational therapists held 27,000 jobs in 2002.

Nature of Work: Recreational therapists, also known as therapeutic recreation specialists, provide a variety of treatment services to individuals with illnesses or disabilities. These include the use of arts and crafts, animals, sports, games, dance and movement, drama, music, and community outings to help reduce depression, stress, and anxiety and to build confidence and independence.

Working Conditions: Recreational therapists work in a variety of settings – hospitals, rehabilitation centers, park and recreation departments, special education programs of school districts, and programs for older adults and people with disabilities. Their work usually takes place in special activity rooms and may involve travel to parks, playgrounds, swimming pools, restaurants, and theaters. Therapists often lift and carry equipment, as well as lead recreational activities. Community-based recreational therapists may work in park and recreation departments, special-education programs for school districts, or programs for older adults and people with disabilities.

Education, Training, Qualifications: The basic entry-level requirement for recreational therapists is a bachelor's degree in therapeutic recreation. However, paraprofessional positions require an associate degree in recreational therapy or a health care related field. An associate degree in recreational therapy; training in art, drama, or music therapy; or qualifying work experience may be sufficient for activity director positions in nursing homes. Most employers want to hire individuals who are certified therapeutic recreation specialists (CTRS). Such individuals must have a bachelor's degree, pass a written certification examination, and complete an internship of at least 360 hours under the supervision of a certified therapeutic recreation specialist.

Earnings: The average annual earnings for therapeutic recreation specialists in 2002 were $30,540. The middle 50 percent earned between $23,180 and $38,620. The median annual earnings for recreational therapists were $25,010 in nursing care facilities.

Key Contacts: For information on careers in recreational therapy, contact:

- **American Therapeutic Recreation Association:** 1414 Prince Street, Suite 204, Alexandria, VA 22314-2853. Website: www.atra-tr.org.

- **National Therapeutic Recreation Society:** 22377 Belmont Ridge Road, Ashburn, VA 20148. Tel. 703-858-0784. Website: www.nrpa. org/content/default.aspx?documentld=530 .

- **National Council for Therapeutic Recreation Certification:** 7 Elmwood Drive, New City, NY 10956. Website: www.nctrc.org.

Registered Nurses (RNs)

✧ **Annual Earnings:** $48,090
✧ **Education/Training:** Associate to bachelor's degrees
✧ **Outlook:** Excellent

Employment Outlook: Registered nurses constitute the largest health care occupation with nearly 2.3 million jobs in 2002. Jobs for registered nurses will grow much faster than for most other occupational groups. This increase responds to the overall growth in health care and the increased demand for new nurses in home health, long-term, and ambulatory care.

Nature of Work: Registered nurses provide for the physical, mental, and emotional needs of sick and injured patients. They observe, assess, and record symptoms, reactions, and progress; assist physicians during treatments and examinations; administer medications; assist in convalescence and rehabilitation; instruct patients and their families in proper care; and help individuals and groups take steps to improve or maintain their health. Hospital nurses form the largest (60 percent) group of nurses. Most are staff nurses, who provide bedside nursing care and carry out medical regimens. One of the fastest growing and most financially rewarding opportunities is for contract nurses who are hired for short-term assignments with different hospitals. Other types of nurses include office nurses, nursing care facility nurses, home health nurses, public health nurses, occupational health nurses (also known as industrial nurses), head nurses or nurse supervisors, and nurse practitioners.

Working Conditions: Most registered nurses w ork in well-lighted, comfortable health care facilities. They also work in a variety of settings as hospital nurses, nursing home nurses, public health nurses, private duty nurses, office nurses, occupational health or industrial nurses, and head nurses or nurse supervisors. Home health and public health nurses travel to patients' homes, schools, community centers, and other sites. Nurses may spend considerable time working and standing. Office, occupational health, and public health nurses are more likely to work regular business hours while other RNs may work in 24-hour care facilities and work nights, weekends, and holidays. Depending on the health care facility, RNs may care for individuals with infectious diseases and maybe exposed to other dangers, such as radiation, accidental needle sticks, chemicals used to sterilize instruments, and anesthetics. In addition, they are vulnerable to back injury when moving patients, shocks from electrical equipment, and hazards posed by gases.

Education, Training, Qualifications: All states require nurses to be licensed. This requirement includes graduation from an accredited nursing school and passing a national licensing examination. Individuals can acquire a nursing education through three types of programs. Nursing graduates can earn an associate degree (ADN), diploma, and bachelor of science degree (BSN) in nursing. The ADN program takes two years and is offered by community and junior colleges. BSN programs take four to five years and are offered by colleges and universities. Diploma programs are offered by hospitals and last two to three years. Licensed graduates of these three programs qualify for entry-level positions as staff nurses.

Earnings: Median annual earnings of full-time salaried registered nurses were $48,090 in 2020. The middle 50 percent earned between $40,140 and $57,490. Median annual earnings in the major industries employing the largest numbers of registered nurses in 2002 were $55,980 in employment services; $49,190 in general medical and surgical hospitals; $45,890 in home health care services; $44,870 in offices of physicians; and $43,850 in nursing care facilities. Many employers offer flexible work schedules, childcare, educational benefits, and bonuses.

Key Contacts: For information on nursing careers, contact:

- **American Association of Colleges of Nursing:** 1 Dupont Circle, NW, Suite 530, Washington, DC 20036. Website: www.aacn.nche. edu.

- **American Nurses Association:** 600 Maryland Avenue, SW, Suite 100 West, Washington, DC 20024-2571. Website: www.nursingworld.org.

- **National League for Nursing:** 61 Broadway, New York, NY 10006. Website: www.nln.org.

Respiratory Therapists

⇨ **Annual Earnings:** $40,220
⇨ **Education/Training:** Associate degree
⇨ **Outlook:** Excellent

Employment Outlook: Employment for respiratory therapists is expected to be very good in the coming decade. The number of jobs is expected to increase substantially due to an increasingly middle-aged and elderly population. Older people are more likely to suffer from cardiopulmonary diseases such as pneumonia, chronic bronchitis, emphysema, and heart disease.

Nature of Work: Respiratory therapists held 112,000 jobs in 2002. More than four out of five jobs were in hospital departments of respiratory care, anesthesiology, or pulmonary medicine. Respiratory therapists treat all sorts of patients, from infants with lung problems to elderly people suffering from lung disease. They provide temporary relief to patients with chronic asthma or emphysema and emergency care for heart failure, stroke, drowning, or shock victims. They most commonly use oxygen or oxygen mixtures, chest physiotherapy, and aerosol medications. They apply oxygen masks, connect patients to ventilators, and regularly check on patients and equipment.

Working Conditions: Respiratory therapists usually work 35-40 hours per week in hospital departments of respiratory care, anesthesiology, or pulmonary medicine. During an emergency, therapists work under a great deal of stress. About 10 percent work with home health agencies, respiratory therapy clinics, and nursing homes. They may work evenings, nights, or weekends. Respiratory therapists employed in home health care must travel frequently to the homes of patients. Much of their work involves standing and walking.

Education, Training, Qualifications: Entry into this field requires postsecondary formal training which is provided by hospitals, medical schools, colleges and universities, trade schools, vocational-technical institutes, and the Armed Forces. Most of the Commission on Accreditation of Allied Health Education Programs (includes 59 entry-level and 319 advanced respiratory therapy programs) last two years and lead to an associate degree. Some are four-year bachelor's degree programs. Technician programs last about one year and award certificates.

Earnings: Median annual earnings for full-time respiratory therapists in 2002 were $40,220. The middle 50 percent earned between $34,430 and $46,130. In general medical and surgical hospitals, median annual earnings of respiratory therapists were $40,390 in 2002. Median annual earnings of respiratory therapy technicians were $34,130 in 2002. The middle 50 percent earned between $28,460 and $41,140.

Key Contacts: For information on respiratory therapist careers, contact:

- **American Association for Respiratory Care:** 9425 N. MacArthur Blvd., Suite 100. Irving, TX 75229. Website: www.aarc.org.

- **The National Board for Respiratory Care, Inc.:** 8310 Nieman Road, Lenexa, KS 66214-1579. Website: www.nbrc.org.

- **Committee on Accreditation of Allied Health Education Programs:** 39 East Wacker Drive, Suite 1970, Chicago, IL 60601. Website: www.caahep.org.

- **Committee on Accreditation for Respiratory Care:** 1248 Harwood Road, Bedford, TX 76021-4244. Website: www.coarc.com.

Surgical Technologists

- ✑ **Annual Earnings:** $31,210
- ✑ **Education/Training:** 9-12 month certificate programs
- ✑ **Outlook:** Good

Employment Outlook: Job opportunities are expected to be favorable. Employment of surgical technologists should grow faster than the average for all occupations in the decade ahead. The number of surgical procedures is expected to rise as the population grows and ages. Technological advances, such as fiber optics and laser technology, will also permit new surgical procedures to be performed.

Nature of Work: Surgical technologists – also called scrubs and surgical or operating room technicians – assist in surgical operations under the supervision of surgeons, registered nurses, or other surgical personnel. Surgical technologists are members of operating room teams, which most commonly include surgeons, anesthesiologists, and circulating nurses. Before an operation, surgical technologists help prepare the operating room by setting up surgical instruments and equipment, sterile drapes, and sterile solutions. They get patients ready for surgery by washing, shaving, and disinfecting incision sites. They transport patients to the operating room, help position them on the operating table, and cover them with sterile surgical "drapes." Technologists also observe patients' vital signs, check charts, and assist the surgical team with putting on sterile gowns and gloves. After an operation, surgical technologists may help transfer patients to the recovery room and clean and restock the operating room.

Working Conditions: Surgical technologists work in clean, well-lighted, cool environments. They must stand for long periods and remain alert during operations. At times they may be exposed to communicable diseases and unpleasant sights, odors, and materials.

Education, Training, Qualifications: Surgical technologists receive formal training through programs offered by community and junior colleges, vocational schools, universities, hospitals, and the military. Most of these programs last from 9 to 24 months and result in a certificate, diploma, or associate degree. In 2002 the Commission on Accreditation of Allied Health Education Programs (CAAHEP) recognized 361 accredited programs. Most employers prefer to hire certified technologists. Technologists advance their careers by specializing in a particular area of surgery, such as neurosurgery or open heart surgery.

Earnings: Median annual earnings of surgical technologists were $31,210 in 2002. The middle 50 percent earned between $26,000 and $36,740. Median annual earnings of surgical technologists in 2002 were $33,790 in offices of physicians and $30,590 in general medical and surgical hospitals.

Key Contacts: For information on a career as a surgical technologist, contact:

- **Association of Surgical Technologists:** 7108-C South Alton Way, Centennial, CO 80112. Website: www.ast.org.

- **Liaison Council on Certification for the Surgical Technologist:** 128 S. Tejon Street, Suite 301, Colorado Springs, CO 80903. Website: www.lcc-st.org.

Veterinary Technologists and Technicians

⇨ **Annual Earnings:** $22,950
⇨ **Education/Training:** Two- to four-year programs
⇨ **Outlook:** Excellent

Employment Outlook: Employment of veterinary technologists and technicians is expected to grow much faster than the average for all occupations during the coming decade. Keen competition is expected for veterinary technologist and technician jobs in zoos, due to expected slow growth in zoo capacity, the low turnover among workers, and high competition for a limited number of openings. As pet owners become more affluent, they are more willing to pay for advanced care of their pets. The rapidly growing number of cat owners should boost the demand for feline medicine, offsetting any reduced demand for veterinary care for dogs. Biomedical facilities, diagnostic laboratories, wildlife facilities, humane societies, animal control facilities, drug or food manufacturing companies, and food safety inspection facilities will provide more jobs for veterinary technologists and technicians.

Nature of Work: Veterinarians use the skills of veterinary technologists and technicians, who perform many of the same duties for a veterinarian that a nurse would for a physician, including routine laboratory and clinical procedures. Veterinary technologists and technicians typically conduct clinical work in a private practice under the supervision of a veterinarian – often performing various medical tests along with treating and diagnosing medical conditions and diseases in animals. They may perform laboratory tests such as urinalysis and blood counts, assist with dental prophylaxis, prepare tissue samples, take blood samples, or assist veterinarians in a variety of tests and analyses in which they often use various items of medical equipment, such as test tubes and diagnostic equipment.

Working Conditions: Veterinary technologists and technologists held about 53,000 jobs in 2002. Most worked in veterinary services. The remainder worked in boarding kennels, animal shelters, stables, grooming shops, zoos, and local, state, and federal agencies.

People who love animals get satisfaction from working with and help them. However, some of the work may be unpleasant, physically and emotionally demanding, and sometimes dangerous. Veterinary technicians sometimes must clean cages and lift, hold, or restrain animals, risking exposure to bites or scratches. The work setting can be noisy. Veterinary technologists and technicians who witness abused animals or who euthanize unwanted, aged, or hopelessly injured animals may experience emotional stress.

Education, Training, Qualifications: Most entry-level veterinary technicians have a two-year degree, usually an associate degree, from an accredited community college program in veterinary technology, in which courses are taught in clinical and laboratory settings using live animals. In 2003, more than 80 veterinary technology programs in 41 states were accredited by the American Veterinary Medical Association. A few colleges offer four-year programs that result in a bachelor's degree in veterinary technology.

Earnings: Median annual earnings of veterinary technologists and technicians were $22,950 in 2002. The middle 50 percent earned between $19,210 and $27,890.

Key Contacts: For information on certification and careers in veterinary technology, contact:

- **American Association for Laboratory Animal Science:** 9190 Crestwyn Hills Drive, Memphis, TN 38125. Website: www.aalas.org.

- **American Veterinary Medical Association:** 1931 N. Meacham Road, Suite 100, Schaumburg, IL 60173-4360. Website: www.avma.org.

- **Association of American Veterinary Medical Colleges:** 1101 Vermont Avenue, NW, Suite 710, Washington, DC 20005. Website: www.aavmc.org.

- **National Association of Veterinary Technicians in America:** P.O. Box 224, Battle Ground, IN 47920. Website: www.navta.net.

5

Computer and Internet Jobs

D ESPITE A GREAT DEAL of talk about the offshoring of information technology jobs to India, China, and the Philippines,
the computer and Internet industries will generate a large
number of jobs within the United States during the coming
decade. Indeed, these remain some of the hottest industries for anyone
wishing to hitch themselves to a very promising career future.

Hot Career Fields

According to the U.S. Department of Labor's most recent occupational
projections to the year 2012, next to health care, the fastest growing
occupations – increasing the number of jobs by over 35 percent – will be
in the computer industry: network systems and data communications
analysts (up 57 percent), computer software engineers (up 46 percent),
database administrators (up 44 percent), computer systems analysts (up
39 percent), network and computer systems administrators (up 37
percent), and computer and information systems managers (up 36

percent). Among the fastest growing industries projected for the period 2002 to 2012, three computer- and Internet- related industries rank in the top 10 for the percentage of annual job growth: software publishers (5.3 percent), computer systems design and related services (4.5 percent), and Internet services, data processing, and other information services (3.9 percent).

The Education Imperative

That's the good news. The bad news affects people without a four-year degree, because most of these growing computer- and Internet-related occupations require at least a bachelor's degree. In fact, entry into these high-demand fields requires a great deal of formal education at the bachelor's level and beyond. Computer software engineers, for example, require at least a bachelor's degree to qualify for the more than 200 certification programs that constitute part of the formal continuing education track for computer software engineers. Given the right education and training in various computer fields, one should experience long-term job security, career advancement, job mobility, and relatively high salaries and generous benefits in these fields. Computer engineers and computer systems analysts in particular rank near the very top on most lists of the 10 or 25 hottest jobs in the decade ahead. If you want to fast-track your career, make good money, and experience long-term job security, these are the fields to be in for the coming decade.

There's also good news here for people with less than a bachelor's degree. Thousands of computer-related job opportunities are available for people without a four-year degree. Many of these jobs require short-term training courses, certification, or a two-year associate degree acquired through a junior or community college. Many of these jobs relate to the serving and maintenance of computers, computer support services, and computer applications. Given the rapidly changing nature of computer technology, individuals in these fields are constantly being retrained in the latest hardware and systems applications. Consequently, the distinction between people with or without a four-year degree becomes less important than the distinction between people with or without the latest training.

Internet Opportunities

The Internet is one of today's hottest, most innovative, and adventuresome occupational frontiers which relies less on formal education credentials and more on demonstrated abilities. We include the Internet with computer occupations because of this emerging field's affinity to the computer industry. But the Internet industry involves numerous occupations and jobs that go beyond just computers and high-tech. When viewed as an electronic form of commerce, the Internet encompasses a broad spectrum of occupations with a high-tech and electronic communication emphasis: engineering, software development, graphic arts, sales, marketing, advertising, writing, and publishing. Because of the multidimensional aspect of the Internet, we're not sure how to best classify Internet-related occupations. What we do know is that this will continue to be a hot job and career arena in the coming decade.

Expanding at an exponential rate, Internet activity is generating a whole new occupational vocabulary reflecting the evolution of the Internet industry and related commerce. Straddling both the computer and Internet worlds, Webmasters occupy one of today's most enviable positions in both the computer and Internet worlds. Their skills are in great demand and they command high salaries – the perfect combination for one of America's best jobs for the future.

Growing and Declining Jobs

As more and more businesses and homes upgrade their computers, use networks, and expand their Internet usage, as well as adapt new applications to work processes, the computer field will experience steady growth. Many of the best paying jobs that also lead to career advancement will be in the computer field.

While fewer jobs will be available at the manufacturing end of the industry – due to the export of low-wage computer manufacturing jobs to developing countries – the largest growth in jobs will take place at the service and application ends of the computer industry: computer engineers, programmers, operations research analysts, and computer systems analysts. We expect continued growth within the field for computer programmers, consultants, salespeople, marketers, educators, technicians, and repairers. New generations of computers will come online and provide increased job opportunities for such computer specialists.

Not all computer jobs will survive the winds of change in this highly volatile field. As the use of computers becomes more widespread at all levels in organizations, many jobs will decline in number, especially for computer operators, word processors, and data entry people.

We also expect the computer field will remain volatile given the highly competitive nature of the computer industry and the large number of small start-up firms challenging the market shares of medium to large computer companies. Many of the routine computer software engineering jobs, which usually require a bachelor's or master's degree and certification, will be increasingly outsourced overseas. Jobs in computer manufacturing will be most volatile. Expect strong performance from Microsoft, Intel, Hewlett Packard, IBM, Dell, and Apple. Software producers will continue to face an extremely competitive market with continuing dominance by Microsoft despite competition from Linux. New jobs will continue to be created in multimedia and on the information highway through commercial on-line services and the Internet.

Given the highly volatile nature of the computer field, individuals working directly in this field should be prepared to change jobs frequently as firms go out of business, downsize, and start up. Surviving and prospering in this field requires constant learning and retraining in the face of short product cycles, many lasting only a few months! This is the classic example of a highly entrepreneurial field that rewards education, hard work, and initiative. Individuals need to be fast on their feet and love what they are doing. Many people in this field may eventually start their own computer companies.

Computer-Control Programmers and Operators

↪ **Annual Earnings:** $30,020
↪ **Education/Training:** Apprenticeships and training programs
↪ **Outlook:** Excellent

Employment Outlook: Computer-control programmers and operators should have excellent job opportunities in the decade ahead. Due to the limited number of people entering training programs, employers are expected to continue to have difficulty finding workers with the necessary skills and knowledge. The demand for computer-control programmers will be negatively affected by the increasing use of software that automatically translates part and product designs into CNC machine tool instructions.

Nature of Work: Computer-control programmers and operators use computer numerically controlled (CNC) machines to cut and shape precision products, such as automobile parts, machine parts, and compressors. CNC machines include machining tools such as lathes, multiaxis spindles, milling machines, and electrical discharge machines (EDM), but the functions formerly performed by human operators are performed by a computer-control module. CNC machines cut away material from a solid block of metal, plastic, or glass – known as a workpiece – to form a finished part. Computer-control programmers and operators normally produce large quantities of one part, although they may produce small batches of one-of-a-kind items. They use their knowledge of the working properties of metals and their skill with CNC programming to design and carry out the operations needed to make machined products that meet precise specifications.

Working Conditions: Most machine shops are clean, well lit, and ventilated. Most modern CNC machines are partially or totally enclosed, minimizing the exposure of workers to noise, debris, and the lubricants used to cool workpieces during machining. Nevertheless, working around high-speed machine tools represents certain dangers, and workers must follow safety precautions. Computer-controlled machine tool operators, metal and plastic, wear protective equipment, such as safety glasses to shield against bits of flying metal and earplugs to dampen machinery noise. Numerical tool and process control programmers work on desktop computers in offices that typically are near, but separate from, the shop floor. These work areas usually are clean, well lit, and free of machine noise. Most computer-control programmers and operators work a 40-hour week. CNC operators increasingly work evening and weekend shifts as companies justify investments in more expensive machinery by extending hours of operation. Overtime is common during peak production periods. Computer-control programmers and operators held nearly 151,000 jobs in 2002, mostly working in machine shops, plastics product manufacturing, or machinery manufacturing.

Education, Training, Qualifications: Computer-control programmers and operators train in various ways – in apprenticeship programs, informally on the job, and in secondary, vocational, or postsecondary schools. Many entrants to these occupations have previously worked as machinists or machine setters, operators, and tenders. Persons interested in becoming computer-control programmers or operators should be mechanically inclined and able to work independently and do highly accurate work.

Earnings: Median hourly earnings of computer-controlled machine tool operators, metal and plastic, were $13.97 in 2002 ($30,020 annual earnings). The middle 50 percent earned between $11.07 and $17.43 an hour ($23,030 and $36,255 annual earnings). Median hourly earnings in the manufacturing industries employing the largest numbers of computer-controlled machine tool operators, metal and plastic, in 2002 were $15.97 in metalworking machinery manufacturing; $15.14 in other fabricated metal product manufacturing; $13.82 in machine shops, turned product, and screw, nut, and bolt manufacturing; $13.08 in motor vehicle parts manufacturing; and $11.00 in plastics product manufacturing. Median hourly earnings of numerical tool and process control programmers were $18.04 in 2002.

Key Contacts: For more information on computer-control programmers and operators, contact:

- **Precision Machined Products Association:** 6700 West Snowville Road, Brecksville, OH 44141-3292. Website: www.pmpa.org.

- **National Tooling and Machining Association:** 9300 Livingston Road, Fort Washington, MD 20744. Website: www.ntma.org.

- **Precision Metalforming Association Educational Foundation:** 6363 Oak Tree Blvd., Independence, OH 44131-2500. Website: www.pmaef.org.

Computer Programmers

⇨ **Annual Earnings:** $60,290
⇨ **Education/Training:** Certificate to BA
⇨ **Outlook:** Good – grow as fast as average

Employment Outlook: The growth of computer programmer jobs is expected to be as fast as average for most occupations in the decade ahead. Jobs for both systems and applications programmers should be most plentiful in data processing service firms, software houses, and computer consulting businesses. These types of establishments are part of computer systems design and related services and software publishers, which are projected to be among the fastest growing industries in the economy in the coming decade.

This growth in computer programmer jobs will not be fast as in the past and it will be slower than that of other computer specialist positions. With the rapid gains in technology, sophisticated computer software now has the capability to write basic code, eliminating the need for more programmers to do this routine work. The consolidation and centralization of systems and applications, developments in packaged software, advances in programming languages and tools, and the growing ability of users to design, write, and implement more of their own programs mean that more of the programming functions can be transferred from programmers to other types of workers. Nonetheless, employers will continue to need programmers who have strong technical skills and who understand an employer's business and its programming requirements. Given the importance of networking and the expansion of client/server, Web-based, and wireless environments, organizations will look for programmers who can support data communications and help to implement commerce and Intranet strategies. Growing emphasis on cyber-security will lead to increased demand for programmers who are familiar with digital security issues and skilled in using appropriate security technology.

Nature of Work: Computer programmers write, update, and maintain the detailed instructions (called programs or software) that list in a logical order the steps that computers must execute. Computer programmers tend to be the "technicians" of the computer field in contrast to the "theoreticians" who occupy positions as computer scientists, computer engineers, and systems analysts. Applications programmers primarily work with software designed for business, engineering, or science. They write software to handle specific applications in their fields as well as modify existing programs. Systems programmers maintain the software that controls the operation of an entire computer system. They often help applications programmers diagnose and resolve related programming problems. The largest number of computer programmers are employed by computer and data processing companies that write and sell software. Others work in a variety of industries and occupational settings, including educational institutions, government agencies, insurance companies, financial institutions, and engineering and management services.

Working Conditions: Programmers usually work a 40-hour week in clean and comfortable offices. They sometimes work longer hours in order to meet deadlines. Given the nature of the technology, many programmers telecommute, working from remote locations via modems. Since they spend most of their time at computer screens and using keyboards, computer programmers are more likely to experience physical problems relating to eyestrain, backaches, and hand and wrist discomfort, such as carpal tunnel syndrome.

Education, Training, Qualifications: Education requirements continue to rise in this career field. While many programmers have four-year college degrees, others primarily have high school, community and junior college, or public and private vocational school educations. However, work experience, computer course training, and proven computer talent count a great deal in this field. But the trend is definitely toward higher levels of formal education and training with a bachelor's degree considered a basic entry-level education requirement. Employers using computers for business applications prefer individuals with college course work in programming and business as well as experience in accounting, management, and other business skills. Programmers need to think logically, demonstrate a high level of analytic skills, and be familiar with several different programming languages rather than specialized in only one language. Prospects should be best for college graduates with knowledge of, and experience working with, a variety of programming languages and tools – including C++ and other object-oriented languages such as Java, as well as newer, domain-specific languages that apply to computer networking, database management, and Internet application development. Obtaining vendor-specific or language-specific certification also can provide a competitive edge. Because demand fluctuates with employers' needs, job seekers should keep up to date with the latest skills and technologies.

Earnings: The median earnings of computer programmers in 2002 were $60,290 a year. The middle 50 percent earned between $45,960 and $78,140 a year. However, these figures disproportionately represent computer programmers with a bachelor's degree or higher. Individuals without a four-year degree generally earn less than the median.

Key Contacts: For information on computer careers, contact:

- **American Society for Information Science and Technology:** 1320 Fenwick Lane, Suite 510, Silver Spring, MD 20910. Website: www. asis.org.

- **Institute for Certification of Computing Professionals:** 2350 East Devon Avenue, Suite 115, Des Plaines, IL 60018. Website: www. iccp.org.

- **Association for Computing Machinery:** 1515 Broadway, New York, NY 10036. Website: www.acm.org.

- **National Workforce Center for Emerging Technologies:** Bellevue Community College, 3000 Landerholm Circle SE, N258, Bellevue, WA 98007. Website: www.nwcet.org.

Computer Service Technicians

⇨ **Annual Earnings:** $36,200
⇨ **Education/Training:** Certificate or associate degree
⇨ **Outlook:** Excellent

Employment Outlook: Employment of computer service technicians (computer repairers) is expected to increase as fast as the average for all occupations in the decade ahead. This is due to the increased dependence of business and residential customers on computers. However, employment growth will be slower than the growth in equipment sales due to the increased reliability and slower progression to obsolescence of computers.

Nature of Work: Computer service technicians install, maintain, troubleshoot, and repair computers and peripheral equipment experiencing mechanical and electronic malfunctions. They wire and connect components, test equipment, and load operating systems and applications. They also may upgrade computers with new boards, replace hard drives, add memory chips, and make other changes to computer hardware. They service mainframe, server, and personal computers; printers; and disc drives. Many also specialize in servicing particular brands of computers and peripherals, such as IBM, Hewlett Packard, Dell, or Apple. Their work primarily involves hands-on repair, maintenance, and installation of computers and related equipment. If they are part of an organization's network administration staff, they must be familiar with the computer networks, software, and operating systems of the organization. Workers who provide technical assistance, in person or by telephone, to computer system users are known as computer support specialists or computer support technicians.

Working Conditions: Computer service technicians primarily work for companies that sell computers or for maintenance service firms. Others work for manufacturers and retailers. Many large organizations have their own staff of computer service technicians to handle in-house networks, software, and operation systems. Computer service technicians normally work a 40-hour week. Some also work evenings, weekends, and holidays, depending on employer or client needs. Daily work routines vary from working in air conditioned and well ventilated shops to servicing computers in clients' offices. About one in eight computer service technicians is self-employed.

Education, Training, Qualifications: Formal education and training are acquired through postsecondary vocational-technical schools, private vocational schools and technical institutes, and junior and community colleges. Employers prefer service technicians who are certified or who have training from associate degree programs, the military, vocational schools, or manufacturers. Many employers prefer hiring individuals who have an A+ certification from the Computing Technology Industry Association. Employers generally provide some training to new technicians on specific systems. Given the rapidly changing technology of computers, computer service technicians receive a great deal of on-the-job training as well as participate in numerous training courses to update their skills.

Earnings: Median hourly earnings of computer service technicians in 2002 was $15.98 or $36,000 a year. The middle 50 percent earned between $12.44 and $20.38. Many self-employed computer service technicians charge on-site hourly rates ranging from $50 to $100 per hour.

Key Contacts: For information on career opportunities for computer service technicians, contact:

- **Association of Computer Support Specialists:** 333 Mamaroneck Avenue, #129, White Plains, NY 10605.

- 218 Huntington Road, Bridgeport, CT 06608. Website: www.acss.org.

- **Computing Technology Industry Association:** 1815 S. Meyers Road, Suite 300, Oakbrook Terrace, IL 60181-5228. Website: www.comptia.org.

- **Electronics Technicians Association:** 5 Depot Street, Greencastle, IN 46135. Website: www.eta-sda.com

- **ComputerWorld:** www.computerworld.com.

- **Apple Computer Technician Training:** www.applecom/support/products/techtrain.html

- **Dell Certified Systems Expert (DCSE) Program:** http://dcse.dell.com.

Computer Support Specialists and Systems Administrators

⇨ **Annual Earnings:** $39,100 and $54,810
⇨ **Education/Training:** Certificate, associate degree, or BS
⇨ **Outlook:** Excellent

Employment Outlook: Employment of computer support specialists is expected to increase faster than the average for all occupations in the decade ahead, as organizations continue to adopt and integrate increasingly sophisticated technology. Employment of systems administrators is expected to increase much faster than average as firms continue to invest heavily in securing computer networks. Demand for computer security specialists will grow as businesses and government continue to invest heavily in cybersecurity, protecting vital computer networks and electronic infrastructures from attack. As businesses continue to expand their electronic commerce in conducting business online, they will increasingly require the services of information technology specialists who can help them use technology to communicate with employees, clients, and consumers. Explosive growth in these areas also is expected to fuel demand for specialists knowledgeable about network, data, and communications security.

Nature of Work: Computer support specialists and systems administrators held about 758,000 jobs in 2002. Of these, about 507,000 were computer support specialists and about 251,000 were network and computer systems administrators. Computer support specialists provide technical assistance, support, and advice to customers and other users. This occupational group includes technical support specialists and help-desk technicians. These troubleshooters interpret problems and provide technical support for hardware, software, and systems. They answer telephone calls, analyze problems using automated diagnostic programs, and resolve recurrent difficulties. Support specialists may work either within a company that uses computer systems or directly for a computer hardware or software vendor. Increasingly, these specialists work for help-desk or support services firms, where they provide computer support to clients on a contract basis.

Network or computer systems administrators design, install, and support an organization's LAN (local-area network), WAN (wide-area network), network segment, Internet, or intranet system. They provide day-to-day on-site administrative support for software users in a variety of work environments, including professional offices, small businesses, government, and large corporations. They maintain network hardware and software, analyze problems, and monitor the network to ensure its availability to system users.

Systems administrators are the information technology employees responsible for the efficient use of networks by organizations. They ensure that the design of an organization's computer set-up allows all of the components, including computers, the network, and software, to fit together and work properly.

In some organizations, computer security specialists may plan, coordinate, and implement the organization's information security.

Working Conditions: Computer support specialists and systems administrators normally work in well lit, comfortable offices or computer laboratories. They usually work about 40 hours a week, but that may include being on call via pager or telephone for rotating evening or weekend work if the employer requires computer support over extended hours. As computer networks expand, more computer support specialists and systems administrators may be able to connect to a customer's computer remotely, using modems, laptops, e-mail, and the Internet, to provide technical support to computer users.

Education, Training, Qualifications: While employers increasingly seek computer support specialists and systems administrators who have a bachelor's degree, these fields are still open, especially at the entry level, to individuals without a four-year degree. Such people need to have some college education, such as a computer-related associate degree. They also need to have certifications and demonstrate practical experience to enter and advance in these high-demand fields. Completion of certification training programs offered by various vendors and product makers, along with relevant computer experience, often substitutes for a four-year degree.

Earnings: Median annual earnings of computer support specialists were $39,100 in 2002. The middle 50 percent earned between $29,760 and $51,680. Median annual earnings of network and computer systems administrators were $54,810. The middle 50 percent earned between $43,290 and $69,530. According to Robert Half International, starting salaries in 2003 ranged from $27,500 to $56,500 for help-desk support staff, and from $51,000 to $67,250 for more senior technical support specialists. For systems administrators, starting salaries in 2003 ranged from $49,000 to $70,250.

Key Contacts: For information on careers as a computer support specialist and systems administrator, contact:

- **Association of Computer Support Specialists:** 333 Mamaroneck Avenue, #129, White Plains, NY 10605.

- **Association of Support Professionals:** 122 Barnard Avenue, Watertown, MA 02472. Website: www.asponline.com.

- **System Administrators Guild:** 2560 Ninth Street, Suite 215, Berkeley, CA 94710. Website: www.sage.org.

- **National Workforce Center for Emerging Technologies:** Bellevue Community College, 3000 Landerholm Circle SE, N258, Bellevue, WA 98007. Website: www.nwcet.org.

Web Developer

⇨ **Annual Earnings:** $50,000
⇨ **Education/Training:** Certificate, associate degree, or BS
⇨ **Outlook:** Good

Employment Outlook: Despite the Internet bubble burst in 2001, the explosive growth of the Internet, intranets, and online commerce make this one of the fastest growing high-tech occupations in the decade ahead. However, times are changing. Like many other computer fields, this one is becoming more and more competitive. Many of these jobs have moved overseas to such cheap high-tech labor markets as India, the Philippines, Egypt, and the Ukraine.

Nature of Work: Web developers, also known as Internet developers and Web designers, primarily design and develop websites. They are involved in the day-to-day development and promotion of websites. Proficient in different programming languages and Web development scripts – HTML, C++, ASP, JavaScript, Perl, and PHP – they assist clients in developing website graphics, content, interactivity, databases, and security features. Many work with large websites involving interactive elements, audio features, animation, and other complex graphics. Much of their work involves debugging computer programs, writing code for pages and functions, and testing programs and pages to make sure they work properly.

Working Conditions: Web developers work in a variety of settings. Many are freelance developers who work from home or are employed by Internet and design companies. While much of their work can be conducted online and from remote locations, some Web developers work on-site with clients, providing them with troubleshooting and training services. Many Web developers work full time for a corporation or agency that has its own websites or sites while others are employed by companies that specialize in developing websites for a variety of clients in business and government.

Education, Training, Qualifications: While nearly 75 percent of Web developers have a bachelor's or master's degree, there are no specific educational and training requirements for this occupational group. Nonetheless, this occupational field is becoming more and more sophisticated, requiring levels of education. Many employers now require Web developers to have a bachelor's degree in computer science as well as certification in particular programming languages. Many schools offer training programs in preparation for certification exams. But one thing is certain – they are constantly on the learning curve in this very dynamic and rapidly changing field. New technologies constantly emerge, from programming languages to new multimedia approaches. Since this is a relatively new and rapidly developing field, many Web developers are self-taught or acquire their skills through on-the-job training. Many also have certifications in various programming languages and applications as well as a two-year associate degree or four-year college degree. It's most important that they be proficient in graphics, XHTML, HTML, XML, ASP, JavaScript Perl PHP, and other Web applications, skills that are acquired on the job or through special training programs.

Earnings: Annual earnings of Web developers can very greatly, depending on whether they work as freelancers or employees. Freelancers may charge clients anywhere from $50 to $100 an hour. Senior developers with a great deal of experience may earn up to $90,000 a year. On average, however, Web developers make around $50,000 a year.

Key Contacts: For information on careers for web developers, contact:

- **Developers.net:** Website: www.developers.net.

- **Web Developer:** Website: www.webdeveloper.com.

- **Internet Society:** 1775 Wiehle Avenue, Suite 102, Reston, VA 20190. Website: www.isoc.org.

Webmaster

- ➪ **Annual Earnings:** $50,000 to $100,000+
- ➪ **Education/Training:** Certificate, associate degree, or BS
- ➪ **Outlook:** Excellent

Employment Outlook: As the number of World Wide Web sites continues to expand and as more and more corporations develop intranets, the position of Webmaster has been in great demand. We expect the demand for Webmasters will be great in the coming decade as more and more businesses, nonprofit organizations, and government agencies further develop Internet and intranet sites. However, like Web developers, this position is becoming more and more competitive as many more people enter this hot career field.

Nature of Work: Webmasters are literally the "persons in charge" of designing, operating, and maintaining the websites of organizations. Because Webmaster is a new position in a rapidly changing industry, the exact nature of a Webmaster's work is difficult to define. In general, Webmasters are responsible for all aspects of a website, including performance issues such as speed of access, and for approving the content of the site. They work closely with Web designers in developing Web pages which are formatted in HTML (HyperText Markup Language) and other sophisticated programming languages. They design sites so they can be easily viewed and used for communicating within the organization and with the public. Much of their work is technical in nature (selecting and importing graphics, coding text, and using software) and involves a great deal of troubleshooting to resolve a variety of Web-related problems. Many Webmasters also are involved with marketing questions which may involve team efforts and working closely with marketing experts and coordinating website efforts of various departments within the organization. They also may be responsible for receiving and answering e-mail.

Working Conditions: Webmasters work in a variety of computer settings that primarily put them behind computer terminals and in meeting rooms where they coordinate work with writers, graphic designers, marketing specialists, and department personnel.

Education, Training, Qualifications: Since this is still a relatively new and rapidly developing occupational frontier, it's difficult to identify specific educational backgrounds and qualifications leading to a Webmaster position. Webmasters come from a variety of technical backgrounds – computer science, mathematics, and engineering. Others may have backgrounds in graphic arts and marketing. Similar to Web developers, Webmasters tend to be very familiar with computer operating systems, programming languages, and computer graphics. Many have bachelor's degrees in computer science, but others may only have a high school diploma, some college, or a two-year degree. More and more schools and colleges now offer certification and degree programs for Webmasters. Webmasters constantly must keep current on the rapid changes taking place in their field.

Earnings: Salary ranges for Webmasters vary greatly, from $50,000 to over $100,000 a year. Many are promoted from computer positions and thus may retain their previous salary level. Since this is a very high demand position at present, it can command a very high salary, depending on the organization and responsibilities involved.

Key Contacts: For more information on the work of Webmasters, contact:

- **World Organization of Webmasters (WOW):** 9580 Oak Avenue Parkway, Suite 7-177, Folsom, CA 95630. Website: www.joinwow. org.

- **International Webmasters Association:** 119 E. Union Street, Suite F, Pasadena, CA 91103-3952. Website: www.iwanet.org.

- **Society of Internet Professionals:** 7321 Victoria Park Avenue, Suite 301, Markham, ON L3R 2Z8, Canada. Website: www.sipgroup.org.

6

Science, Math, Engineering, and Technology Jobs

WHILE THE U.S. ECONOMY is by no means experiencing a shortage of scientists and engineers, nonetheless, job opportunities for scientists and engineers should be good to excellent throughout the coming decade. Like others, we assume the U.S. economy will continue to move in the direction of more science and technology. The electronics revolution will continue unabated as it spreads through all areas of life. More and more money is expected to be invested by both government and private industry in research and development in order to develop a more internationally competitive economy.

While decreased defense spending in the 1990s did have an adverse effect on some scientific and engineering jobs tied to defense industries, the overall picture for the coming decade looks good, especially for those in the biological sciences, chemistry, mathematics, geology, meteorology, and civil, electronics, and mechanical engineering. As more public money is spent on developing national security and a more adequate infrastructure of roads, bridges, airports, tunnels, rapid transit, and water supply and sewage systems, opportunities for engineering technicians should improve considerably. Assuming manufacturing industries will continue to grow in the decade ahead, opportunities for mechanical engineering technicians should be good. The future especially looks good for electronics and environmental engineering technicians.

Drafters

⇨ **Annual Earnings:** $37,330
⇨ **Education/Training:** Technical training to associate degree
⇨ **Outlook:** Good – about average

Employment Outlook: Employment of drafters is expected to grow more slowly than the average for occupations in the coming decade. Industrial growth and increasingly complex design problems associated with new products and manufacturing processes will increase the demand for drafting services. Drafters also are beginning to break out of the traditional drafting role and increasingly do work traditionally performed by engineers and architects, thus also increasing demand for drafters. However, the greater use of CADD equipment by drafters, as well as by architects and engineers, should limit demand for less skilled drafters, resulting in slower-than-average overall employment growth.

Nature of Work: Drafters prepare technical drawings and plans used by production and construction workers to build everything from manufactured products, such as toys, toasters, industrial machinery, and spacecraft, to structures, such as houses, office buildings, and oil and gas pipelines. Their drawings provide visual guidelines, show the technical details of the products and structures, and specify dimensions, materials, and procedures. Drafters fill in technical details, using drawings, rough sketches, specifications, codes, and calculations previously made by engineers, surveyors, architects, or scientists.

Working Conditions: Most drafters work a standard 40-hour week; only a small number work part time. Drafters usually work in comfortable offices furnished to accommodate their tasks. Because they spend long periods in front of computer terminals doing detailed work, drafters may be susceptible to eyestrain, back discomfort, and hand and wrist problems.

Education, Training, Qualifications: Employers prefer applicants who have completed postsecondary school training in drafting, which is offered by technical institutes, community colleges, and some four-year colleges and universities. Employers are most interested in applicants with well-developed drafting and mechanical-drawing skills; knowledge of drafting standards, mathematics, science, and engineering technology; and a solid background in computer-aided design and drafting techniques.

Earnings: Earnings for drafters vary by specialty and level of responsibility. Median annual earnings of architectural and civil drafters were $37,330 in 2002. The middle 50 percent earned between $30,170 and $45,5000. Median annual earnings of mechanical drafters were $40,730 in 2002. The middle 50 percent earned between $32,100 and $51,950. Median annual earnings of electrical and electronics drafters were $41,090 in 2002. The middle 50 percent earned between $32,060 and $53,440.

Key Contacts: Information on training and certification for drafting and related fields is available from:

- **Accrediting Commission of Career Schools and Colleges of Technology:** 2101 Wilson Blvd., Suite 302, Arlington, VA 22201. Website: www.accsct.org.

- **American Design Drafting Association:** 105 E. Main Street, Newbern, TN 38059. Website: www.adda.org.

Electrical and Electronics Installers and Repairers

⇨ **Annual Earnings:** $41,120
⇨ **Education/Training:** Postsecondary training
⇨ **Outlook:** Good

Employment Outlook: Overall employment of electrical and electronics installers and repairers is expected to grow more slowly than the average for all occupations in the decade ahead, but varies by occupational specialty. Average employment growth is projected for electrical and electronics installers and repairers of commercial and industrial equipment. Employment of motor vehicle electronic equipment installers and repairers also is expected to grow as fast as the average. Employment of electric motor, power tool, and related repairers is expected to growth more slowly than average. Employment of electrical and electronic installers and repairers of transportation equipment is expected to grow more slowly than the average, due to declining industry employment in rail transportation, aerospace product and parts manufacturing, and ship- and boatbuilding. Employment of electrical and electronics installers and repairers of powerhouse, substation, and relay is expected to decline slightly.

Nature of Work: Electrical and electronics installers and repairers install, maintain, and repair complex pieces of electronic equipment used in business, government, and other organizations. The nature of their work varies depending on their occupational specialty. In 2,000 electrical and electronics installers and repairers held about 173,000 jobs in their occupational specialties:

- Electrical and electronics repairers,
  commercial and industrial equipment   85,000
- Electric motor, power tool, and related repairers   31,000
- Electrical and electronics repairers,
  powerhouse, substation, and relay   21,000
- Electrical and electronics installers and
  repairers, motor vehicles   18,000
- Electrical and electronics installers and
  repairers, transportation equipment   18,000

Many repairers worked for utilities, building equipment contractors, machinery and equipment repair shops, wholesalers, the federal government, retailers of automotive parts and accessories, rail transportation companies, and manufacturers of electrical, electronic, and transportation equipment.

Working Conditions: Many electrical and electronics installers and repairers work on factory floors, where they are subject to noise, dirt, vibration, and heat. Bench technicians work primarily in repair shops, where the surroundings are relatively quiet, comfortable, and well lighted. Installers and repairers may have to do heavy lifting and work in a variety of positions. They follow safety guidelines and often wear protective goggles and hardhats.

Education, Training, Qualifications: Knowledge of electrical equipment and electronics is necessary for employment. Many applicants gain this knowledge through programs lasting one to two years at vocational schools or community colleges, although some less skilled repairers may have only a high school diploma. Entry-level repairers may work closely with more experienced technicians who provide technical guidance. Various organizations provide certification, including ACES International, the Consumer Electronics Association, the Electronics Technicians Association International, and the International Society of Certified Electronics Technicians. Repairers may specialize

– in industrial electronics, for example. To receive certification, repairers must pass qualifying exams corresponding to their level of training and experience.

Earnings: Median hourly earnings of electrical and electronics repairers, commercial and industrial equipment, were $19.77 in 2002 ($41,120 per year). Median hourly earnings of electric motor, power tool, and related repairers were $15.49 in 2002 ($32,200 per year). Median hourly earnings of electrical and electronics repairers, powerhouse, substation, and relay, were $24.95 in 2002 ($51,900). Median hourly earnings of electronics installers and repairers, motor vehicles, were $12.51 in 2002 ($26,000 per year). Median hourly earnings of electrical and electronics repairers, transportation equipment, were $18.56 in 2002 ($38.600 per year).

Key Contacts: For information on careers and certification, contact the following organizations:

- **Association of Communications and Electronics Schools:** 5241 Princess Anne Road, Suite 110, Virginia Beach, VA 23462. Website: www.acesinternational.org.

- **Consumer Electronics Association:** 2500 Wilson Blvd., Arlington, VA 22201-3834. Website: www.ce.org.

- **Electronics Technicians Association International:** 5 Depot Street, Greencastle, IN 46135. Website: www.eta-sda.org.

- **International Society of Certified Electronics Technicians:** 3608 Pershing Avenue, Fort Worth, TX 76107-4527. Website: www.iscet. org.

Electricians

⇨ **Annual Earnings:** $41,400
⇨ **Education/Training:** Apprenticeship program (3-5 years)
⇨ **Outlook:** Good

Employment Outlook: Job opportunities for electricians are expected to be good. Numerous openings will arise each year as experienced electricians leave the occupation. In addition, many potential workers may choose not to enter training programs because they prefer work that is less strenuous and has more comfortable working conditions. Employment of electricians is expected to grow faster than the average for all occupations in the coming decade. As the population and economy grow, more electricians will be needed to install and maintain electrical devices and wiring in homes, factories, offices, and other structures. New technologies also are expected to continue to stimulate the demand for these workers.

Nature of Work: Electricians install, connect, test, and maintain electrical systems for a variety of purposes, including climate control, security, and communications. They also may install and maintain the electronic controls for machines in business and industry. Although most electricians specialize in construction or maintenance, a growing number do both. Electricians work with blueprints when they install electrical systems in factories, office buildings, homes, and other structures. Blueprints indicate the locations of circuits, outlets, load centers, panel boards, and other equipment. Electricians must follow the National Electric Code and comply with state and local building codes when they install these systems. Maintenance work varies greatly, depending on where the electrician is employed. Maintenance electricians spend much of their time doing preventive maintenance. They periodically inspect equipment, and locate and correct problems before breakdowns occur. Electricians use hand tools such as screwdrivers, pliers, knives, hacksaws, and wire strippers. They also use a variety of power tools as well as testing equipment such as oscilloscopes, ammeters, and test lamps.

Working Conditions: Electricians held about 659,000 jobs in 2002. More than one-quarter of wage and salary workers were employed in the construction industry. The remainder worked as maintenance electricians outside the construction industry. About one in 10 electricians was self-employed.

Electricians' work is sometimes strenuous. They bend conduits, stand for long periods, and frequently work on ladders and scaffolds. Their working environment varies, depending on the type of job. Some may work in dusty, dirty, hot, or wet conditions, or in confined areas, ditches, or other uncomfortable places. Electricians risk injury form electrical shock, falls, and cuts. Most electricians work a standard 40-hour week, although overtime may be required. Those in maintenance work may work nights or weekends, and be on call.

Education, Training, Qualifications: Most people learn the electrical trade by completing an apprenticeship program lasting three to five years. Apprenticeship gives trainees a thorough knowledge of all aspects of the trade and generally improves their ability to find a job. Although electricians are more likely to be trained through apprenticeship than are workers in other construction trades, some still learn their skills informally on the job. Others train to be residential electricians in a three-year program. Apprenticeship programs may be sponsored by joint training committees made up of local unions of the International Brotherhood of Electrical Workers and local chapters of the National Electrical Contractors Association; company management committees of individual electrical contracting companies; or local chapters of the Associated Builders and Contractors and the Independent Electrical Contractors Association. The typical large apprenticeship program provides at least 144 hours of classroom instruction and 2,000 hours of on-the-job-training each year. Those who do not enter a formal apprenticeship program can begin to learn the trade informally by working as helpers for experienced electricians.

Earnings: In 2002, median hourly earnings of electricians were $19.90 ($41,400 per year). The middle 50 percent earned between $14.95 and $26.50. Median hourly earnings in the industries employing the largest numbers of electricians in 2002 were:

- Motor vehicle parts manufacturing $28.72
- Local government $21.15
- Building equipment contractors $19.54
- Nonresidential building construction $19.36
- Employment services $15.46

Depending on experience, apprentices usually start at between 40 and 50 percent of the rate paid to fully trained electricians.

Key Contacts: For details about apprenticeships or other work opportunities in this trade, contact the offices of the state employment service, the state apprenticeship agency, local electrical contractors or firms that employ maintenance electricians, or local union-management electrician apprenticeship committees. For information about union apprenticeship programs, contact:

- **National Joint Apprenticeship Training Committee:** 301 Prince George's Blvd., Upper Marlboro, MD 20774. Website: www.njatc.org.

- **National Electrical Contractors Association:** 3 Bethesda Metro Center, Suite 1100, Bethesda, MD 20814. Website: www.necanet.org.

- **International Brotherhood of Electrical Workers:** 1125 15th Street, NW, Washington, DC 20005. Website: www.ibew.org.

For information about independent apprenticeship programs, contact:

- **Independent Electrical Contractors, Inc.:** 4401 Ford Avenue, Suite 1100, Alexandria, VA 22302. Website: www.ieci.org.

- **Associated Builders and Contractors:** Workforce Development Department, 4250 North Fairfax Drive, 9th Floor, Arlington, VA 22203. Website: www.abc.org.

- **National Association of Home Builders:** 1201 15th Street NW, Washington, DC 20005. Website: www.nahb.org.

- **Home Builders Institute:** 1201 15th Street, NW, Washington, DC 20005. Website: www.hbi.org.

Engineering Technicians

↔ **Annual Earnings:** $36,850 to $51,650
↔ **Education/Training:** Associate degree
↔ **Outlook:** Excellent

Employment Outlook: Overall employment of engineering technicians is expected to increase about as fast as average for all occupations in the coming decade. Competitive pressures will force companies to improve and update manufacturing facilities and product designs, resulting in more jobs for engineering technicians. However, the growing use of advanced technologies, such as computer simulation and computer-aided design and drafting will continue to increase productivity and limit job growth.

Nature of Work: Engineering technicians use the principles and theories of science, engineering, and mathematics to solve technical problems in research and development, manufacturing, sales, construction, inspection, and maintenance. Their work is more limited in scope and more practically oriented than that of scientists and engineers. Many engineering technicians assist engineers and scientists, especially in research and development. Others work in quality control – inspecting products and processes, conducting tests, or collecting data. In manufacturing, they may assist in product design, development, or production. Most engineering technicians specialize in certain areas, learning skills and working in the same disciplines as engineers. Occupational titles, therefore, tend to reflect those of engineers. Engineering technicians held 478,000 jobs in 2002 in the following occupational fields:

- Electrical and electronic engineering technicians   204,000
- Civil engineering technicians   92,000
- Industrial engineering technicians   62,000
- Mechanical engineering technicians   55,000
- Electro-mechanical technicians   31,000

- Environmental engineering technicians   19,000
- Aerospace engineering and operations technicians   15,000

Working Conditions: Most engineering technicians work at least 40 hours a week in laboratories, offices, or manufacturing or industrial plants, or on construction sites. Some may be exposed to hazards from equipment, chemicals, or toxic materials.

Education, Training, Qualifications: Although it may be possible to qualify for certain engineering technician jobs without formal training, most employers prefer to hire someone with a least a two-year associate degree in engineering technology. Training is available at technical institutes, community colleges, extension divisions of colleges and universities, and public and private vocational-technical schools, and in the Armed Forces.

Earnings: Median annual earnings of engineering technicians vary by specialty:

- Aerospace engineering and operations technicians $51,650
- Electrical and electronic engineering technicians $42,950
- Industrial engineering technicians $41,910
- Mechanical engineering technicians $41,280
- Electro-mechanical technicians $38,120
- Civil engineering technicians $37,720
- Environmental engineering technicians $36,850

Key Contacts: For information on training and certification of engineering technicians, contact:

- **National Institute for Certification in Engineering Technologies (NICET):** 1420 King Street, Alexandria, VA 22314-2794. Website: www.nicet.org.

- **Accreditation Board for Engineering and Technology, Inc.:** 111 Market Place, Suite 1050, Baltimore, MD 21202. Website: www.abet.org.

Laser Technicians

> ⇨ **Annual Earnings:** $39,000
> ⇨ **Education/Training:** Associate degree
> ⇨ **Outlook:** Excellent

Employment Outlook: Job opportunities for laser technicians are expected to be excellent in the decade ahead. The increased use of laser technology in industry, including the fast-growing field of fiber optics, will generate numerous job opportunities for laser technicians. Expect increased demand for laser technicians in entertainment, defense, medicine, construction, manufacturing, and telecommunications.

Nature of Work: Laser technicians, also known as laser/electro-optics technicians (LEOTs), work in a variety of occupational settings – manufacturing, medicine, research, communication, military, and defense – where they build, operate, repair, install, and test lasers, fibers, and systems that use lasers. Working under the direct supervision of scientists or engineers, they calculate measurements and clear, inspect, adjust, and operate lasers. Some laser technicians primarily work with semiconductor systems relating to computers and telecommunications. Others primarily work with gas-type systems in the fields of robotics, manufacturing, and medicine.

Working Conditions: Laser technicians work in clean and well-equipped laboratories and assembly areas. When working on delicate electronic and optical assemblies, laser technicians work in environmentally controlled areas, known as "clean rooms," where temperature, humidity, and dust content of air is carefully controlled. The work requires a great deal of attention to detail and special safety precautions since the work can be dangerous, especially in handling hazardous manufacturing materials (dye solutions, gas-filled discharge tubes, high-voltage power sources) and working with dangerous laser beams.

Education, Training, Qualifications: Laser technicians need a certificate or associate degree in electrical or electronic technology. Many laser technicians complete a two-year associate degree in laser/electro-optics technology, which is offered by some community colleges. These institutions usually work closely with employers who hire directly from these programs. Some laser technicians receive training in laser technology through the Armed Forces.

Earnings: The median annual earnings of laser technicians were around $39,000 in 2002. Starting salaries begin at $23,000.

Key Contacts: For information on laser technology jobs and careers, including training programs, contact:

- **Laser Institute of America:** 13501 Ingenuity Drive, Suite 128, Orlando, FL 32826. Website: www.laserinstitute.org.

- **Laser and Electro-Optics Society:** 445 Hoes Lane, Piscataway, NJ 08855-1331. Website: www.i-leos.org.

Marine Service Technicians

⇨ **Annual Earnings:** $28,000
⇨ **Education/Training:** High school diploma and training
⇨ **Outlook:** Good

Employment Outlook: Employment opportunities for marine service technicians, also known as marine mechanics, should be good in the decade ahead, assuming the economy continues to grow. During good economic times, when boat ownership increases, the demand for marine services technicians increases accordingly. In many parts of the country this is often a seasonal job. The best opportunities are found in affluent marine-oriented communities where boating is a year round activity.

Nature of Work: Marine service technicians primarily test, service, and repair powerboats and sailboats. They work on both inboard and outboard engines, electrical and plumbing systems, fuel and water pumps, transmissions, rigging, masts, sails, navigation equipment, propellers, steering gear, sanitation systems, and hulls. They work with metal, wood, and fiberglass materials. Some marine service technicians are trained to service particular brands of two- and four-stroke cycle engines as well as particular types of vessels. Mechanics work on engines, transmissions, propellers, and navigational systems. Fiberglass/wood technicians focus on cleaning and repairing damaged boat hulls. Painters mix and apply paint or gel coats to boats with hand and spray equipment.

Working Conditions: Marine service technicians work in a variety of repair shops, marinas, and boat yards. Working conditions will vary depending on the particular employer.

Education, Training, Qualifications: Most employers prefer applicants with a high school diploma. They also seek candidates who have completed marine service technician training programs. Some trade schools, career and technical schools, and community colleges offer six-month to two-year programs for marine service technicians. Employers also may send marine service technicians to special training programs offered by equipment manufacturers or distributors which may last up to two weeks.

Earnings: The median annual earnings of marine service technicians in 2002 were around $28,000. Keep in mind, however, that this is a seasonal job in many parts of the country.

Key Contacts: For more information on certification and careers for marine service technicians, contact:

- **Marine Retailers Association of America:** P.O. Box 1127, Oak Park, IL 60304. Website: www.mraa.com.

- **National Marine Electronics Association:** 7 Riggs Avenue, Severna Park, MD 21146. Website: www.nmea.org.

- **Association of Marine Technicians:** 455 Knollwood Terrace, Roswell, GA 30075-3416. Website: www.am-tech.org.

- **National Marine Manufacturers Association:** 200 E. Randolph Drive, Suite 5100, Chicago, IL 60601. Website: www.nmma.org.

- **Marine Advanced Technology Education Center:** Monterey Peninsula College, 980 Fremont Street, Monterey, CA 93940. Website: www.marinetech.org.

Science Technicians

- ➭ **Annual Earnings:** $28,800 to $60,000
- ➭ **Education/Training:** Certificate, associate degree, or BA
- ➭ **Outlook:** Good to excellent

Employment Outlook: Job opportunities for science technicians are expected to increase as fast as the average for all occupations in the decade ahead. Continued growth of scientific and medical research, particularly related to biotechnology, as well as the development and production of technical products, should stimulate demand for science technicians.

Nature of Work: Science technicians use the principles and theories of science and mathematics to solve problems in research and development and to investigate, invent, and help improve products. Their jobs are more practically oriented than those of scientists. They set up, operate, and maintain laboratory instruments, monitor experiments, make observations, calculate and record results, and often develop conclusions. They must keep detailed logs of all of their work-related activities. They make extensive use of computers, computer-interfaced equipment, robotics, and high-technology industrial applications such as biological engineering. They encompass a variety of occupations such as agricultural technicians, biological technicians, chemical technicians, nuclear technicians, and petroleum technicians.

Working Conditions: Science technicians work in a variety of settings. Many work indoors, usually in laboratories, and have regular hours. Others, such as agricultural and petroleum technicians, work outdoors, sometimes in remote locations, and may be exposed to hazardous conditions. Chemical technicians sometimes work with toxic chemicals, nuclear technicians may be exposed to radiation, and biological technicians sometimes work with disease-causing organisms or radioactive agents.

Education, Training, Qualifications: Science technicians have at least two years of specialized training. Many junior and community colleges offer associate degrees in specific technology or a more general education in science and mathematics. Many science technicians have a bachelor's degree in science or mathematics, or have had science and math courses in four-year colleges. Some companies offer formal or on-the-job training for science technicians.

Earnings: The median annual earnings for science technicians ranged from $28,800 to $60,000 in 2002. The median hourly earnings of science technicians in 2002 were as follows for various occupations:

- Nuclear technicians $28.84
- Forensic science technicians $19.73
- Geological and petroleum technicians $18.96
- Chemical technicians $18.00
- Environmental science and protection
  technicians, including health $16.98
- Biological technicians $15.73
- Forest and conservation technicians $14.90
- Agricultural and food science technicians $13.74

In 2003, the average annual salary in nonsupervisory, supervisory, and managerial positions in the federal government was $30,440 for biological science technicians; $44,068 for physical science technicians; $55,374 for geodetic technicians; $40,781 for hydrologic technicians; and $52,585 for meteorological technicians.

Key Contacts: For information on career opportunities for chemical technicians, contact:

- **American Chemical Society:** Education Division, Career Publications, 1155 16th Street, NW, Washington, DC 20036. Website: www.acs. org.

- **American Academy of Forensic Sciences:** P.O. Box 669, Colorado Springs, CO 80901. Website: www.aafs.org.

- **Society of American Foresters:** 5400 Grosvenor Lane, Bethesda, MD 20814. Website: www.safnet.org.

Semiconductor Technicians

↪ **Annual Earnings:** $28,000
↪ **Education/Training:** Certificate to associate degree
↪ **Outlook:** Good

Employment Outlook: Job opportunities for semiconductor technicians are expected to be good in the decade ahead despite the fact that many of these jobs are increasingly being outsourced abroad. Like many other jobs, future opportunities for semiconductor technicians **depend on the continuing growth of the economy**

Nature of Work: Semiconductor technicians primarily design, produce, and test electronic semiconductors (computer chips, microchips, integrated circuits). Working under the supervision of engineers, they produce the microchips that go into electronic devices, such as computers, cameras, cars, cell phones, microwave ovens, pagers, and video games. In addition to producing these chips, they monitor the manufacturing process, maintain equipment, and work in teams.

Working Conditions: Semiconductor technicians primarily work in clean and well organized laboratories. They work in "fabs" and "clean rooms" that are designed to prevent any dust from coming into contact with microchips. Much of their work involves standing and working behind computer terminals and equipment.

Education, Training, Qualifications: Semiconductor technicians receive training through vocational education programs and community colleges. While some semiconductor technicians only have a high school education, employers increasingly prefer hiring individuals with a two-year associate degree in electronics technology or related field.

Earnings: The median annual earnings for semiconductor technicians was around $28,000 in 2002.

Key Contacts: For information on jobs for semiconductor technicians, contact:

- **International Society of Certified Electronic Technicians:** 3608 Pershing Avenue, Fort Worth, TX 76107-4527. Website: www.iscet. org.

- **Semiconductor Equipment and Materials International:** 1401 K Street, NW, Suite 601, Washington, DC 20005. Website: www.semi. org.

- **Semiconductor Industry Association:** 181 Metro Drive, Suite 450, San Jose, CA 95110. Website: www.semichips.org.

7

Government, Legal, and Public Safety Jobs

T HE PUBLIC AND LEGAL SECTORS offer numerous job and career opportunities for people without a four-year degree. Employing more than 22 million people at the federal, state, and local levels, the public sector is an enormous complex. Despite efforts to downside government, the size of government continues to increase in response to population growth and the demand for improved public services, from schools and highways to parks and public safety.

While education remains the largest public sector complex, most professional jobs in education require at least a four-year degree. Many other jobs, especially administrative and maintenance in nature, only require a high school diploma and on-the-job training. Many of the medical and health care jobs outlined in Chapter 4 are actually performed in local, state, and federal government hospitals and health care facilities.

The public safety complex is especially receptive to hiring individuals without a four-year degree. From police and fire protection to courts and legal offices, the public safety arena is enormous in size, and it continues to grow in response to important public safety and security issues.

The jobs outlined in this chapter represent only a few of many attractive opportunities open to anyone without a four-year degree. If your interests include government, public safety, and law, or if you're oriented toward public service, be sure to explore the many exciting opportunities available through government and the justice system. Many of these jobs offer excellent salaries, benefits, advancement, and long-term job security.

Correctional Officers

⇨ **Annual Earnings:** $32,670
⇨ **Education/Training:** High school or two years experience
⇨ **Outlook:** Excellent

Employment Outlook: Job opportunities for correctional officers are expected to be excellent in the decade ahead. The need to replace correctional officers who transfer to other occupations, retire, or leave the labor force, coupled with rising employment demand, will generate thousands of job openings each year. In the past, some local and state corrections agencies have experienced difficulty in attracting and keeping qualified applicants, largely due to relatively low salaries and the concentration of jobs in rural locations. This situation is expected to continue.

Correctional officers held about 476,000 jobs in 2002. About three of every five jobs were in state correctional institutions such as prisons, prison camps, and youth correctional facilities. Most of the remaining jobs were in city or county jails or other institutions run by local governments. About 16,000 jobs for correctional officers were in federal correctional institutions, and about 16,000 jobs were in privately owned and managed prisons.

There are about 118 jail systems in the United States that house over 1,000 inmates, all of which are located in urban areas. A significant number work in jails and other facilities located in law enforcement agencies throughout the country. However, most correctional officers work in institutions located in rural areas with smaller inmate populations than those in urban jails.

Nature of Work: Correctional officers are responsible for overseeing individuals who have been arrested and are awaiting trial or who have been convicted of a crime and sentenced to serve time in a jail, reformatory, or penitentiary. They maintain security and inmate accountability to prevent disturbances, assaults, or escapes. Officers have no law enforcement responsibilities outside the institution where they work. Police and sheriffs' departments in county and municipal jails or precinct station houses employ many correctional officers. Correctional officers in the U.S. jail system admit and process more than 11 million people per year, with about 500,000 offenders in jail at any given time. When individuals are first arrested, the jail staff may not know their true identity or criminal record, and violent detainees may be placed in the general population. This is the most dangerous phase of the incarceration process for correctional officers.

Most correctional officers are employed in large jails or state or federal prisons, watching over the approximately one million offenders who are incarcerated at any given time. In addition to jails and prisons, a relatively small number of correctional officers oversee individuals being held by the U.S. Immigration and Naturalization Service before they are released or deported, or they work for correctional institutions that are run by private for-profit organizations. While both jails and prisons can be dangerous places to work, prison populations are more stable than jail populations, and correctional officers in prisons know the security and custodial requirements of the prisoners with whom they are dealing.

Working Conditions: Working in a correctional institution can be stressful and hazardous. Every year, a number of correctional officers are injured in confrontations with inmates. Correctional officers may work indoors or outdoors. Some correctional institutions are well lighted, temperature controlled and ventilated, while others are old, overcrowded, hot and noisy. Correctional officers usually work an eight-hour day, five days a week, on rotating shifts. Prison and jail security must be provided around the clock, which often means that officers work all hours of the day and night, weekends, and holidays. In addition, officers may be required to work paid overtime.

Education, Training, Qualifications: Most institutions require correctional officers to be at least 18 to 21 years of age and a U.S. citizen; have a high school education or its equivalent; demonstrate job stability – usually by accumulating two years of work experience; and have no felony convictions. Promotion prospects may be enhanced through obtaining a postsecondary education.

Correctional officers must be in good health. Candidates for employment are generally required to meet formal standards of physical fitness, eyesight, and hearing. Applicants are typically screened for drug abuse, subject to background checks, and required to pass a written examination. Good judgment and the ability to think and act quickly are indispensable.

Federal, state, and some local departments of corrections provide training for correctional officers. Some states have regional training academies which are available to all local agencies. All states and local correctional agencies provide on-the-job training at the conclusion of formal instruction, including legal restrictions and interpersonal relations. Many systems require firearms proficiency and self-defense skills. Officer trainees typically receive several weeks or months of training in an actual job setting under the supervision of an experienced officer. However, specific entry requirements and on-the-job training vary widely from agency to agency.

Academy trainees generally receive instruction on a number of subjects, including institutional policies, regulations, and operations, as well as custody and security procedures. As a condition of employment, new federal correctional officers must undergo 200 hours of formal training within the first year of employment. They must also complete 120 hours of specialized training at the U.S. Federal Bureau of Prisons residential training center at Glynco, Georgia within the first 60 days after appointment. Experienced officers receive annual in-service training to keep abreast of new developments and procedures.

Some correctional officers are members of prison tactical response teams, which are trained to respond to disturbances, riots, hostage situations, forced-cell moves, and other potentially dangerous confrontations. Team members receive training and practice with weapons, chemical agents, forced-entry methods, crisis management, and other tactics.

Earnings: Median annual earnings of correctional officers and jailers were $32,670 in 2002. The middle 50 percent earned between $25,950 and $42,620. The highest 10 percent earned more than $52,370. Median annual earnings in the public sector were $40,900 in the federal government; $33,260 in state government; and $31,380 in local government. In addition to typical benefits, correctional officers employed in the public sector usually are provided with uniforms or a clothing allowance to purchase their own uniforms. Civil service systems or merit boards cover officers employed by the federal government and most state governments. Their retirement coverage entitles them to retire at age 50 after 20 years of service or at any age with 25 years of service.

Key Contacts: Information about correctional jobs in a jail setting is available from:

- **American Jail Association:** 1135 Professional Court, Hagerstown, MD 21740. Website: www.corrections.com/aja.

Information on obtaining a position as a correctional officer with the federal government is available from the Office of Personnel Management (OPM) through a telephone-based system. Consult your telephone directory under U.S. Government for a local number or call 703-724-1850 (**not** a toll-free number) or Federal Relay Service 800-877-8339.

Two Internet sites may be useful to obtain information about opportunities at the federal level:

- **Federal Bureau of Prisons**   www.bop.gov
- **Office of Personnel Management**   www.usajobs.opm.gov

Court Reporters

⇨ **Annual Earnings:** $41,550
⇨ **Education/Training:** Technical training to associate degree
⇨ **Outlook:** Good to excellent

Employment Outlook: Employment of court reporters is projected to grow about as fast as the average for occupations in the coming decade. Demand for court reporter services will be spurred by the continuing need for accurate transcription of proceedings in courts and in pretrial depositions and by the growing need to create captions for live or prerecorded television and to provide other realtime transcription services for people with hearing loss. Despite the good job prospects, fewer people are going into this profession, creating a shortage of court reporters – particularly stenographic typists – and making job opportunities very good to excellent.

Court reporters held about 18,000 jobs in 2002. About 50 percent worked for state and local governments, a reflection of the large number of court reporters working in courts, legislatures, and various agencies. Most of the remaining wage and salary workers worked for court reporting agencies. Eleven percent of court reporters were self-employed.

Nature of work: Court reporters typically take verbatim reports of speeches, conversations, legal proceedings, meetings, and other events when written accounts of spoken words are necessary for correspondence, records, or legal proof. Court reporters play a critical role not only in judicial proceedings, but at every meeting where the spoken word must be preserved as a written transcript. They are responsible for ensuring a complete, accurate, and secure legal record. In addition to preparing and protecting the legal record, many court reporters assist judges and attorneys in a variety of ways, such as organizing and searching for information in the official record or making suggestions to judges and attorneys regarding courtroom administration and procedure. Increasingly, court reporters are providing closed-captioning and realtime transcription services that enable deaf and hard of hearing people to know what is being said – in classrooms, movie theaters, TV broadcasts, meetings, court proceedings, and other venues.

There are two main methods of court reporting: stenotyping and voice writing. Using a stenotype machine, stenotypists document all statements made in official proceedings. The machine allows them to press multiple keys at a time to record combinations of letters representing sounds, words, or phrases. These symbols are then recorded on computer disks or CD-ROM, which are then translated and displayed as text in a process called computer-aided transcription. The other method of court reporting is called voice writing. Using the voice-writing method, a court reporter speaks directly into a stenomask – a hand-held mask containing a microphone with a voice silencer. As the reporter repeats the testimony into the recorder, the mask and silencer prevent the reporter from being heard during testimony. Voice writers record everything that is said by judges, witnesses, attorneys, and other parties to a proceeding, including gestures and emotional reactions.

In addition to recording official proceedings in the courtroom, court reporters may take depositions for attorneys in offices and document proceedings of meetings, conventions, and other private activities. Still others capture the proceedings taking place in government agencies at all levels, from the U.S. Congress to state and local government bodies. Court reporters, both stenotypists and voice writers, who specialize in captioning live television programming for people with hearing loss are known as stenocaptioners. They work for television networks or cable stations, captioning news, emergency broadcasts, sporting events, and other programming. With CART and broadcast captioning, the level of understanding gained by a person with hearing loss depends entirely on the skill of the stenocaptioner. In an emergency, such as a tornado or a hurricane, hearing impaired people's safety may depend entirely on the accuracy of information provided in the form of captioning. People learning English as a second language also use captions to facilitate their English skills.

Working Conditions: The majority of court reporters work in comfortable settings, such as offices of attorneys, courtrooms, legislatures, and conventions. An increasing number of court reporters work from home-based offices as independent contractors, or freelancers. Work in this occupation presents few hazards, although sitting in the same position for long periods can be tiring, and workers can suffer wrist, back, neck, or eye problems due to strain. Workers also risk repetitive motion injuries such as carpal tunnel syndrome. In addition, the pressure to be accurate and fast can be stressful. Many official court reporters work a standard 40-hour week. Self-employed court reporters, or freelancers, usually work flexible hours, including part time, evenings, and weekends, or they can work on an on-call basis.

Education, Training, Qualifications: The amount of training required to become a court reporter varies with the type of reporting chosen. It usually takes less than a year to become a voice writer. In contrast, the average length of time it takes to become a stenotypist is 33 months. Training is offered by about 160 postsecondary vocational and technical schools and colleges. The National Court Reporters Association (NCRA) has approved about 82 programs, all of which offer courses in stenotype computer-aided transcription and realtime reporting. NCRA-approved programs require students to capture a minimum of 225 words per minute, a federal government requirement as well. Some states require court reporters to be notary publics. Others require the certified court reporter (CCR) designation, for which a reporter must pass a state certification test administered by a board of examiners. Additional certifications that demonstrate higher levels of competency may be earned. In addition to possessing speed and accuracy, court reporters must have excellent listening skills, as well as good English grammar, vocabulary, and punctuation skills. Voice writers must learn to listen and speak simultaneously and very quickly, while also identifying speakers and describing peripheral activities in the courtroom or deposition room. They must be aware of business practices and current events as well as the correct spelling of names of people, places, and events that may be mentioned in a broadcast or court proceedings. For those who work in courtrooms, an expert knowledge of legal terminology and criminal and appellate procedure is essential. Because capturing proceedings requires the use of computerized stenography or speech recognition equipment, court reporters must be knowledgeable about computer hardware and software applications.

Earnings: Court reporters had median annual earnings of $41,550 in 2002. The middle 50 percent earned between $29,770 and $55,360. The highest paid 10 percent earned more than $73,440. Median annual earnings in 2002 were $40,720 for court reporters working in local government. Both compensation and compensation methods for court reporters vary with type of reporting job, the experience of the reporter, the level of certification achieved, and the region of the country the reporter works in. Official court reporters earn a salary and a per-page fee for transcripts. Many salaried court reporters supplement their income by doing additional freelance work. Freelance court reporters are paid per job and receive a per-page fee for transcripts. Communication access realtime translation (CART) providers are paid hourly. Stenocaptioners receive a salary and benefits of they work as employees of a captioning company; stenocaptioners working as independent contractors are paid hourly.

Key Contacts: State employment service offices can provide information about job openings for court reporters. For information about careers, training, and certification in court reporting, contact any of the following sources:

- **National Court Reporters Association:** 8224 Old Courthouse Road, Vienna, VA 22182. Website: www.ncraonline.org.

- United States Court Reporters Association: P.O. Box 465, Chicago, IL 60690-0465. Website: www.uscra.org.

- National Verbatim Reporters Association: 207 Third Avenue, Hattiesburg, MS 39401. Website: www.nvra.org.

Firefighters

- ↻ **Annual Earnings:** $36,200
- ↻ **Education/Training:** High school diploma plus examination
- ↻ **Outlook:** Good

Employment Outlook: Prospective firefighters are expected to face keen competition for available job openings. Many people are attracted to firefighting because it is challenging and provides the opportunity to perform an essential public service, a high school education is usually sufficient for entry, and a pension is guaranteed upon retirement after 20 years.

Employment figures include only paid career firefighters – they do not include volunteer firefighters, who perform the same duties and may comprise the majority of firefighters in a residential area. According to the United States Fire Administration, nearly 70 percent of fire companies are staffed by volunteer firefighters. Paid career firefighters held about 282,000 jobs in 2002. First-line supervisors/managers of firefighting and prevention workers held about 63,000 jobs; and fire inspectors held about 14,000.

About 9 out of 10 firefighting workers were employed by municipal or county fire departments. Some large cities have thousands of career firefighters, while many small towns have only a few. Most of the remainder worked in fire departments on federal and state installations, including airports. Private firefighting companies employ a small number of firefighters and usually operate on a subscription basis.

In response to the expanding role of firefighters, some municipalities have combined fire prevention, public fire education, safety, and emergency medical services into a single organization commonly referred to as a public safety organization. Some local and regional fire departments are being consolidated into countywide establishments in order to reduce administrative staffs and cut costs, and to establish training standards and work procedures.

Nature of Work: Firefighters are frequently the first emergency personnel at the scene of a traffic accident or medical emergency and may be called upon to put out a fire, treat injuries, or perform other vital functions. During duty hours, firefighters must be prepared to respond immediately to a fire or any other emergency that arises. Because fighting fires is dangerous and complex, it requires organization and teamwork. At every emergency scene, firefighters perform specific duties. At fires, they connect hose lines to hydrants, operate a pump to send water to high pressure hoses, and position ladders to enable them to deliver water to the fire. They also rescue victims and provide emergency medical attention as needed, ventilate smoke-filled areas, and attempt to salvage the contents of buildings. Sometimes they remain at the site of a disaster for days at a time, rescuing trapped survivors and assisting with medical treatment.

Firefighters work in a variety of settings, including urban and suburban areas, airports, chemical plants, other industrial sites, and rural areas such as grasslands and forests. In addition, some firefighters work in hazardous materials units that are trained for the control, prevention, and clean-up of oil spills and other hazardous materials incidents. Workers in urban and suburban areas, airports, and industrial sites typically use conventional firefighting equipment and tactics, while forest fires and major hazardous materials spills call for different methods.

In national forests and parks, forest fire inspectors spot fires from watchtowers and report their findings to headquarters. Forest rangers patrol to ensure campers comply with fire regulations. When fires break out, crews of firefighters are brought in to suppress the blaze using heavy equipment, hand tools, and water hoses. Forest firefighting, like urban firefighting, can be rigorous work. One of the most effective means of battling the blaze is by creating fire lines through cutting down trees and digging out grass and all other combustible vegetation, creating bare land in the path of the fire that deprives it of fuel. Elite firefighters, called smoke jumpers, parachute from airplanes to reach otherwise inaccessible areas. This can be extremely hazardous because the crews have no way to escape if the wind shifts and causes the fire to burn toward them.

Between alarms, firefighters clean and maintain equipment, conduct practice drills and fire inspections, and participate in physical activities.

Working Conditions: Firefighters spend much of their time at fire stations, which usually have features common to a residential facility like a dormitory. When an alarm sounds, firefighters respond rapidly, regardless of the weather or hour. Firefighting involves risk of death or injury from sudden cave-ins of floors, toppling walls, traffic accidents when responding to calls and exposure to flames and smoke. Firefighters may also come in contact with poisonous, flammable, or explosive gases and chemicals, as well as radioactive or other hazardous materials that may have immediate or long-term effects on their health. For these reasons, they must wear protective gear that can be very heavy and hot.

Work hours of firefighters are longer and vary more widely than hours of most other workers. Many work more than 50 hours a week, and sometimes they may work even longer. In some agencies, they are on duty for 24 hours, then off for 48 hours, and receive an extra day off at intervals. In others, they work a day shift of 10 hours for three or four days, a night shift of 14 hours for three or four nights, have three or four days off, and then repeat the cycle. In addition, firefighters often work extra hours at fires and other emergencies and are regularly assigned to work holidays. Fire lieutenants and fire captains often work the same hours as the firefighters they supervise.

Education, Training, Qualifications: Applicants for municipal fire-fighting jobs generally must pass a written exam; tests of strength, physical stamina, coordination, and agility; and a medical examination that includes drug screening. Examinations are generally open to persons who are at least 18 years of age and have a high school education or its equivalent. Those who receive the highest scores in all phases of testing have the best chances of appointment. The completion of community college courses in fire science may improve an applicant's chances for appointment. In recent years, an increasing proportion of entrants to this occupation have had some postsecondary education.

As a rule, entry-level workers in large fire departments are trained for several weeks at the department's training center or academy. Through classroom instruction and practical training, the recruits study firefighting techniques, fire prevention, hazardous material control, local building codes, and emergency medical procedures, including first aid and cardiopulmonary resuscitation. They also learn how to use axes, chain saws, fire extinguishers, ladders, and other firefighting and rescue equipment. After successfully completing this training, they are assigned to a fire company, where they undergo a period of probation.

A number of fire departments have accredited apprenticeship programs lasting up to five years. These programs combine formal, technical instruction with on-the-job training under the supervision of experienced firefighters. A number of colleges offer courses leading to two- or four-year degrees in fire engineering or fire science. Many fire departments offer incentives such as tuition reimbursement or higher pay for completing advanced training.

Among the personal qualities firefighters need are mental alertness, self-discipline, courage, mechanical aptitude, endurance, strength, and a sense of public service. Initiative and good judgment are also extremely important because firefighters make quick decisions in emergencies. Because members of a crew live and work closely together under conditions of stress and danger for extended periods, they must be dependable and able to get along well with others.

Earnings: Median hourly earnings of firefighters were $17.42 in 2002 ($36,200 per year). The highest 10 percent earned more than $28.22. Median earnings were $17.92 in local government, $15.96 in the Federal Government, and $13.58 in state government. Supervisors, managers, and inspectors earn higher salaries. Firefighters who average more than a certain number of hours a week are required to be paid overtime. Almost all fire departments provide protective clothing (helmets, boots, and coats) and breathing apparatus, and may also provide dress uniforms. Firefighters are generally covered by pension plans, often providing retirement at half pay after 25 years of service or if disabled in the line of duty.

Key Contacts: Information about a career as a firefighter may be obtained from local fire departments and from:

- **International Association of Fire Fighters:** 1750 New York Avenue, NW., Washington, DC 20006. Website: www.iaff.org.

- **U.S. Fire Administration:** 16825 South Seton Avenue, Emmitsburg, MD 21727. Website: www.usfa.fema.gov.

Information about firefighter professional qualifications and a list of colleges offering two- or four-year degree programs in fire science or fire prevention may be obtained from:

- **National Fire Academy:** 16825 South Seton Avenue, Emmitsburg, MD 21727. Website: www.usfa.fema.gov/fire-service/nfa/nfa.shtm.

Paralegals and Legal Assistants

⇨ **Annual Earnings:** $37,950
⇨ **Education/Training:** Associate to four-year degree
⇨ **Outlook:** Good to excellent

Employment Outlook: Paralegals and legal assistants are projected to grow faster than average for all occupations in the decade ahead. Some employment growth stems from law firms and other employers with legal staffs increasingly hiring paralegals to lower the cost and increase the availability of legal services. Additional job openings will arise as people leave the occupation. Despite projections of fast employment growth, competition for jobs should continue as many people enter the profession; however, highly skilled, formally trained paralegals with prior experience have excellent employment potential.

Private law firms will continue to be the largest employers of paralegals, but a growing array of other organizations, such as corporate legal departments, insurance companies, real estate and title insurance firms, and banks hire paralegals. Demand for paralegals is also expected to grow as an increasing population requires legal services, especially in areas such as intellectual property, health care, international, elder, criminal, and environmental law. A growing number of experienced paralegals are expected to establish their own businesses. Job opportunities for paralegals will expand in the public sector as well. Community legal-aid programs, which provide assistance to the poor, aged, minorities, and middle-income families, will employ additional paralegals to minimize expenses and serve the most people. Federal, state and local government agencies, consumer organizations, and the courts also should continue to hire paralegals in increasing numbers. Paralegals who provide some of the same legal services as lawyers at a lower cost, tend to fare relatively better in difficult economic conditions.

Nature of Work: While lawyers assume ultimate responsibility for legal work, they often delegate many of their tasks to paralegals. In fact, paralegals – also called legal assistants – continue to assume a growing range of tasks in the nation's legal offices and perform some of the same tasks as lawyers. Nevertheless, they are still prohibited from carrying out duties which are considered to be the practice of law, such as setting legal fees, giving legal advice, and presenting cases in court.

One of a paralegal's most important tasks is helping lawyers prepare for closings, hearings, trials, and corporate meetings. Paralegals investigate the facts of cases and ensure that all relevant information is considered. They also identify appropriate laws, judicial decisions, legal articles, and other materials that are relevant to assigned cases. After they analyze and organize the information, paralegals may prepare written reports that attorneys use in determining how cases should be handled. If attorneys decide to file lawsuits on behalf of clients, paralegals may help prepare the legal arguments, draft pleadings and motions to be filed with the court, obtain affidavits, and assist attorneys during trials. Paralegals also organize and track files of all important case documents and make them available and easily accessible to attorneys. In addition to this preparatory work, paralegals help draft contracts, mortgages, separation agreements, and trust instruments. They may also assist in preparing tax returns and planning estates. Tasks vary – depending on the employer.

Working Conditions: Paralegals employed by corporations and government usually work a standard 40-hour week. Although most paralegals work year-round, some are temporarily employed during busy times of the year, then released as the workload diminishes. Paralegals who work for law firms sometimes work very long hours when they are under pressure to meet deadlines. Some law firms reward such loyalty with bonuses and additional time off. Paralegals do most of their work at desks in offices and law libraries. Occasionally, they travel to gather information and perform other duties.

Education, Training, Qualifications: There are several ways to become a paralegal. The most common in through a community college paralegal program that leads to an associate degree. The other common method of entry, mainly for those who have a college degree, is through a certification program that leads to a certificate in paralegal studies. A small number of schools also offer bachelor's and master's degrees in paralegal studies. Some employers train paralegals on the job, hiring college graduates with no legal experience or promoting experienced legal secretaries. Other entrants have experience in a technical field that is useful to law firms, such as a background in tax preparation for tax and estate practice, criminal justice, or nursing or health administration for personal injury practice.

Formal paralegal training programs are offered by an estimated 600 colleges and universities. Approximately 250 paralegal programs are approved by the American Bar Association (ABA). Although this approval is neither required nor sought by many programs, graduation from an ABA-approved program can enhance one's employment opportunities. Paralegal programs include two-year associate's degree and four-year bachelor's degree programs, and certificate programs that can take only a few months to complete. Many paralegal training programs include an internship in which students can gain practical experience by working for several months in a private law firm, office of a public defender or attorney general, bank, corporate legal department, legal-aid organization, or government agency. Experience gained in internships is an asset when seeking a job after graduation. Although most employers do not require certification, earning a voluntary certificate from a professional society may offer advantages in the labor market. Familiarity with operation and application of computers in legal research and litigation support as well as the ability to write also are increasingly important.

Earnings: Earnings of paralegals and legal assistants vary greatly. Salaries depend on education, training, experience, type and size of employer, and geographic location of the job. In general, paralegals who work for large law firms or in large metropolitan areas earn more than those who work for smaller firms or in less populated regions. In addition to a salary, many paralegals receive bonuses. In 2002, full-time, wage and salary paralegals and legal assistants had median annual earnings, including bonuses, of $37,950. The top 10 percent earned more than $61,150. Median annual earnings in the industries employing the largest' numbers of paralegals in 2002 were as follow: federal government, $53,770; legal services, $36,780; local government, $36,030; and state government, $34,750.

Key Contacts: General information on a career as a paralegal can be obtained from:

- **Standing Committee on Paralegal Assistants:** American Bar Association, 321 North Clark Street, Chicago, IL 60610. Website: www.abanet.org/legalservices/legalassistants/home.html.

For information on the Certified Legal Assistant exam, schools that offer training programs in a specific state, and standards and guidelines for paralegals, contact:

- **National Association of Legal Assistants, Inc.:** 1516 South Boston Street, Suite 200, Tulsa, OK 74119. Website: www.nala.org.

For information on a career as a paralegal, schools that offer training programs, job postings for paralegals, the Paralegal Advanced Competency Exam, and local paralegal associations, contact:

- **National Federation of Paralegal Associations:** 2517 Eastlake Avenue East, Suite 200, Seattle, WA 98102. Website: www.paralegals. org.

Information on paralegal training programs, including the pamphlet *How to Choose a Paralegal Education Program,* may be requested from:

- **American Association for Paralegal Education:** 407 Wekiva Springs Road, Suite 241, Longwood, FL 32779. Website: www.aafpe. org.

Private Detectives and Investigators

- ➪ **Annual Earnings:** $32,300
- ➪ **Education/Training:** High school diploma plus some college
- ➪ **Outlook:** Good

Employment Outlook: Private detectives and investigators held about 48,000 jobs in 2002. About a third were self-employed, including many who held a second job as a self-employed private detective. Almost a fifth of the jobs were found in investigation and security services, including private detective agencies, while another fifth were in department or other general merchandise stores. The rest worked mostly in state and local government, legal services firms, employment services, insurance carriers, and credit intermediation and related activities, including banks and other depository institutions. Employment of private detectives is expected to grow faster than average for all occupations. However, keen competition is expected because private detective and investigative careers attract many qualified people, including relatively young retirees from law enforcement and military careers.

Nature of Work: Private detectives and investigators use many means to determine the facts in a variety of matters. To carry out investigations, they may use various types of surveillance or searches. To verify facts, such as an individual's place of employment or income, they make phone calls or visit a subject's workplace. In other cases, especially those involving missing persons and background checks, investigators often interview people to gather as much information as possible about an individual. In all cases, private detectives and investigators assist attorneys, businesses, and the public with a variety of legal, financial, and personal problems. They also provide assistance in civil liability and personal injury cases, insurance claims and fraud, child custody, and protection cases. Increasingly, they are hired to investigate individuals to prove or disprove infidelity.

Working Conditions: Private detectives and investigators often work irregular hours because of the need to conduct surveillance and contact people who are not available during normal working hours. Early morning, evening, weekend, and holiday work is common. Many detectives and investigators spend time away from their offices conducting interviews or doing surveillance – often for long periods in a car or van. Some work in their office most of the day conducting computer searches and making phone calls.

When working on a case away from the office, the environment might range from plush boardrooms to seedy bars. Store and hotel detectives work in the businesses they protect. Investigators generally work alone, but they sometimes work with others during surveillance or when following a subject in order to avoid detection by the subject. Some of the work involves confrontation, so the job can be stressful and dangerous. Some situations call for the investigator to be armed, such as certain bodyguard assignments for corporate executives or celebrities. In most cases however, a weapon is not necessary because the purpose of their work is gathering information and not law enforcement or criminal apprehension. Owners of investigative agencies have the added stress of having to deal with demanding and sometimes distraught clients.

Education, Training, Qualifications: There are no formal education requirements for most private detective and investigator jobs, although many private detectives have college degrees. Private investigators and detectives typically have previous experience in other occupations. Some work initially for insurance or collection companies or in the private security business. Many investigators enter the field after serving in law enforcement, the military, government auditing and investigative positions, or federal intelligence jobs. These individuals often can apply their prior work experience in a related investigative field. A few enter the occupation directly after graduation from college, generally with an associate or bachelor's degree in criminal justice or police science.

The majority of states and the District of Columbia require private detectives and investigators to be licensed. Licensing requirements vary widely, but convicted felons cannot receive a license in most states and a growing number of states are enacting mandatory training programs for private detectives and investigators. For private detective and investigator jobs most employers look for individuals with ingenuity, persistence, and assertiveness. A candidate must not be afraid of confrontation, should communicate well, and should be able to think on his or her feet. Good interviewing and interrogation skills also are important and are usually acquired in earlier careers in law enforcement or other fields. Because the courts often are the ultimate judge of a properly conducted investigation, the investigator must be able to present the facts in a manner the jury will believe. Training in subjects such as criminal justice is helpful to aspiring private detectives and investigators.

Earnings: Median annual earnings of salaried private detectives and investigators were $29,980 in 2002. The highest 10 percent earned more than $57,370. Median annual earnings were $29,030 in investigation and security services and $22,250 in department stores. Earnings of private detectives and investigators vary greatly depending upon their employer, specialty, and the geographic area in which they work.

Key Contacts: For information on a career as a legal investigator, contact:

- **National Association of Legal Investigators:** 908 21st St., Sacramento, CA 95814-3118. Website: www.nalionline.org.

For information on local licensing requirements, contact your state Department of Public Safety, State Division of Licensing, or local or state police headquarters.

8

Building and
Construction Jobs

THE BUILDING AND CONSTRUCTION trades offer numerous job opportunities for people without a four-year degree. These jobs are especially plentiful in communities experiencing population and housing growth. Indeed, in many parts of the country experiencing a housing boom, it's difficult to find people in these trades.

The building and construction trades have always been cyclical occupational fields. When economic times are good, individuals in these fields have plenty of work, and their skills command top dollar. However, during recessions many of these workers have difficulty finding full-time employment, and many leave their trade for other types of employment.

Working in these trades often involves hard work, uncomfortable working conditions, stressful projects, and unpredictable employment. Many people drop out of these trades because of unhappy experiences. Given the constant turnover of employees in the building and construction trades, opportunities regularly open for skilled and enterprising workers. But if you are very skilled and enjoy this type of work, you'll find excellent opportunities in the building and construction trades.

Many people without a four-year degree enter these trades because entry into the trades is based more on interests, skills, and on-the-job training than on education requirements. Many individuals with or without a high school diploma initially break into the building and construction trades through apprenticeship programs through which they acquire the necessary skills and experience to advance into their respective trades.

Brickmasons, Blockmasons, and Stonemasons

⇨ **Annual Earnings:** $41,800
⇨ **Education/Training:** Experience and vocational education
⇨ **Outlook:** Excellent

Employment Outlook: Employment opportunities for brickmasons, blockmasons, and stonemasons are expected to be excellent in the decade ahead. Many openings will result from the need to replace workers who retire, transfer to other occupations, or leave these trades for other reasons. There may be fewer applicants than needed because many potential workers prefer to work under less strenuous, more comfortable conditions. Employment in these trades is expected to increase about as fast as the average for all occupations as population and business growth create a need for new houses, industrial facilities, schools, hospitals, offices, and other structures. Employment of brickmasons, blockmasons, and stonemasons, like that of many other construction workers, is sensitive to changes in the economy. When construction activity falls, these workers can experience periods of unemployment.

Nature of Work: Brickmasons, blockmasons, and stonemasons work in closely related trades creating attractive, durable surfaces, and structures. The work varies in complexity, from laying a simple masonry walkway to installing an ornate exterior on a highrise building. Breakmasons and blockmasons – who often are called simply bricklayers – build and repair walls, floors, partitions, fireplaces, chimneys, and other structures with bricks, precast masonry panels, concrete block, and other masonry materials. Some brickmasons specialize in installing firebrick linings in industrial furnaces. Stonemasons build stone walls, as well as set stone exteriors and floors. They work with two types of stone – natural cut stone, such as marble, granite, and limestone, and artificial stone made from concrete, marble chips, or other masonry materials. Stonemasons usually work on nonresidential structures, such as houses of worship, hotels, and office buildings.

Working Conditions: Brickmasons, blockmasons, and stonemasons usually work outdoors and are exposed to the elements. They stand, kneel, and bend for long periods and often have to lift heavy materials. Common hazards include injuries from tools and falls from scaffolds, but these can often be avoided when proper safety equipment is used and safety practices are followed.

Education, Training, Qualifications: Most brickmasons, blockmasons, and stonemasons pick up their skills informally, observing and learning from experienced workers. Many others receive training in vocational education schools or from industry-based programs that are common throughout the country. Another way to learn these skills is through an apprenticeship program, which generally provides the most thorough training. Individuals who learn the trade on the job usually start as helpers, laborers, or mason tenders. These workers carry materials, move scaffolds, and mix mortar.

Earnings: Median hourly earnings of brickmasons and blockmasons in 2002 were $20.11 (around $41,800 in annual earnings). The middle 50 percent earned between $15.36 and $25.32. Median hourly earnings in the industries employing the largest number of brickmasons in 2002 were:

- Nonresidential building construction $22.12
- Foundation, structure, and building
  exterior contractors $20.26

Median hourly earnings of stonemasons in 2002 were $16.36. The middle 50 percent earned between $12.06 and $20.76.

Earnings for workers in these trades can be reduced on occasion because poor weather and downturns in construction activity limit the time they can work.

Key Contacts: For information on the work of brickmasons, blockmasons, or stonemasions, contact:

- **Associated Builders and Contractors:** Workforce Development Department, 4250 N. Fairfax Drive, 9th Floor, Arlington, VA 22203.

- **International Masonry Institute:** Apprenticeship and Training, The James Brice House, 42 East Street, Annapolis, MD 21401. Website: www.imiweb.org.

- **Associated General Contractors of America, Inc.:** 333 John Carlyle Street, Suite 200, Alexandria, VA 22314. Website: www.agc.org.

- **Brick Industry Association:** 11490 Commerce Park Drive, Reston, VA 22091-1525. Website: www.brickinfo.org.

- **National Association of Home Builders:** 1201 15th Street, NW, Washington, DC 20005. Website: www.nahb.org.

- **National Concrete Masonry Association:** 13750 Sunrise Valley Drive, Herndon, VA 20171-4662. Website: www.ncma.org.

Carpenters

➪ **Annual Earnings:** $34,200
➪ **Education/Training:** On-the-job training
➪ **Outlook:** Excellent

Employment Outlook: Job opportunities for carpenters are expected to be excellent in the coming decade, largely due to the numerous openings arising each year as experienced carpenters leave this large occupation. Because there are no strict training requirements for entry, many people with limited skills take jobs as carpenters but eventually leave the occupation because they dislike the work or cannot find steady employment. Employment of carpenters is expected to grow about as fast as average for all occupations. Construction activity should increase in response to new housing and commercial and industrial plants and the need to renovate and modernize existing structures. The demand for larger homes with more amenities and for second homes will continue to rise, especially as the baby boomers reach their peak earning years and can afford to spend more on housing. Carpenters can experience periods of unemployment because of the short-term nature of many construction projects and the cyclical nature of the construction industry.

Nature of Work: Carpenters are involved in many different kinds of construction activity. They cut, fit, and assemble wood and other materials for the construction of buildings, highways, bridges, docks, industrial plants, boats, and many other structures. Carpenters' duties vary by type of employer. Builders increasingly are using specialty trade contractors who, in turn, hire carpenters who specialize in just one or two activities. Such activities include setting forms for concrete construction, erecting scaffolding, or doing finishing work, such as interior and exterior trim. However, a carpenter directly employed by a general building contractor often must perform a variety of the tasks associated with new construction, such as framing walls and partitions, putting in doors and windows, building stairs, laying hardwood floors, and hanging kitchen cabinets. Carpenters employed outside the construction industry perform a variety of installation and maintenance work. They may replace panes of glass, ceiling tiles, and doors, as well as repair decks, cabinets, and other furniture.

Working Conditions: As is true of other building trades, carpentry work is sometimes strenuous. Prolonged standing, climbing, bending, and kneeling often are necessary. Carpenters risk injury working with sharp or rough materials, using sharp tools and power equipment, and working in situations where they might slip or fall. Additionally, many carpenters work outdoors. Some carpenters change employers each time they finish a construction job. Others alternate between working for a contractor and working as contractors themselves on small jobs.

Education, Training, Qualifications: Carpenters learn their trade through on-the-job training, as well as formal training programs. Most pick up skills informally by working under the supervision of experienced workers. Many acquire skills through vocational education. Others participate in employer training programs or apprenticeships. Most employers recommend an apprenticeship as the best way to learn carpentry. Apprenticeship programs are administered by local point union-management committees of the United Brotherhood of Carpenters and Joiners of America, the Associated General Contractors, Inc., and the National Association of Home Builders.

Earnings: Median hourly earnings of carpenters were $16.44 ($34,200 in annual earnings). The middle 50 percent earned between $12.59 and $21.91 an hours. Median hourly earnings in the industries employing the largest numbers of carpenters in 2002 were:

- Nonresidential building construction $18.31
- Building finishing contractors $17.30
- Residential building construction $16.02
- Foundation, structure and building exterior
  contractors $16.01

Earnings can be reduced on occasion, because carpenters lose work time in bad weather and during recessions when jobs are unavailable. Some carpenters are members of the United Brotherhood of Carpenters and Joiners of America.

Key Contacts: For information on training opportunities and carpentry in general, contact:

- **Associated Builders and Contractors:** Workforce Development Department, 4250 N. Fairfax Drive, 9th Floor, Arlington, VA 22203.

- **Associated General Contractors of America, Inc.:** 333 John Carlyle Street, Alexandria, VA 22314. Website: www.agc.org.

- **National Association of Home Builders:** 1201 15th Street, NW, Washington, DC 20005. Website: www.nahb.org.

- **United Brotherhood of Carpenters and Joiners of America:** 50 F Street, NW, Washington, DC 20001. Website: www.carpenters.org.

Construction and Building Inspectors

> **Annual Earnings:** $41,620
> **Education/Training:** Experience, certificate, associate degree
> **Outlook:** Good

Employment Outlook: Employment of construction and building inspectors is expected to grow about as fast as the average for all occupations in the coming decade. Growing concern for public safety and improvements in the quality of construction should continue to stimulate demand for construction and building inspectors. In addition to the expected employment growth, some job openings will arise from the need to replace inspectors who transfer to other occupations or leave the labor force. Inspectors are involved in all phases of construction, including maintenance and repair work, and are therefore less likely to lose jobs when new construction slows during recessions. As the population grows and the volume of real estate transactions increases, greater emphasis on home inspections should result in strong demand for home inspectors.

Nature of Work: There are many types of specialized inspectors related to the construction and repair processes: building, plan, electrical, elevator, mechanical, plumbing, public works, home inspectors, and specification. Construction and building inspectors examine the construction, alteration, or repair of buildings, highways and streets, sewer and water systems, dams, bridges, and other structures to ensure compliance with building codes and ordinances, zoning regulations, and contract specifications. Building codes and standards are the primary means by which building construction is regulated in the United States for health and safety of the general public. Building inspectors inspect the structural quality and general safety of buildings. Some specialize in such areas as structural steel or reinforced concrete structures. Home inspectors conduct inspections of newly built or previously owned homes. Home inspection has become a standard practice in the home purchasing process. Although inspections are primarily visual, inspectors may use tape measures, survey instruments, metering devices, and test equipment such as concrete strength measurers. They keep a log of their work, take photographs, file reports, and, if necessary, act on their findings. Many inspectors also investigate construction or alterations being done without proper permits.

Working Conditions: Construction and building inspectors usually work alone. However, several may be assigned to large, complex projects, particularly because inspectors tend to specialize in different areas of construction. Although they spend considerable time inspecting construction worksites, inspectors also spend time in a field office reviewing blueprints, answering letters or telephone calls, writing reports, and scheduling inspections. Inspection sites are dirty and may be cluttered with tools, materials, or debris. Inspectors may have to climb ladders or many flights of stairs, or crawl around in tight spaces. Although their work generally is not considered hazardous, inspectors, like other construction workers, wear hard hats and adhere to other safety requirements while at a construction site. Inspectors normally work regular hours. However, they may work additional hours during periods when a lot of construction is taking place.

Education, Training, Qualifications: Although requirements very considerably depending upon where one is employed, construction and building inspectors should have a thorough knowledge of construction materials and practices in either a general area, such as structural or heavy construction, or in a specialized area, such as electrical or plumbing systems, reinforced concrete, or structural steel. Applicants for construction or building inspection jobs need several years of experience as a construction manager, supervisor, or craftworker. Many inspectors previously worked as carpenters, electricians, plumbers, or pipefitters. Because inspectors must possess the right mix of technical knowledge, experience, and education, employers prefer applicants who have formal training as well as experience. Most employers require at least a high school diploma or equivalent, even for workers with considerable experience. Construction and building inspectors usually receive much of their training on the job, although they must learn building codes and standards on their own. Most states and cities require some type of certification for employment. To become certified, inspectors with substantial experience and education must pass stringent examinations on code requirements, construction techniques, and materials.

Earnings: Median annual earnings for construction and building inspectors were $41,620 in 2002. The median hourly earnings were $20.01. The middle 50 percent earned between $15.81 and $25.05. Median annual earnings in the industries employing the largest numbers of construction and building inspectors in 2002 were:

- Local government $42,260
- Architectural, engineering, and related services $40,770
- State government $39,610

Generally, building inspectors, including plan examiners, earn the highest salaries. Salaries in large metropolitan areas are substantially higher than those in small jurisdictions.

Key Contacts: For information on careers and certification, contact the following organizations:

- **International Code Council:** 5203 Leesburg Pike, Suite 600, Falls Church, VA 22041. Website: www.iccsafe.org.

- **Association of Construction Inspectors:** 1224 North Nokomis NE, Alexandria, MN 56308. Website: www.iami.org/aci.

- **International Association of Electrical Inspectors:** 901 Waterfall Way, Suite 602, Richardson, TX 75080-7702. Website: www.iaei.com.

- **American Society of Home Inspectors:** 932 Lee Street, Suite 101, Des Plaines, IL 60016. Website: www.ashi.org.

- **National Association of Certified Home Inspectors:** 1220 Valley Forge Road, Building 47, P.O. Box 987, Valley Forge, PA 19482-0987. Website: www.nachi.org.

- **National Association of Home Inspectors:** 4248 Park Glen Road, Minneapolis, MN 55416. Website: www.nahi.org.

Drywall Installers, Ceiling Tile Installers, and Tapers

> ⇨ **Annual Earnings:** $33,700
> ⇨ **Education/Training:** Experience and apprenticeships
> ⇨ **Outlook:** Good

Employment Outlook: Job opportunities for drywall installers, ceiling tile installers, and tapers are expected to be good in the decade ahead – to grow faster than the average for all occupations, reflecting increases in new construction and remodeling projects. In addition to jobs involving traditional interior work, drywall workers will find employment opportunities in the installation of insulated exterior wall systems, which are becoming increasingly popular. Many jobs will open up each year because of the need to replace workers who transfer to other occupations or leave the labor force. Some drywall installers, ceiling title installers, and tapers with limited skills leave the occupation when they find that they dislike the work or fail to attain steady employment. Since most of their work is done indoors, these workers lose less work time because of inclement weather than do some other construction workers. Nevertheless, they may be unemployed between construction projects and during downturns in construction activity.

Nature of Work: There are two kinds of drywall workers – installers and tapers – although many workers do both types of work. Installers, also called applicators or hangers, fasten drywall panels to the inside framework of residential houses and other buildings. Tapers, or finishers, prepare these panels for painting by taping and finishing joints and imperfections. Ceiling tile installers, or acoustical carpenters, apply or mount acoustical tiles or blocks, strips, or sheets of shock-absorbing materials to ceilings and walls of buildings to reduce reflection of sound or to decorate rooms. Lathers fasten metal or rockboard lath to walls, ceilings, and partitions of buildings. Lath forms the support base for plaster, fireproofing, or acoustical materials.

Working Conditions: As in many other construction trades, the work sometimes is strenuous. Drywall installers, ceiling tile installers, and tapers spend most of the day on their feet, either standing, bending, or kneeling. Some tapers use stilts to tape and finish ceiling and angle joints. Installers have to lift and maneuver heavy panels. Hazards include falls from ladders and scaffolds and injuries from power tools and from working with sharp materials. Because sanding a joint compound to a smooth finish creates a great deal of dust, some finishers wear masks for protection.

Education, Training, Qualifications: Most drywall installers, ceiling tile installers, and tapers start as helpers and learn their skills on the job. Installer helpers start by carrying materials, lifting and holding panels, and cleaning up debris. Within a few weeks they learn to measure, cut, and install materials. Eventually they become fully experienced workers. Some drywall installers, ceiling tile installers, and tapers learn their trade in an apprenticeship program. The United Brotherhood of Carpenters and Joiners of America, in cooperation with local contractors, administers an apprenticeship program both in drywall installation and finishing and in acoustical carpentry. Apprenticeship programs consist of at least three years, or 6,000 hours, of on-the-job training and 144 hours a year of related classroom instruction. In addition, local affiliates of the Associated Builders and Contractors and the

National Association of Home Builders conduct training programs for nonunion workers. The International Union of Painters and Allied Trades conducts an apprenticeship program in drywall finishing that lasts two to three years. Employers prefer high school graduates who are in good physical condition, but they frequently hire applicants with less education. High school or vocational school courses in carpentry provide a helpful background for drywall work. Drywall installers, ceiling tile installers, and tapers with a few years of experience and with leadership ability may become supervisors. Some workers start their own contracting businesses.

Earnings: In 2002, the median hourly earnings of drywall and ceiling tile installers were $16.21 (annual earnings of $33,700). The middle 50 percent earned between $12.43 and $21.50. The median hourly earnings in the industries employing the largest numbers of drywall and ceiling tile installers in 2002 were:

- Building finishing contractors $16.50
- Nonresidential building construction $14.66

In 2002, median hourly earnings of tapers were $18.75. The middle 50 percent earned between $14.57 and $24.68 an hour. Trainees usually started at about half the rate paid to experienced workers and received wage increases as they became more highly skilled.

Key Contacts: For information about work opportunities in drywall application and finishing and ceiling tile installation, contact local drywall installation and ceiling tile installation contractors, a local of the building unions, a local joint union-management apprenticeship committee, a state or local chapter of the Associated Builders and Contractors, or the nearest office of the state employment service or apprenticeship agency.

For details about job qualifications and training programs in drywall application and finishing and ceiling tile installation, contact:

- **Associated Builders and Contractors:** 1300 North 17th Street, Arlington, VA 22009.

- **National Association of Home Builders:** 1201 15th Street, NW, Washington, DC 20005. Website: www.nahb.org.

- **Home Builders Institute:** 1201 15th Street, NW, Washington, DC 20005. Website: www.hbi.org.

- **International Union of Painters and Allied Trades:** 1750 New York Avenue, NW, Washington, DC 20006. Website: www.iupat.org.

■ **United Brotherhood of Carpenters and Joiners of America:** 50 F Street, NW, Washington, DC 20001. Website: www.carpenters.org.

Glaziers

⇨ **Annual Earnings:** $31,600
⇨ **Education/Training:** Experience and apprenticeship programs
⇨ **Outlook:** Excellent

Employment Outlook: Job opportunities are expected to be excellent for glaziers, largely due to the numerous openings arising each year as experienced glaziers leave the occupation. In addition, many potential workers may choose not to enter this occupation because they prefer work that is less strenuous and has more comfortable working conditions. Employment of glaziers is expected to grow about as fast as the average for all occupations in the coming decade, as a result of growth in residential and commercial construction. Demand for glaziers will be spurred by the continuing need to modernize and repair existing structures and the popularity of glass in bathroom and kitchen design. The need to improve glass performance related to insulation, privacy, safety, condensation control, and noise reduction also is expected to contribute to the demand for glaziers in both residential and nonresidential remodeling. Glaziers held 49,000 jobs in 2002.

Nature of Work: Glaziers are responsible for selecting, cutting, installing, replacing, and removing glass. They generally work on one of several types of projects. Residential glazing involves work such as replacing glass in home windows; installing glass mirrors, shower doors, and bathtub enclosures; and fitting glass for tabletops and display cases. On commercial interior projects, glaziers install items such as heavy, often etched, decorative room dividers or security windows. Glazing projects also may involve replacement of streetfront windows for establishments such as supermarkets, auto dealerships, or banks. In the construction of large commercial buildings, glaziers build metal framework extrusions and install glass panels or curtain walls.

Working Conditions: Glaziers often work outdoors, sometimes in inclement weather. At times, they work on scaffolds at great heights. They do a considerable amount of bending, kneeling, lifting, and standing. Glaziers may be injured by broken glass or cutting tools, by falls from scaffolds, or by improperly lifting heavy glass panels.

Education, Training, Qualifications: Many glaziers learn the trade informally on the job. They usually start as helpers, carrying glass and cleaning up debris in glass shops. They often practice cutting on discarded glass. After a while, they are given an opportunity to cut glass for a job. Eventually, helpers assist experienced workers on simple installation jobs. By working with experienced glaziers, they eventually acquire the skills of a fully qualified glazier. Employers recommend that glaziers learn the trade through a formal apprenticeship program that lasts three to four years. Apprenticeship programs, which are administered by the National Glass Apprenticeship and local union-management committees or local contractors' associations, consist of on-the-job training and a minimum of 144 hours of classroom instruction or home study each year. On the job, apprentices learn to use the tools and equipment of the trade; handle, measure, cut, and install glass and metal framing; cut and fit moldings; and install and balance glass doors.

Earnings: In 2002, median hourly earnings of glaziers were $15.20 ($31,600 per year). The middle 50 percent earned between $11.56 and $20.53. Median hourly earnings in the industries employing the largest numbers of glaziers in 2002 were:

- Advertising and related services $48,070
- Local government $42,000
- Business, professional, labor, political
  and similar organizations $39,330
- Colleges, universities, and professional schools $36,820

Glaziers covered by union contracts generally earn more than their nonunion counterparts. Apprentice wage rates usually start at between 40 and 50 percent of the rate paid to experienced glaziers and increase as they gain experience in the field.

Key Contacts: For more information about glazier apprenticeships or work opportunities, contact local glazing or general contractors, a local of the International Union of Painters and Allied Trades, a local joint union-management apprenticeship agency, or the nearest office of the state employment service or state apprenticeship agency. For information about the work and training of glaziers, contact:

- **International Union of Painters and Allied Trades:** 1750 New York Avenue, NW, Washington, DC 20006. Website: www.iupat.org.

- **National Glass Association:** Education and Training Department, 8200 Greensboro Drive, Suite 302, McLean, VA 22102-3881. Website: www.glass.org.

- **Associated Builders and Contractors:** Workforce Development Department, 4250 N. Fairfax Drive, 9th Floor, Arlington, VA 22203.

Hazardous Materials Removal Workers

➭ **Annual Earnings:** $32,500
➭ **Education/Training:** High school diploma and training
➭ **Outlook:** Good

Employment Outlook: Job opportunities are expected to be good for hazardous materials removal workers. The occupation is characterized by a relatively high rate of turnover, resulting in a number of job openings each year. Many potential workers are not attracted to this occupation, because they prefer work that is less strenuous and has safer working conditions. Employment of hazardous materials removal workers is expected to grow much faster than the average for all occupations in the decade ahead, reflecting increasing concern for a safe and clean environment. Special-trade contractors will have strong demand for the largest segment of these workers, namely, asbestos abatement and lead abatement workers; lead abatement should offer particularly good opportunities. Mold remediation is an especially rapidly growing part of the occupation at the present time, but it is unclear whether its rapid growth will continue. Employment of decontamination technicians, radiation safety technicians, and decommissioning and decontamination workers is expected to grow in response to increased pressure for safer and cleaner nuclear and electric generator facilities.

Nature of Work: Hazardous materials workers identify, remove, package, transport, and dispose of various hazardous materials, including asbestos, lead, and radioactive and nuclear materials. The removal of hazardous materials, or "hazmats," from public places and the environment also is called abatement, remediation, and decontamination. Hazardous materials removal workers use a variety of tools and equipment, depending on the work at head. Equipment ranges form brooms to personal protective suits that completely isolate workers from the hazardous materials. The equipment required varies with the threat of contamination and can include disposable or reusable coveralls, gloves, hardhats, shoe covers, safety glasses or goggles, chemical-resistant clothing, face shields, and devices to protect one's hearing. Most workers also are required to wear respirators while working, to protect them from airborne particles. Asbestos abatement workers and lead abatement workers remove asbestos, lead, and other materials from buildings scheduled to be renovated or demolished. Using a variety of hand and power tools, such as vacuums and scrapers, these workers remove the asbestos and lead from surfaces. Emergency and disaster response workers clean up hazardous materials after train derailments and trucking accidents. These workers also are needed when an immediate cleanup is required, as would be the case after an attack by biological or chemical weapons. Decommissioning and decontamination workers remove and treat radioactive materials generated by nuclear facilities and power plants. Treatment, storage, and disposal workers transport and prepare materials for treatment or disposal. Nearly 38,000 hazardous materials removal workers held jobs in 2002.

Working Conditions: Hazardous materials removal workers function in a highly structured environment, to minimize the danger they face. Each phase of an operation is planned in advance, and workers are trained to deal with safety breaches and hazardous situations. Crews and supervisors take every precaution to ensure that the worksite is safe. Whether they work in asbestos, mold, or lead abatement or in radioactive decontamination, hazardous materials removal workers must stand, stoop, and kneel for long periods. Some must wear fully enclosed personal protective suits for several hours at a time. These workers face different working conditions, depending on their area of expertise. Although many work a standard 40-hour week, overtime and shift work are common, especially in asbestos and lead abatement. Hazardous materials removal workers may be required to travel outside their normal working areas in order to respond to emergencies.

Education, Training, Qualifications: No formal education beyond a high school diploma is required for a person to become a hazardous materials removal worker. Federal regulations require an individual to have a license to work in the occupation, although, at present, there are few laws regulating mold removal. Most employers provide technical training on the job, but a formal 32- to 40-hour training program must be completed if one is to be licensed as an asbestos abatement and lead abatement worker or a treatment, storage, and disposal worker. For decommissioning and decontamination workers employed at nuclear facilities, training is more extensive. Workers in all fields are required to take refresher courses every year in order to maintain their license. Because much of the work is done in buildings, a background in construction is helpful.

Earnings: In 2002, median hourly earnings of hazardous materials removal workers were $15.61 ($32,500 per year). The middle 50 percent earned between $12.37 and $22.18 per hour. The median hourly earnings in remediation and other waste management services, the largest industries employing hazardous materials removal workers, were $14.92 in 2002. Treatment, storage, and disposal workers usually earn slightly more than asbestos abatement and lead abatement workers. Decontamination and decommissioning workers and radiation protection technicians, though constituting the smallest group, tend to earn the highest wages.

Key Contacts: For more information on hazardous materials removal workers, including information on training, contact:

- **Laborers-AGC Education and Training Fund:** 37 Deerfield Road, P.O. Box 37, Pomfret, CT 06259. Website: www.laborerslearn.org.

Insulation Workers

↪ **Annual Earnings:** $28,900
↪ **Education/Training:** Experience and apprenticeships
↪ **Outlook:** Excellent

Employment Outlook: Job opportunities are expected to be excellent for insulation workers. Because there are no strict training requirements for entry, many people with limited skills work as insulation workers for a short time and then move on to other types of work, creating many job openings. Employment of insulation workers should grow as fast as average for all occupations in the coming decade, due to growth in residential and commercial construction. Demand for efficient use of energy to heat and cool buildings will create an increased demand for these workers in the construction of new residential, industrial, and commercial buildings. Insulation workers in the construction industry may experience periods of unemployment because of the short duration of many construction projects.

Nature of Work: Insulation workers cement, staple, wire, tape, or spray insulation. When covering a steam pipe, for example, insulation workers measure and cut sections of insulation to the proper length, stretch it open along a cut that runs the length of the material, and slip it over the pipe. They fasten the insulation with adhesive, staples, tape, or wire bands. When covering a wall or other flat surface, workers may use a hose to spray foam insulation onto a wire mesh that provides a rough surface to which the foam can cling and which adds strength to the finished surface. In attics or exterior walls of uninsulated buildings, workers blow in loose-fill insulation. In new construction or on major renovations, insulation workers staple fiberglass or rock-wool batts to exterior walls and ceilings before drywall, paneling, or plaster walls are put in place. Insulation workers use common handtools – trowels, brushes, knives, scissors, saws, pliers, and stapling guns. They use power saws to cut insulating materials, welding machines to join sheet metal or secure clamps, and compressors to blow or spray insulation.

Working Conditions: Insulation workers generally work indoors. They spend most of the workday on their feet, either standing, bending, or kneeling. Sometimes they work from ladders or in tight spaces. The work requires more coordination than strength. Insulation work often is dusty and dirty, and the summer heat can make the insulation worker very uncomfortable. Minute particles from insulation materials, especially when blown, can irritate the eyes, skin, and respiratory system. Workers must follow strict safety guidelines to protect themselves from the dangers of insulating irritants. They keep work areas well ventilated; wear protective suites, masks, and respirators; and take decontamination showers when necessary.

Education, Training, Qualifications: Most insulation workers learn their trade informally on the job, although some complete formal apprenticeship programs. For entry-level jobs, insulation contractors prefer high school graduates who are in good physical condition and licensed to drive. Applicants seeking apprenticeship positions should have a high school diploma or its equivalent and be at least 18 years old. Trainees who learn on the job receive instruction and supervision from experienced insulation workers. Trainees begin with simple tasks, such as carrying insulation or holding material while it is fastened in place. On-the-job training can take up to two years, depending on the nature of the work.

Earnings: In 2002, median hourly earnings of insulation workers were $13.91 ($28,900 per year). The middle 50 percent earned between $10.58 and $18.36 per hour.

Key Contacts: For information on training programs or other work opportunities in this trade, contact a local insulation contractor, the nearest office of the state employment service or apprenticeship agency, or the following organizations:

- **National Insulation Association:** 99 Canal Center Plaza, Suite 222, Alexandria, VA 22314. Website: www.insulation.org.

- **Insulation Contractors Association of America:** 1321 Duke Street, Suite 303, Alexandria, VA 22314. Website: www.insulate.org.

Painters and Paperhangers

⇨ **Annual Earnings:** $29,100
⇨ **Education/Training:** Experience and apprenticeships
⇨ **Outlook:** Good

Employment Outlook: Job prospects should be good as thousands of painters and paperhangers transfer to other occupations or leave the labor force each year. Because there are no strict training requirements for entry, many people with limited skills work as painters or paperhangers for a short time and then move on to other types of work. Employment of painters and paperhangers is expected to grow about as fast as average for all occupations in the decade ahead, reflecting increases in the level of new construction and in the supply of buildings and others structures that require maintenance and renovation.

Nature of Work: Painters apply paint, stain, varnish, and other finishes to buildings and other structures. They choose the right paint or finish for the surface to be covered, taking into account durability, ease of handling, method of applications, and customers' wishes. Painters first prepare the surfaces to be covered. This may require removing the old cost of paint by stripping, sanding, wire brushing, burning, or water and abrasive blasting. Painters also wash walls and trim to remove dirt and grease, fill nail holes and cracks, sandpaper rough spots, and brush off dust. When working on tall buildings, painters erect scaffolding, including "swing stages," scaffolds suspended by ropes, or cables attached to the roof hood.

Paperhangers cover walls and ceilings with decorative wall coverings made of paper, vinyl, or fabric. They first prepare the surface to be covered by applying "sizing," which seals the surface and makes the covering stick better. When redecorating, they may first remove the old covering by soaking, steaming, or applying solvents. When necessary, they patch holes and take care of other imperfections before handing the new wall covering. After the surface has been prepared, paperhangers must prepare the paste or other adhesive. Then they measure the area to be covered, check the covering for flaws, cut the covering into strips of the proper size, and closely examine the pattern in order to match it when the strips are hung. The next step is to brush or roll the adhesive onto the back of the covering and then place the strips on the wall or ceiling, making sure the pattern is matched, the strips are hung straight, and the edges are butted together to make tight, closed seams. They finally smooth the strips to remove bubbles and wrinkles, trim the top and bottom with a razor knife, and wipe off any excess adhesive.

Working Conditions: Most painters and paperhangers work 40 hours a week or less; about one-quarter have variable schedules or work part time. Painters and paperhangers must stand for long periods. Their jobs also require a considerable amount of climbing and bending. These workers must have stamina, because much of the work is done with their arms raised overhead. Painters often work outdoors but seldom in wet, cold, or inclement weather. These workers risk injury from slipping or falling off ladders and scaffolds. They sometimes may work with materials that can be hazardous if masks are not worn or if ventilation is poor. Some painting jobs can leave a worker covered with paint. In some cases, painters may work in a sealed self-contained suit to prevent inhalation of, or contact with, hazardous materials.

Education, Training, Qualifications: Painting and paperhanging are learned through apprenticeships or informal, on-the-job instruction. Although training authorities recommend completion of an apprenticeship program as the best way to become a painter or paperhanger, most painters learn the trade informally on the job as a helper to an experienced painter. Limited opportunities for informal training exist for paperhangers because few paperhangers need helpers. The apprenticeships for painters and paperhangers consists of two to four years of on-the-job training, in addition to 144 hours of related classroom instruction each year. Apprentices receive instruction in color harmony, use and care of tools and equipment, surface preparation, application techniques, paint mixing and matching, characteristics of different finishes, blueprint reading, wood finishing, and safety. Painters and paperhangers may advance to supervisory or estimating jobs with painting and decorating contractors. Many establish their own painting and decorating businesses.

Earnings: The median annual earnings of painters (construction and maintenance) were $13.98 ($29,100 annually). The middle 50 percent earned between $11.08 and $18.00 an hour. Median hourly earnings in the industries employing the largest numbers of painters in 2002 were:

- Local government $17.46
- Residential building construction $14.01
- Building finishing contractors $14.00
- Lessors of real estate $11.62

In 2002, median earnings for paperhangers were $15.22. The middle 50 percent earned between $11.52 and $20.38.

Earnings for painters may be reduced on occasion because of bad weather and the short-term nature of many construction jobs. Hourly wage rates for apprentices usually start at 40 to 50 percent of the rate for experienced workers and increase periodically.

Key Contacts: For information about the work of painters and paperhangers, contact local painting and decorating contractors, a local of the International Union of Painters and Allied Trades, a local joint union-management apprenticeship committee, or an office of the state apprenticeship agency or employment services:

- **International Union of Painters and Allied Trades:** 1750 New York Avenue, NW, Washington, DC 20006. Website: www.iupat.org.

- **Associated Builders and Contractors:** Workforce Development Department, 4250 N. Fairfax Drive, 9th Floor, Arlington, VA 22203.

- **Painting and Decorating Contractors of America:** 11960 Westline Industrial Drive, Suite 201, St. Louis, MO 63146-3209. Website: www.pdca.org.

Pipelayers, Plumbers, Pipefitters, and Steamfitters

- ➪ **Annual Earnings:** $28,500 and $40,200
- ➪ **Education/Training:** Apprenticeship
- ➪ **Outlook:** Excellent

Employment Outlook: Job opportunities are expected to be excellent, as demand for skilled pipelayers, plumbers, pipefitters, and steamfitters is expected to outpace the supply of workers trained in these crafts. Many potential workers may prefer work that is less strenuous and has more comfortable working conditions. Employment of individuals in these trades is expected to grow about as fast as the average for all occupations in the coming decade. Demand for plumbers will stem from building renovation, including the growing use of sprinkler systems; repair and maintenance of existing residential systems; and maintenance activities for places having extensive systems of pipes, such as power plants, water and wastewater treatment plants, pipelines, office buildings, and factories. Employment of pipelayers, plumbers, pipefitters, and steamfitters generally is less sensitive to changes in economic conditions than is employment of some other construction trades. Even when construction activity declines, maintenance, rehabilitation, and replacement of existing piping systems, as well as the increasing installation of fire sprinkler systems, provide many jobs for pipelayers, plumbers, pipefitters, and steamfitters.

Nature of Work: Although pipelaying, plumbing, pipefitting, and steam-fitting sometimes are considered a single trade, workers generally specialize in one of the four areas. Pipelayers lay clay, concrete, plastic, or cast-iron pipe for drains, sewers, water mains, and oil or gas lines. Before laying the pipe, pipelayers prepare and grade the trenches either manually or with machines. Plumbers install and repair the water, waste disposal, drainage, and gas systems in homes and commercial and industrial buildings. Plumbers also install plumbing fixtures – bathtubs, showers, sinks, and toilets – and appliances such as dishwashers and water heaters. Pipefitters install and repair both high- and low-pressure pipe systems used in manufacturing, in the generation of electricity, and in heating and cooling buildings. They also install automatic controls that are increasingly being used to regulate these systems. Some pipefitters specialize in only one type of system. Steamfitters, for example, install pipe systems that move liquids or gases under high pressure. Sprinkler fitters install automatic fire sprinkler systems in buildings.

Working Conditions: Because pipelayers, plumbers, pipefitters, and steamfitters frequently must lift heavy pipes, stand for long periods, and sometimes work in uncomfortable or cramped positions, they need physical strength as well as stamina. They also may have to work outdoors in inclement weather. In addition, they are subject to possible falls from ladders, cuts from sharp tools, and burns from hot pipes or soldering equipment. Pipelayers, plumbers, pipefitters, and steamfitters engaged in construction generally work a standard 40-hour week. Those involved in maintenance services under contract may have to work evening or weekend shifts, as well as be on call. These maintenance workers may spend quite a bit of time traveling to and from worksites.

Education, Training, Qualifications: Virtually all pipelayers, pipe-fitters, plumbers, and steamfitters undergo some type of apprenticeship training. Many apprenticeship programs are administered by local union management committees made up of members of the United Association of Journeymen and Apprentices of the Plumbing and Pipefitting Industry of the United States and Canada, and local employers who are members of either the Mechanical Contractors Association of America, the National Association of Plumbing-Heating-Cooling Contractors, or the National Fire Sprinkler Association. Nonunion training and apprenticeship programs are administered by local chapters of the Associated Builders and Contractors, the National Association of Plumbing-Heating-Cooling Contractors, the American Fire Sprinkler Association, or the Home Builders Institute of the National Association of Home Builders. Apprenticeships – both union and nonunion – consist of four or five years of on-the-job training, in addition to at least 144 hours per year of related classroom instruction. As apprentices gain experience, they learn how to work with various types of pipe and how to install different piping systems and plumbing fixtures.

Earnings: Pipelayers, plumbers, pipefitters, and steamfitters are among the highest paid construction occupations. In 2002, median annual earnings of pipelayers were $13.70 ($28,500 per year). The middle 50 percent earned between $10.96 and $13.70. Also, in 2002, median hourly earnings of plumbers, pipefitters, and steamfitters were $19.31 ($40,200 per year). The middle 50 percent earned between $14.68 and $25.87. Median hourly earnings in the industries employing the largest numbers of plumbers, pipefitters, and steamfitters in 2002 were:

- Nonresidential building construction $19.65
- Building equipment contractors $19.52
- Utility system construction $17.81
- Ship and boat building $16.62
- Local government $16.21

Apprentices usually are paid about 50 percent of the wage rate paid to experienced pipelayers, plumbers, pipefitters, and steamfitters.

Key Contacts: For information on apprenticeship opportunities for pipelayers, plumbers, pipefitters, and steamfitters, contact:

- **United Association of Journeymen and Apprentices of the Plumbing, Pipefitting, Sprinkler Fitting Industry of the United States and Canada:** 901 Massachusetts Avenue, NW, Washington, DC 20001. Website: www.ua.org.

For more informaton about training programs for pipelayers, plumbers, pipefitters, and steamfitters, contact:

- **Associated Builders and Contractors:** Workforce Development Department, 4250 North Fairfax Drive, 9th Floor, Arlington, VA 22203.

- **National Association of Home Builders:** 1201 15th Street, NW, Washington, DC 20005. Website: www.nahb.org.

- **Home Builders Institute:** 1201 15th Street, NW, Washington, DC 20005. Website: www.hbi.org.

For general information about the work of pipelayers, plumbers, and pipefitters, contact:

- **Mechanical Contractors Association of America:** 1385 Piccard Drive, Rockville, MD 20850. Website: www.mcaa.org.

- **National Association of Plumbing-Heating-Cooling Contractors:** 180 S. Washington Street, P.O. Box 6808, Falls Church, VA 22040. Website: www.phccweb.org.

For general information about the work of sprinkler fitters, contact:

- **American Fire Sprinkler Association, Inc.:** 9696 Skillman Street, Suite 300, Dallas, TX 75243-8264. Website: www.firesprinkler.org.

- **National Fire Sprinkler Association:** P.O. Box 1000, Patterson, NY 12563. Website: www.nfsa.org.

Sheet Metal Workers

⇨ **Annual Earnings:** $35,600
⇨ **Education/Training:** Apprenticeship
⇨ **Outlook:** Good

Employment Outlook: Employment opportunities are expected to be good for sheet metal workers in the construction industry and in construction-related sheet metal fabrication, reflecting both employment growth and openings arising each year as experienced sheet metal workers leave the occupation. In addition, many potential workers may prefer work that is less strenuous and that has more comfortable working conditions, thus limiting the number of applicants for sheet metal jobs. Opportunities should be particularly good for individuals who acquire apprenticeship training.

Employment of sheet metal workers in construction is expected to grow about as fast as the average for all occupations in the decade ahead. This will be in response to growth in the demand for sheet metal installations as more industrial, commercial, and residential structures are built. The need to install energy-efficient air-conditioning, heating, and ventilation systems in the increasing stock of old buildings and to perform other types of renovation and maintenance work also should boost employment.

Nature of Work: Sheet metal workers make, install, and maintain heating, ventilation, and air-conditioning duct systems; roofs; siding; rain gutters; downspouts; skylights; restaurant equipment; outdoor signs; railroad cars; tailgates; customized precision equipment; and many other products made form metal sheets. They also may work with fiberglass and plastic materials. Although some workers specialize in fabrication, installation, or maintenance, most do all three jobs. Sheet metal workers do both construction-related sheet metal work and mass production of sheet metal products in manufacturing.

Sheet metal workers held about 205,000 jobs in 2002. Nearly two-thirds of all sheet metal workers were found in the construction industry. Of those employed in construction, almost half worked for plumbing, heating, and air-conditioning contractors; most of the rest worked for roofing and sheet metal contractors.

Working Conditions: Sheet metal workers usually work a 40-hour week. Those who fabricate sheet metal products work in shops that are well-lighted and well-ventilated. However, they stand for long periods and lift heavy materials and finished pieces. Sheet metal workers must follow safety practices because working around high-speed machines can be dangerous. They also are subject to cuts from sharp metal, burns from soldering and welding, and falls from ladders and scaffolds. They usually wear safety glasses but must not wear jewelry or loose-fitting clothing that could easily be caught in a machine. Those performing installation work do considerable bending, lifting, standing, climbing, and squatting, sometimes in close quarters or in awkward positions.

Education, Training, Qualifications: Apprenticeship generally is considered to be the best way to learn this trade. The apprenticeship program consists of four to five years of on-the-job training and an average of 200 hours per year of classroom instruction. Apprenticeship programs may be administered by local joint committees composed of the Sheet Metal Workers' International Association and local chapters of the Sheet Metal and Air-Conditioning Contractors National Association. On the job, apprentices learn the basics of pattern layout and how to cut, bend, fabricate, and install sheet metal. In the classroom, apprentices learn drafting, plan and specification reading, trigonometry and geometry applicable to layout work, the use of computerized equipment, welding, and the principles of heating, air-conditioning, and ventilating systems.

Some people pick up the trade informally, usually by working as helpers to experienced sheet metal workers. Most sheet metal workers in large-scale manufacturing receive on-the-job training, with additional classwork or in-house training when necessary.

Earnings: In 2002, median hourly earnings of sheet metal workers were $16.62 ($35,600 per year). The middle 50 percent earned between $12.15 and $23.03. The median hourly earnings of the largest industries employing sheet metal workers in 2002 were:

- Federal government $19.73
- Building equipment contractors $17.47
- Building finishing contractors $16.77

- Foundation, structure, and building exterior
  contractors $15.48
- Architectural and structural metals
  manufacturing $14.60

Apprentices normally start at about 40 to 50 percent of the rate paid to experienced workers.

Key Contacts: For more information on apprenticeships or other work opportunities, contact local sheet metal contractors or heating, refrigeration, and air-conditioning contractors; a local of the Sheet Metal Workers International Association; a local of the Sheet Metal and Air-Conditioning Contractors National Association; a local joint union-management apprenticeship committee; or the nearest office of your state employment service or apprenticeship agency.

For general and training information about sheet metal workers, contact:

- **International Training Institute for the Sheet Metal and Air Conditioning Industry:** 601 N. Fairfax Street, Suite 240, Alexandria, VA 22314. Website: www.sheetmetal-iti.org.

- **Sheet Metal and Air Conditioning Contractors National Association:** 4201 Lafayette Center Drive, Chantilly, VA 20151-1209. Website: www.smacna.org.

- **Sheet Metal Workers International Association:** 1750 New York Avenue, NW, Washington, DC 20006. Website: www.smwia.org.

Structural and Reinforcing Iron and Metal Workers

- ➪ **Annual Earnings:** $40,700
- ➪ **Education/Training:** Apprenticeships
- ➪ **Outlook:** Good to excellent

Employment Outlook: Employment of structural and reinforcing iron and metal workers is expected to grow about as fast as the average for all occupations in the decade ahead, largely on the basis of continued growth in industrial and commercial construction. The rehabilitation, maintenance, and replacement of a growing number of older buildings, factories, power plants, highways, and bridges is expected to create employment opportunities. The number of job openings fluctuates from year to year with economic conditions and the level of construction activity.

Nature of Work: Structural and reinforcing iron and metal workers place and install iron or steel girders, columns, and other construction materials to form buildings, bridges, and other structures. They also position and secure steel bars or mesh in concrete forms in order to reinforce the concrete used in highways, buildings, bridges, tunnels, and other structures. In addition, they repair and renovate older buildings and structures. Even though the primary metal involved in this work is steel, these workers often are known as ironworkers.

Working Conditions: Structural and reinforcing iron and metal workers usually work outside in all kinds of weather. However, those who work at great heights do not work during wet, icy, or extremely windy conditions. Because the danger of injuries due to falls is great, ironworkers use safety devices such as safety belts, scaffolding, and nets to reduce risk. Some ironworkers fabricate structural metal in fabricating shops, which usually are located away from the construction site. These workers usually work a 40-hour week. They held about 107,000 jobs in 2002.

Education, Training, Qualifications: Most employers recommend a three- or four-year apprenticeship consisting of on-the-job training and evening classroom instruction as the best way to learn this trade. Apprenticeship programs usually are administered by committees made up of representatives of local unions of the International Association of Bridge, Structural, Ornamental and Reinforcing Iron Workers or the local chapters of contractors' associations. Ironworkers must be at least 18 years old. A high school diploma is preferred by employers and local apprenticeship committees.

Earnings: In 2002, median hourly earnings of structural iron and steel workers in all industries were $19.55 ($40,700 per year). The middle 50 percent earned between $14.45 and $26.00. In 2002, median hourly earnings of reinforcing iron and rebar workers in all industries were $17.66. Median hourly earnings of structural iron and steel workers in 2002 employed by foundation, structure, and building exterior contractors were $21.35 and in nonresidential building construction, $16.98. According to the International Association of Bridge, Structural, Ornamental, and Reinforcing Iron Workers, average hourly earnings, including benefits, for structural and reinforcing metal workers who belonged to a union and worked full time were 34 percent higher than the hourly earnings of nonunion workers.

Key Contacts: For information on apprenticeships or other work opportunities, contact local general contractors; a local of the International Association of Bridge, Structural, Ornamental, and Reinforcing Iron Workers Union; a local iron workers' joint union-management apprenticeship committee; a local or state chapter of the Associated Builders and Contractors or the Associated General Contractors; or the nearest office of your state employment service or apprenticeship agency.

For apprenticeship information, contact:

- **International Association of Bridge, Structural, Ornamental, and Reinforcing Iron Workers:** Apprenticeship Department, 1750 New York Avenue, NW, Suite 400, Washington, DC 20006.

For general information about ironworkers, contact either of the following sources:

- **Associated Builders and Contractors:** Workforce Development Department, 4250 N. Fairfax Drive, 9th Floor, Arlington, VA 22203

- **Associated General Contractors of America:** 333 John Carlyle Street, Suite 200, Alexandria, VA 22314. Website: www.agc.org.

9

Sports, Entertainment, and Media Jobs

EW JOB AND CAREER FIELDS have such a mass appeal as sports, entertainment, and the media. Many people would love to get paid playing their favorite sport, starring in a movie, or being before the television camera. Others would like to become a famous artist, musician, singer, or designer.

In many respects, these fields generate a disproportionate number of glamor jobs that place primary emphasis on special skills rather than education. Talented and entrepreneurial individuals without a four-year degree, who demonstrate a great deal of creativity and imagination, will find many opportunities in these fields.

Be forewarned, however, that jobs in sports, entertainment, and media often pay much less than expected. While the top talent in these fields earn top dollar, many others working in these fields struggle for years on a part-time basis as they attempt to acquire experience and connections for making a rewarding career in a field that allows them to pursue their passions. If you have the necessary talent and drive, you'll find numerous job opportunities in these exciting fields.

Actors

▷ **Annual Earnings:** $23,470
▷ **Education/Training:** High school diploma to college degree
▷ **Outlook:** Good

Employment Outlook: Employment of actors is expected to grow about as fast as the average for all occupations in the decade ahead. Although a growing number of people will aspire to enter this profession, many will leave the field early because the work – when it is available – is hard, the hours are long, and the pay is low. Competition for jobs will be stiff, in part because the large number of highly trained and talented actors auditioning for roles generally exceeds the number of parts that become available. Only performers with the most stamina and talent will find regular employment.

In 2002, actors (including producers and directors) held about 139,000 jobs, primarily in motion picture and video, performing arts, and broadcast industries. Because many others were between jobs, the total number of actors available for work was higher. Employment in the theater is cyclical – higher in the fall and spring seasons – and concentrated in New York and other major cities with large commercial houses for musicals and touring productions. Actors may find work in summer festivals, on cruise lines, and in theme parks. Many smaller, nonprofit professional companies, such as repertory companies, dinner theaters, and theaters affiliated with drama schools, acting conservatories, and universities, provide employment opportunities for local amateur talent and professional entertainers.

Nature of Work: Actors express ideas and create images in theater, film, radio, television, and other performing arts media. They interpret a writer's script to entertain, inform, or instruct an audience. Although the most famous actors work in film, network television, or theater in New York or Los Angeles, far more work in local or regional television studios, theaters, or film production companies, preparing advertising, public relations, or independent, small-scale movie productions. Actors perform in stage, radio, television, video, or motion picture productions. They also work in cabarets, nightclubs, theme parks, and in "industrial" films produced for training purposes. Most actors struggle to find steady work; only a few ever achieve recognition as stars. Some actors do voiceover and narration work for advertisements, animated features, books on tape, and other electronic media. They also teach in high school or university drama departments, acting conservatories, or public programs.

Working Conditions: Actors work under constant pressure. Many face stress from the continual need to find their next job. To succeed, actors need patience and commitment to their craft. Actors strive to deliver flawless performances while working under undesirable and unpleasant conditions. Acting assignments typically are short term – ranging from one day to a few months – which means that actors frequently experience long periods of unemployment between jobs. The uncertain nature of the work results in unpredictable earnings and intense competition for even the lowest-paid jobs. Often, actors must hold other jobs in order to sustain a living.

When performing, actors typically work long, irregular hours. For example, stage actors may perform one show at night while rehearsing another during the day. They might even travel with a show when it tours the country. Movie actors may work on location, sometimes under adverse weather conditions, and may spend considerable time in their trailers or dressing rooms waiting to perform their scenes. Actors who perform in a television series often appear on camera with little or no preparation time, because scripts tend to be revised frequently or even written moments before taping. Evening and weekend work is a regular part of a stage actor's life. On weekends, more than one performance may be held per day.

Education, Training, Qualifications: Persons who become actors follow many paths. Employers generally look for people with the creative instincts, innate talent, and intellectual capacity to perform. Actors should possess a passion for performing and enjoy entertaining others. Most aspiring actors participate in high school or college plays, work in college radio stations, or perform with local community theater groups. Local and regional theater experience and work in summer stock, on cruise lines, or in theme parks help many young actors hone their skills and earn qualifying credits toward membership in one of the actors' unions.

Formal dramatic training, either through an acting conservatory or a university program, generally is necessary; however, some people successfully enter the field without it. College courses in radio and television broadcasting, communications, film, theater, drama or dramatic literature are helpful. Actors, regardless of experience level, may pursue workshop training through acting conservatories or by being mentored by a drama coach. Actors also research roles so that they can grasp concepts quickly during rehearsals and understand the story's setting and background. Sometimes actors learn a foreign language or train with a dialect coach to develop an accent to make their characters more realistic. Actors need talent, creative ability, and training that will enable them to portray different characters. A wide range of related skills, such as singing, dancing, skating, juggling, or miming are especially useful. Physical appearance, such as the right size, weight, or features, often is one of the deciding factors in being selected for particular roles.

Earnings: Median annual earnings of salaried actors were $23,470 in 2002. The middle 50 percent earned between $15,320 and $53,320. The highest 10 percent earned more than $106,360. According to Equity, the minimum weekly salary for actors in Broadway productions as of June 2003 was $1,354. Actors in off-Broadway productions received minimums ranging from $479 to $557 a week – depending on the seating capacity of the theater. Some well-known actors – stars – earn well above the minimum; their salaries are many times the figures cited, creating the false impression that all actors are highly paid. For example, of the nearly 100,000 members of the Screen Actors' Guild, only about 50 might be considered stars.

Key Contacts: For general information about theater arts and a list of accredited college-level programs contact:

- **National Association of Schools of Theatre:** 11250 Roger Bacon Drive, Suite 21, Reston, VA 20190. Website: http://nast.arts-accredit. org.

For general information on actors, contact any of the following:

- **Actors Equity Association:** 165 West 46th Street, New York, NY 10036. Website: www.actorsequity.org.

- **Screen Actors Guild:** 5757 Wilshire Blvd., Los Angeles, CA 90036-3600. Website: www.sag.org.

- **American Federation of Television and Radio Artists – Screen Actors Guild:** 260 Madison Avenue, New York, NY 10016-2401. Website: www.aftra.org.

Athletes, Coaches, Umpires, and Related Workers

⇨ **Annual Earnings:** Varies greatly
⇨ **Education/Training:** Experience and training
⇨ **Outlook:** Good

Employment Outlook: Employment of athletes, coaches, umpires, and related workers is expected to increase about as fast as the average for all occupations in the decade ahead. Employment will grow as the general public continues to increasingly participate in organized sports as a form of entertainment, recreation, and physical conditioning. Job growth also will be driven by the growing numbers of baby boomers approaching retirement, during which they are expected to become more active participants of leisure-time activities, such as golf and tennis, and require instruction. The large numbers of the children of baby boomers in high schools and colleges also will be active participants in athletics and require coaches and instructors.

Expanding opportunities are expected for coaches and instructors, as a higher value is being placed upon physical fitness in our society. Competition for professional athlete jobs will continue to be extremely intense. Opportunities should be best for persons seeking part-time umpire, referee, and other sports official jobs at the high school level, but competition is expected for higher paying jobs at the college level, and even greater competition for jobs in professional sports. Competition should be very keen for jobs as scouts, particularly for professional teams, since the number of available positions is limited.

Nature of Work: We are a nation of sports fans and sports players. Some of those who participate in amateur sports dream of becoming paid professional athletes, coaches, or sports officials, but very few beat the long and daunting odds of making a full-time living from professional athletics. Even though the chances of employment as a professional athlete are slim, there are many opportunities for at least a part-time job related to athletics as a coach, instructor, referee, or umpire in amateur athletics and in high schools, colleges, and universities.

Athletes and sports competitors compete in organized, officiated sports events to entertain spectators. The events in which they compete include both team sports – such as baseball, basketball, football, hockey, and soccer – and individual sports – such as golf, tennis, and bowling. In addition to competing in athletic events, athletes spend many hours practicing skills and teamwork under the guidance of a coach or sports instructor. Most athletes spend hours in hard practice every day. They also spend additional hours viewing videotapes, in order to critique their own performances and techniques and to scout their opponents' tendencies and weaknesses to gain a competitive advantage.

Coaches organize, instruct, and teach amateur and professional athletes in the fundamentals of individual and team sports. In individual sports, instructors may sometimes fill this role. Coaches train athletes for competition by holding practice sessions to perform drills and improve the athletes' skills and stamina. Coaches also are responsible for managing the team during both practice sessions and competitions, and for instilling good sportsmanship, a competitive spirit, and teamwork. They may also select, store, issue, and inventory equipment, materials, and supplies.

Sports instructors teach professional and nonprofessional athletes on an individual basis. They organize, instruct, train, and lead athletes of indoor and outdoor sports such as bowling, tennis, golf, and swimming. Because activities are as diverse as weight lifting, gymnastics, and scuba diving, and may include self-defense training such as karate, instructors tend to specialize in one or a few types of activities.

Umpires, referees, and other sports officials officiate at competitive athletic and sporting events. They observe the play, detect infractions of rules, and impose penalties established by the sports' rules and regulations. The job is highly stressful because officials are often required to make a decision in a matter of a split second, sometimes resulting in strong disagreement among competitors, coaches, or spectators.

Professional scouts evaluate the skills of both amateur and professional athletes to determine talent and potential. As a sports intelligence agent, the scout's primary duty is to seek out top athletic candidates for the team he or she represents, ultimately contributing to team success.

Athletes, coaches, umpires, and related workers held about 158,000 jobs in 2002. Coaches and scouts held 130,000 jobs; athletes, 15,000; and umpires, referees, and other sports officials, 14,000. Large proportions of athletes, coaches, umpires, and related workers worked part time – about 37 percent, while 17 percent maintained variable schedules. About 27 percent of workers in this occupation were self-employed, earning prize money or fees for lessons, scouting, or officiating assignments, and many other coaches and sports officials, although technically not self-employed, have such irregular or tenuous working arrangements that their working conditions resemble self-employment.

Working Conditions: Irregular work hours are the trademark of the athlete. They are common for coaches, as well as umpires, referees, and other sports officials. Athletes, coaches, umpires, and related workers often work Saturdays, Sundays, evenings, and holidays. Athletes and full-time coaches usually work more than 40 hours a week for several months during the sports season. Athletes, coaches, and sports officials who participate in competitions that are held outdoors may be exposed to all weather conditions of the season. Athletes, coaches, and some sports officials frequently travel to sporting events by bus or airplane. Many athletes are susceptible to physical injuries.

Education, Training, Qualifications: Education and training requirements for athletes, coaches, umpires, and related workers vary greatly by the level and type of sport. Regardless of the sport or occupation, jobs require immense overall knowledge of the game, usually acquired through years of experience at lower levels. Athletes usually begin competing in sports while in elementary or middle school and continue through high school and sometime college. They play in amateur tournaments and on high school and college teams, where the best attract the attention of professional scouts.

For sports instructors, certification is highly desirable for those interested in becoming a tennis, golf, karate, or any other kind of instructor. Often, one must be at least 18 years old and CPR certified.

Each sport has specific requirements for umpires, referees, and other sports officials. Referees, umpires, and other sports officials often begin their careers by volunteering for intramural, community, and recreational league competitions.

Standards are stringent for officials in professional sports. For umpire jobs in professional baseball, for example, a high school diploma or equivalent is usually sufficient, plus 20/20 vision and quick reflexes. To qualify for the professional ranks, however, prospective candidates must attend professional umpire training school.

Earnings: Median annual earnings of athletes were $45,320 in 2002. The lowest 10 percent earned less than $14,090, and the highest 10 percent earned more than $145,600. Similar to actors, the very top paid professionals made millions. Median annual earnings of umpires and related workers were $20,540 in 2002. The middle 50 percent earned between $16,210 and $29,490. Median annual earnings of coaches and scouts were $27,880 in 2002. The middle 50 percent earned between $17,890 and $42,250.

Key Contacts: For information about sports officiating for team and individual sports, contact:

- **National Association of Sports Officials:** 2017 Lathrop Avenue, Racine, WI 53405. Website: www.naso.org.

Artists and Related Workers

▷ **Annual Earnings:** Varies greatly
▷ **Education/Training:** Training and experience
▷ **Outlook:** Good

Employment Outlook: Employment of artists and related workers is expected to grow about as fast as the average in the decade ahead. Because the arts attract many talented people with creative ability, the number of aspiring artists continues to grow. Consequently, competition for both salaried jobs and freelance work in some areas is expected to be keen. The need for artists to illustrate and animate materials for magazines, journals, and other printed or electronic productions will spur demand for illustrators and animators of all types. Growth in the motion picture and video industries will provide new job opportunities for illustrators, cartoonists, and animators. Competition for most jobs, however, will be strong, because job opportunities are relatively few and the number of people interested in these positions usually exceeds the number of available openings.

Nature of Work: Artists create art to communicate ideas, thoughts, or feelings. They use a variety of methods – painting, sculpting, or illustration – and an assortment of materials, including oils, watercolors, acrylics, pastels, pencils, pen and ink, plaster, clay, and computers. Artists generally fall into one of three categories: *Art directors* formulate design concepts and presentation approaches for visual communications media. *Fine artists, including painters, sculptors, and illustrators*, create original artwork, using a variety of media and techniques and display their work in museums, commercial art galleries, corporate collections, and private homes; some of their artwork may be commissioned. *Multimedia artists and animators* create special effects, animation, or other visual images on film, or video, or with computers or other electronic media. They primarily work in motion picture and video industries, advertising, and computer systems design services.

Working Conditions: Many artists work in fine- or commercial-art studios located in office buildings, warehouses, or lofts. Others work in private studios in their homes. Some fine artists share studio space. Studio surroundings usually are well lighted and ventilated; however, fine arts may be exposed to fumes from glue, paint, ink, and other materials and to dust or other residue from filings, splattered paint, or spilled fluids. Artists employed by publishing companies, advertising agencies, and design firms generally work a standard workweek. Self-employed artists can set their own hours, but may spend much time and effort selling their artwork to potential customers or clients and building a reputation. Artists held about 149,000 jobs in 2002. More than half were self-employed.

Of the artists who were not self-employed, many worked in advertising and related services; newspaper, periodical, book, and software publishers; motion picture and video industries; specialized design services; and computer systems design and related services. Some self-employed artists offered their services to advertising agencies, design firms, publishing houses, and other businesses on a contract or freelance basis.

Education, Training, Qualifications: Training requirements for artists vary by specialty. Although formal training is not strictly necessary for fine artists, it is very difficult to become skilled enough to make a living without some training. Independent schools of art and design offer post-secondary studio training in the fine arts leading to an Associate in Art or a Bachelor in Fine Arts degree. Typically, these programs focus more intensively on studio work than do the academic programs in a university setting. Illustrators learn drawing and sketching skills through training in art programs and through extensive practice. Evidence of appropriate talent and skill, displayed in an artist's portfolio, is an important factor used by art directors, clients, and others in deciding whether to hire an individual or to contract out work.

Earnings: Median annual earnings of salaried art directors were $61,850 in 2002. Median annual earnings of salaried fine artists, including painters, sculptors, and illustrators, were $35,260 in 2002. Median annual earnings of salaried multimedia artists and animators were $43,980 in 2002. Earnings for self-employed artists vary widely. Some charge only a nominal fee while they gain experience and build a reputation for their work. Others, such as well-established freelance fine artists and illustrators, can earn more than salaried artists. Many, however, find it difficult to rely solely on income earned from selling paintings or other works of art.

Key Contacts: For general information about art and design and a list of accredited college-level programs, contact:

- **National Association of Schools of Art and Design:** 11250 Roger Bacon Drive, Suite 21, Reston, VA 20190. Website: http://nasad.arts-accredit.org.

For information on careers in medical illustration, contact:

- **Association of Medical Illustrators:** 5475 Mark Dabling Blvd., Suite 108, Colorado Springs, CO 80918. Website: www.ami.org.

Broadcast and Sound Engineering Technicians and Radio Operators

⇨ **Annual** $27,760 to $36,970
⇨ **Education/Training:** Technical school to college training
⇨ **Outlook:** Good

Employment Outlook: People seeking entry-level jobs as technicians in broadcasting are expected to face strong competition in major metropolitan areas, where pay generally is higher and the number of qualified job seekers typically exceeds the number of openings. Overall employment of broadcast and sound engineering technicians and radio operators is expected to grow about as fast as the average for all occupations in the decade ahead. Job growth in radio and television broadcasting will be limited by consolidation of ownership of radio and television stations, and by labor-saving technical advances such as computer-controlled programming and remotely controlled transmitters. Projected job growth varies among detailed occupations in this field. For example, employment of broadcast technicians is expected to grow about as fast as the average for all occupations in the decade ahead, as improved technology enhances the capabilities of technicians to produce higher quality radio and television programming. Employment of radio operators is expected to decline as more stations operate transmitters that control programming remotely. Employment of audio and video equipment technicians and sound engineering technicians is expected to grow faster than the average for all occupations.

Nature of Work: Broadcast and sound engineering technicians and radio operators set up, operate, and maintain a wide variety of electrical and electronic equipment involved in almost any radio or television broadcast, concert, play, musical recording, television show, or movie. There are many specialized occupations within the field. *Audio and video equipment technicians* set up and operate audio and video equipment, including microphones, sound speakers, video screens, projectors, video monitors, recording equipment, connecting wires and cables, sound and mixing boards, and related electronic equipment for concerts, sports events, meetings and conventions, presentations, and news conferences. *Broadcast technicians* set up, operate, and maintain equipment that regulates the signal strength, clarity, and range of sounds and colors of radio or television broadcasts. *Sound engineering technicians* operate machines and equipment to record, synchronize, mix, or reproduce music, voices, or sound effects in recording studios, sporting arenas, theater productions, or movie and video productions. *Radio operators* mainly receive and transmit communications using a variety of tools. They also are responsible for repairing equipment.

Broadcast and sound engineering technicians and radio operators held about 93,000 jobs in 2002 in the following occupations:

- Audio and video equipment technicians   42,000
- Broadcast technicians   35,000
- Sound engineering technicians   13,000
- Radio operators   3,000

Working Conditions: Broadcast and sound engineering technicians and radio operators generally work indoors in pleasant surroundings. However, those who broadcast news and other programs from locations outside the studio may work outdoors in all types of weather.

Technicians at large stations and the networks usually work a 40-hour week under great pressure to meet broadcast deadlines, and may occasionally work overtime. Those who work on motion pictures may be on a tight schedule and may work long hours to meet contractual deadlines.

Education, Training, Qualifications: The best way to prepare for a broadcast and sound engineering technician job is to obtain technical school, community college, or college training in electronics, computer networking, or broadcast technology. In the motion picture industry, people are hired as apprentice editorial assistants and work their way up to more skilled jobs. Employers in the motion picture industry usually hire experienced freelance technicians on a picture-by-picture basis. Reputation and determination are important in getting jobs.

Beginners learn skills on the job from experienced technicians and supervisors. They often begin their careers in small stations and, once experienced, move on to larger ones. Large stations usually hire only technicians with experience.

Audio and video equipment technicians generally need a high school diploma. Many recent entrants have a community college degree or various other forms of postsecondary degrees, although that is not always a requirement.

Earnings: Television stations usually pay higher salaries than do radio stations; commercial broadcasting usually pays more than public broadcasting; and stations in large markets pay more than those in small markets.

Median annual earnings of broadcast technicians in 2002 were $27,760. The middle 50 percent earned between $18,860 and $45,200. Median annual earnings of sound engineering technicians in 2002 were $36,350. The middle 50 percent earned between $24,330 and $57,350. Median annual earnings of audio and video equipment technicians in 2002 were $31,110. The middle 50 percent earned between $22,670 and $43,950. Median annual earnings of radio operators in 2002 were $31,530. The middle 50 percent earned between $24,000 and $41,430.

Key Contacts: For career information and links to employment resources, contact:

- **National Association of Broadcasters:** 1771 N Street, NW, Washington, DC 20036. Website: www.nab.org.

- **Society of Broadcast Engineers:** 9247 North Meridian Street, Suite 305, Indianapolis, IN 46260. Website: www.sbe.org.

Designers

⇨ **Annual Earnings:** Varies from $19,480 to $52,260
⇨ **Education/Training:** Experience to bachelor's degree
⇨ **Outlook:** Good to excellent

Employment Outlook: Overall employment of designers is expected to grow about as fast as the average for all occupations in the decade ahead as the economy expands and consumers, businesses, and manufacturers continue to rely on the services provided by designers. However, designers in most fields – with the exception of floral design – are expected to face keen competition for available positions. Many talented individuals are attracted to careers as designers. Individuals with little or no formal education in design, as well as those who lack creativity and perseverance, will find it very difficult to establish and maintain a career in this occupation. Among the design specialties, graphic designers are projected to provide the most new jobs. Demand for graphic designers should increase because of the rapidly expanding market for Web-based information and expansion of the video entertainment market, including television, movies, video, and made-for-Internet outlets. Rising demand for interior design of private homes, offices, restaurants and other retail establishments, and institutions that care for the rapidly growing elderly population should spur employment growth of interior designers. New jobs for floral designers are expected to stem mostly from the relatively high replacement needs in retail florists that result from comparatively low starting pay and limited opportunities for advancement. Increased demand for industrial designers will stem from continued emphasis on the quality and safety of products, demand for new products that are easy and comfortable to use, and the development of high-technology products in medicine, transportation, and other fields.

Nature of Work: Designers are people with a desire to create. They combine practical knowledge with artistic ability to turn abstract ideas into formal designs for the merchandise we buy, the clothes we wear, the website we use, the publications we read, and the living and office space we inhabit. Designers usually specialize in a particular area of design, such as automobiles, industrial or medical equipment, home appliances, clothing and textiles, floral arrangements, publications, websites, logos, signage, movie or TV credits, interiors of homes or office buildings, merchandise displays, or movie, television, and theater sets. *Commercial and industrial designers* develop countless manufactured products, including airplanes, cars, children's toys, computer equipment, furniture, home appliances, and medical, office, and recreational equipment. *Fashion designers* design clothing and accessories. *Floral designers* cut and arrange live, dried, or artificial flowers and foliage into designs, according to the customer's order. *Graphic designers* plan, analyze, and create visual solutions to communications problems. *Interior designers* enhance the function, safety, and quality of interior spaces of private homes, public buildings, and business or international facilities, such as offices, restaurants, retail establishments, hospitals, hotels, and theaters. *Merchandise displayers and window dressers, or visual merchandisers,* plan and erect commercial displays, such as those in windows and interiors of retail stores or at trade exhibitions. *Set and exhibit designers* create sets for movie, television, and theater productions and design special exhibition displays.

Designers held about 532,000 jobs in 2002. Approximately one-third were self-employed. Employment was distributed as follows:

- Graphic designers   212,000
- Floral designers   104,000
- Merchandise displayers and window trimmers   77,000
- Interior designers   60,000
- Commercial and industrial designers   52,000
- Fashion designers   15,000
- Set and exhibit designers   12,000

Working Conditions: Working conditions and places of employment vary. Designers employed by manufacturing establishments, large corporations, or design firms generally work regular hours in well-lighted and comfortable settings. Designers in small design consulting firms, or those who freelance, generally work on a contract, or job, basis. They frequently adjust their workday to suit their clients' schedules and deadlines, meeting with the clients during evening or weekend hours when necessary. Consultants and self-employed designers tend to work longer hours and in smaller, more congested, environments. Designers may transact business in their own offices or studios, or in clients' homes or offices. They also may travel to other locations, such as showrooms, design centers, clients' exhibit sites, and manufacturing facilities.

Education, Training, Qualifications: Creativity is crucial in all design occupations. People in this field must have a strong sense of the esthetic – an eye for color and detail, a sense of balance and proportion, and an appreciation for beauty. A good portfolio – a collection of examples of a person's best work – often is the deciding factor in getting a job.

While a bachelor's degree is required for most entry-level design positions, many other positions, such a floral design and visual merchandising, primarily require experience and talent. Interior design is the only design field subject to government regulation. Passing the National Council for Interior Design qualification examination is required for registration or licensure. In fashion design, employers seek individuals with a two- or four-year degree who are knowledgeable in the areas of textiles, fabrics, and ornamentation, and about trends in the fashion world. Most floral designers learn their skills on the job. Formal training for some design professions is available in two- and three-year professional schools that award certificates or associate degrees in design. Employers increasingly expect new designers to be familiar with computer-aided design software as a design tool. Beginning designers usually receive on-the-job training and normally need one to three years of training before they can advance to higher level positions.

Earnings: Median annual earnings for commercial and industrial designers were $52,260 in 2002. The middle 50 percent earned between $39,240 and $67,430. Median annual earnings for fashion designers were $51,290 in 2002. The middle 50 percent earned between $35,550 and $75,970. Median annual earnings for floral designers were $19,480 in 2002. The middle 50 percent earned between $15,880 and $23,560. Median annual earnings for graphic designers were $36,680 in 2002. The middle 50 percent earned between $28,140 and $48,820. Median annual earnings for interior designers were $39,180 in 2002. The middle 50 percent earned between $29,070 and $53,060. Median annual earnings of merchandise displayers and window dressers were $22,550 in 2002. The middle 50 percent earned between $18,320 and $29,070. Median annual earnings for set and exhibit designers were $33,870 in 2000. The middle 50 percent earned between $24,780 and $46,350. The American Institute of Graphic Arts reported 2002 median annual earnings for staff-level graphic designers was $40,000. Senior designers with supervisory and decision-making responsibilities made $55,000. Solo designers, who freelanced or worked under contract to another company, reported median earnings of $55,000.

Key Contacts: For information about graphic, communication, or inter-action design careers, contact:

- **American Institute of Graphic Arts:** 164 Fifth Avenue, New York, NY 10010. Website: www.aiga.org.

For information on degree, continuing education, and licensure programs in interior design and interior design research, contact:

- **American Society of Interior Designers:** 608 Massachusetts Avenue, NE, Washington, DC 20002-6006. Website: www.asid.org.

For a list of schools with accredited programs in interior design, contact:

- **Foundation for Interior Design Education Research:** 146 Monroe Center, NW, Suite 1318, Grand Rapids, MI 49503. Website: www. fider.org.

For information on careers, continuing education, and certification programs in the interior design specialty of residential kitchen and bath design, contact:

- **National Kitchen and Bath Association:** 687 Willow Grove Street, Hackettstown, NJ 07840. Website: www.nkba.org/student.

For information about careers in floral design, contact:

- **Society of American Florists:** 1601 Duke Street, Alexandria, VA 22314. Website: www.safnow.org.

Desktop Publishers

- ⮑ **Annual Earnings:** $31,620
- ⮑ **Education/Training:** Certificate and on-the-job training
- ⮑ **Outlook:** Excellent

Employment Outlook: Employment of desktop publishers is expected to grow faster than the average for all occupations in the decade ahead as more page layout and design work is performed in-house using computers and sophisticated publishing software. Desktop publishing is replacing much of the pre-press work done by compositors and typesetters, enabling organizations to reduce costs while increasing production speeds.

Desktop publishers held about 35,000 jobs in 2002. Two out of three worked in newspaper, periodical, book, and directory publishing, and printing and related support activities; the rest worked in a wide variety of industries. Firms in the publishing industry employ most desktop publishers. These firms publish newspapers, periodicals (magazines and journals), books, directories and mailing lists, and greeting cards. A large number of desktop publishers also work for printing and related support activities firms, which print a wide range of products – newspapers, books, labels, business cards, stationery, inserts, catalogs, pamphlets, and advertisements – while business form establishments print material such as sales receipts, and business forms and perform support activities such as data imaging and bookbinding. Establishments in printing and related support activities typically perform custom composition. Desktop publishing jobs are found throughout the country. However, most jobs are in large metropolitan areas.

Nature of Work: Using computer software, desktop publishers format and combine text, numerical data, photographs, charts, and other visual graphic elements to produce publication-ready material. Depending on the nature of a particular project, desktop publishers may write and edit text, create graphics to accompany text, convert photographs and drawings into digital images, design page layouts, create proposals, develop presentations and advertising campaigns, typeset and do the color separation, and translate electronic information into film or other traditional forms. Personal computers enable desktop publishers to perform publishing tasks that would otherwise require complicated equipment and human effort. Advances in computer software and printing technology continue to change and enhance desktop publishing work. Instead of receiving a typed text manuscript (hard copy) from customers, desktop publishers get the material over the Internet or on a computer disk.

Working Conditions: Desktop publishers usually work in clean, air-conditioned office areas with little noise. They generally work an eight-hour day, five days a week. Some workers work night shifts, weekends, and holidays. Desktop publishers often are subject to stress and the pressures of short deadlines and tight work schedules. Like other workers who spend long hours working in front of a computer monitor, they may be susceptible to eyestrain, back discomfort, and hand and wrist problems.

Education, Training, Qualifications: Most workers qualify for jobs as desktop publishers by taking classes or completing certificate programs at vocational schools, colleges, or through the Internet. Programs range in length, but the average certificate program takes approximately one year. However, some desktop publishers train on-the-job to develop the necessary skills. The length of on-the-job training varies by company. An internship or part time desktop publishing assignment is another way to gain experience as a desktop publisher. Students interested in pursuing a career in desktop publishing may obtain an associate's degree in applied science or a bachelor's degree in graphic arts, graphic communications, or graphic design. Although formal training is not always required, those with certificates or degrees will have the best job opportunities. Most employers prefer to hire people who have at least a high school diploma and who possess good communication skills, basic computer skills, and a strong work ethic.

Earnings: Earnings for desktop publishers vary according to level of experience, training, location, and size of firm. Median annual earnings in the industries employing the largest numbers of these workers were $35,140 in printing and related support activities; $26,050 for newspaper, periodical, book and directory publishers. The middle 50 percent earned between $24,030 and $41,280.

Key Contacts: Details about apprenticeship and other training programs may be obtained from local employers such as newspapers and printing shops. For information on careers and training in printing, desktop publishing, and graphic arts, contact either of the following sources:

- **Association for Suppliers of Printing, Publishing, and Converting Technologies:** 1899 Preston White Drive, Reston, VA 20191. Website: www.npes.org/education/index.html.

- **Graphic Arts Information Network:** 200 Deer Run Road, Sewickley, PA 15143. Website: www.gain.net.

Gaming Services

- ➪ **Annual Earnings:** Varies from $14,090 to $39,290
- ➪ **Education/Training:** High school or GED plus training
- ➪ **Outlook:** Excellent

Employment Outlook: With demand for gaming showing no sign of waning, employment in gaming services occupations is projected to grow faster than the average for all occupations in the decade ahead. Even during the recent downturn in the economy, profits at casinos have risen. With many states benefiting from casino gambling in the form of tax revenue or compacts with Indian tribes, additional states are rethinking their opposition to legalized gambling and will likely approve the building of more casinos and other gaming formats in the coming decade. The increase in gaming reflects growth in the population and in its disposable income, both of which are expected to continue.

Nature of Work: Legalized gambling in the United States today includes casino gaming, state lotteries, parimutuel wagering on contests such as horse or dog racing, and charitable gaming. Gaming, the playing of games of chance, is a multibillion-dollar industry that is responsible for the creation of a number of unique service occupations. Gaming services occupations held 192,000 jobs in 2002:

- Gaming dealers   78,000
- Gaming supervisors   39,000
- Slot key persons   21,000
- Gaming and sports book writers & runners   14,000
- All other gaming service workers   40,000

Gaming services workers are found mainly in the traveler accommodation and gaming industries. Most are employed in commercial casinos, including land-based or riverboats in 11 states. The largest number works in land-based casinos in Nevada, and the second largest group works in similar establishments in New Jersey. Mississippi, which boasts the greatest number of riverboat casinos in operation, employs the most workers in that venue. In addition, 23 states have Indian casinos. Legal lotteries are held in 40 states and the District of Columbia, and parimutuel wagering is legal in 41 states.

Like nearly every business establishment, casinos have workers who direct and oversee day-to-day operations. *Gaming supervisors* oversee the gaming operations and personnel in an assigned area. They circulate among the tables and observe the operations to ensure that all of the stations and games are covered for each shift. Some gaming occupations demand specially acquired skills – dealing blackjack, for example – that are unique to casino work. Others require skills common to most businesses, such as the ability to conduct financial transactions. *Slot key persons*, also called slot attendants or slot technicians, coordinate and supervise the slot department and its workers. *Gaming and sportsbook writers and runners* assist in the operations of games such as bingo and keno, in addition to taking bets on sporting events. *Gaming dealers* operate table games such as craps, blackjack, and roulette. Standing or sitting behind the table, dealers provide dice, dispense cards to players, or run the equipment.

Working Conditions: The atmosphere in casinos is generally filled with fun and often considered glamorous. However, casino work can also be physically demanding. Most occupations require that workers stand for long periods; some require the lifting of heavy items. The "glamorous" atmosphere exposes casino workers to certain hazards, such as cigarette, cigar, and pipe smoke. Noise from slot machines, gaming tables, and chattering workers and patrons may be distracting to some, although workers wear protective headgear in areas where loud machinery is used to count money.

Education, Training, Qualifications: There usually are no minmum educational requirements for entry-level gaming jobs, although most employers prefer a high school diploma or GED. However, entry-level gaming services workers are required to have a license issued by a regulatory agency, such as a state casino control board or commission. Each casino establishes its own requirements for education, training, and experience. Almost all provide some in-house training in addition to requiring certification. Many institutions of higher learning give training toward certification in gaming, as well as offering an associate's, bachelor's, or master's degree in a hospitality-related field.

Earnings: Wage earnings for gaming services workers vary according to occupation, level of experience, training, location, and size of the gaming establishment. The following were median earnings for various gaming services occupations in 2002:

- Gaming supervisors $39,290
- Slot key persons $22,870
- Gaming and sports book writers & runners $18,660
- Gaming dealers $14,090

Key Contacts: For additional information on careers in gaming, visit your public library and your state gaming regulatory agency or casino control commission. Information on careers in gaming also is available from:

- **American Gaming Association**: 555 13th Street, NW, Suite 1010 East, Washington, DC 20004. Website: www.americangaming.org.

Musicians, Singers, and Related Workers

- ⇨ **Annual Earnings:** $36,290
- ⇨ **Education/Training:** Experience, training, and college
- ⇨ **Outlook:** Good

Employment Outlook: Competition for jobs for musicians, singers, and related workers is expected to be keen. The vast number of persons with the desire to perform will exceed the number of openings. Overall employment of musicians, singers, and related workers is expected to grow about as fast as the average for all occupations in the decade ahead. Most new wage and salary jobs for musicians will arise in religious organizations. Slower-than-average growth is expected for self-employed musicians, who generally perform in nightclubs, concert tours, and other venues.

Musicians, singers, and related workers held about 215,000 jobs in 2002. Almost 40 percent worked part-time, and more than one-third were self-employed. Many found jobs in cities in which entertainment and recording activities are concentrated, such as New York, Los Angeles, Chicago, and Nashville. Musicians, singers, and related workers are employed in a variety of settings. Of those who earn a wage or salary, more than one-half are employed by religious organizations and one-fourth by performing arts companies, such as professional orchestras, small chamber music groups, musical theater companies, and ballet troupes. Musicians and singers also perform in nightclubs and restaurants and for weddings and other events. Well-known musicians and groups may perform in concerts, appear on radio and television broadcasts, and make recordings and music videos. The Armed Forces also offers careers in their bands and smaller musical groups.

Nature of Work: Musicians, singers, and related workers play musical instruments, sing, compose or arrange music, or conduct groups in instrumental or vocal performances. They may perform solo or as part of a group. Although most of these entertainers play for live audiences, many perform exclusively for recording or production studios. Regardless of the setting, musicians, singers, and related workers spend considerable time practicing, alone and with their band, orchestra, or other musical ensemble.

Musicians often gain their reputation or professional standing in a particular kind of music or performance. However, *instrumental musicians* who learn several related instruments, such as flute and clarinet, and who can perform equally well in several musical styles, have better employment opportunities. *Singers* are often classified according to their voice range – soprano, contralto, tenor, baritone, or bass – or the type of music they sing, such as opera, rock, popular, folk, rap, or country and western. *Music directors* and *conductors* lead groups of musicians. These leaders usually audition and select the musicians, choose the music most appropriate for their talents and abilities – as well as the situation or audience, and direct rehearsals and performances. *Composers* create original music such as symphonies, operas, sonatas, radio and television jingles, film scores, or popular songs. Although most composers and songwriters practice their craft on instruments and transcribe the notes with pen and paper, some use computer software to compose and edit their music. *Arrangers* transcribe and adapt musical compositions to a particular style for orchestras, bands, choral groups, or individuals. Components of music – including tempo, volume, and the mix of instruments needed – are arranged to express the composer's message. While some arrangers write directly into a musical composition, others use computer software to make changes.

Working Conditions: Musicians typically perform at night and on weekends. They spend much of their remaining time practicing or in rehearsal. Full-time musicians with long-term employment contracts, such as those with symphony orchestras or television and film production companies, enjoy steady work and less travel. Nightclub, solo, or recital musicians frequently travel to perform in a variety of local settings and may tour nationally or internationally. Because many musicians find only part-time or intermittent work, experiencing unemployment between engagements, they often supplement their income with other types of jobs. The stress of constantly looking for work leads many musicians to accept permanent, full-time jobs in other occupations, while working only part time as musicians.

Although they usually work indoors, some perform outdoors for parades, concerts, and dances. In some nightclubs and restaurants, smoke and odors may be present, and lighting and ventilation may be inadequate.

Education, Training, Qualifications: Aspiring musicians begin studying an instrument at an early age. They may gain valuable experience playing in a school or community band or orchestra or with a group of friends. Participation in school musicals or choirs provides good early training and experience. Although there are no mandated credentials such as certificates or degrees required, and a few musicians gain success through natural talent and hard work, formal training is helpful and necessary for most people. Formal training may be obtained through private study with an accomplished musician, in a college or university music program, or in a music conservatory.

Young people considering careers in music should have musical talent, versatility, creativity, poise, and a good stage presence. Because quality performance requires constant study and practice, self-discipline is vital. Musicians who play in concerts or in nightclubs and those who tour must have physical stamina to endure frequent travel and an irregular performance schedule. Musicians and singers must always make their performances look effortless; therefore, preparation and practice are important. They also must be prepared to face the anxiety of intermittent employment and of rejection when auditioning for work.

Earnings: Median annual earnings of salaried musicians and singers were $36,290 in 2002. The middle 50 percent earned between $18,660 and $59,970. Median earnings were $43,060 in performing arts companies and $18,160 in religious organizations. Earnings often depend upon the number of hours and weeks worked, a performer's professional reputation, and the setting. The most successful musicians earn performance or recording fees that far exceed the median earnings.

Key Contacts: For general information about music and music teacher education and a list of accredited college-level programs, contact:

- **National Association of Schools of Music:** 11250 Roger Bacon Drive, Suite 21, Reston, VA 20190. Website: http://nasm.arts-accredit. org.

Photographers

⮑ **Annual Earnings:** $24,040
⮑ **Education/Training:** Experience to associate degree
⮑ **Outlook:** Good

Employment Outlook: Photographers can expect keen competition for job openings because the work is attractive to many people. Employment of photographers is expected to increase about as fast as the average for all occupations in the decade ahead. Demand for portrait photographers should increase as the population grows. Job growth, however, will be constrained somewhat by the widespread use of digital photography and the falling price of digital equipment.

Photographers held about 130,000 jobs in 2002. More than half were self-employed, a much higher proportion than the average for all occupations. Some self-employed photographers have contracts with advertising agencies, magazines, or other places to do individual projects at a predetermined fee, while others operate portrait studios or provide photographs to stock photo agencies. Most salaried photographers work in portrait or commercial photography studios. Newspapers, magazines, television broadcasters, and advertising agencies employ most of the rest. Most photographers work in metropolitan areas.

Nature of Work: Photographers produce and preserve images that paint a picture, tell a story, or record an event. To create commercial quality photographs, photographers need both technical expertise and creativity. Producing a successful picture requires choosing and presenting a subject to achieve a particular effect, and selecting the appropriate equipment. Photographers use either a traditional camera that records images on film that is developed into prints or a digital camera that electronically records images. Some photographers send their film to laboratories for processing and printing. Other photographers, especially those who use black and white film or who require special effects, prefer to develop their own film. Using computers and specialized software, photographers also can manipulate and enhance the scanned or digital image to create the desired effect. Some photographers specialize in areas such as portrait, commercial and industrial, scientific, news, or fine art photography. Self-employed, or freelance, photographers may license the use of their photographs through stock photo agencies or contract with clients or agencies to provide photographs as necessary.

Working Conditions: Working conditions for photographers vary considerably. Photographers employed in government and advertising agencies usually work a five-day, 40-hour week. On the other hand, news photographers often work long, irregular hours and must be available to work on short notice. Many photographers work part-time or variable schedules. Portrait photographers usually work in their own studios but also may travel to take photographs at the client's location, such as a school, a company office, or a private home. News and commercial photographers frequently travel locally, stay overnight on assignments, or travel to distant places for long periods. Some photographers work in uncomfortable or even dangerous surroundings, especially news photographers covering accidents, natural disasters, civil unrest, or military conflicts. Many photographers must wait long hours in all kinds of weather for an event to take place and stand or walk for long periods while carrying heavy equipment. News photographers often work under strict deadlines. Self-employment allows greater autonomy; however, income can be uncertain and the continuous, time-consuming search for new clients can be stressful.

Education, Training, Qualifications: Employers usually seek applicants with a "good eye," imagination, and creativity, as well as a good technical understanding of photography. Many community and junior colleges, vocational-technical institutes, private trade and technical schools, and universities offer photography courses. Qualifications required vary widely depending on the type of photography position sought. Experience gained through an internship or as an assistant to an experienced photographer is useful and can substitute for formal training for many positions. A degree from a community or junior college will strengthen an applicant's job chances. Entry-level positions in photojournalism or in industrial or scientific photography generally require a college degree in journalism or photography.

Photographers who operate their own businesses, or freelance, need business skills as well as talent. These individuals must know how to prepare a business plan; submit bids; write contracts; market their work; hire models, if needed; get permission to shoot on locations that normally are not open to the public; obtain releases to use photographs of people; license and price photographs; secure copyright protection for their work; and keep financial records. Some photographers teach at technical schools, film schools, or universities.

Earnings: Median annual earnings of salaried photographers were $24,040 in 2002. The middle 50 percent earned between $17,740 and $34,910. The highest 10 percent earned more than $49,920. Median hourly earnings in the industries employing the largest numbers of salaried photographers were $15.12 for newspapers and periodicals and $10.51 for other professional or scientific services. Salaried photographers – more of whom work full-time –

tend to earn more than those who are self-employed. Because most freelance photographers purchase their own equipment, they incur considerable expense acquiring and maintaining cameras and accessories.

Key Contacts: Career information on photography is available from:

- **Professional Photographers of America, Inc.:** 229 Peachtree Street NE, Suite 2200, Atlanta, GA 30303. Website: www.ppa.com.

- **National Press Photographers Association, Inc.:** 3200 Croasdaile Drive, Suite 306, Durham, NC 27705. Website: www.nppa.org.

Public Relations Specialists

- ⇨ **Annual Earnings:** $41,710
- ⇨ **Education/Training:** Internships or associate degree
- ⇨ **Outlook:** Excellent

Employment Outlook: Employment of public relations specialists is expected to increase faster than the average for all occupations in the coming decade. Keen competition will likely continue for entry-level public relations jobs, as the number of qualified applicants is expected to exceed the number of job openings. Many people are attracted to this profession due to the high-profile nature of the work. While college graduates who combine a degree in journalism, public relations, advertising, or another communications-related field with a public relations internship or other work experience will have the best opportunities, individuals without a four-year degree can also succeed in this field.

Public relations specialists held about 158,000 jobs in 2002. Public relations specialists are concentrated in service-providing industries such as advertising and related services; health care and social assistance; educational services; and government. Others worked for communications firms, financial institutions, and government agencies. About 11,000 public relations specialists were self-employed. Public relations specialists are concentrated in large cities, where press services and other communications facilities are readily available and many businesses and trade associations have their headquarters. Cities such as New York, Los Angeles, San Francisco, Chicago, and Washington, DC have a disproportionate number of such firms. There is a trend, however, for public relations jobs to be dispersed throughout the country – closer to clients.

Nature of Work: Public relations specialists – also referred to as communications specialists and media specialists – serve as advocates for businesses, nonprofit associations, universities, hospitals and other organizations, and build positive relationships with the public. Public relations specialists handle organizational functions such as media, community, consumer, industry, and governmental relations; political campaigns; interest-group representation; conflict mediation; or employee and investor relations. They help an organization and its public adapt mutually to each other. Informing the general public, interest groups, and stockholders of an organization's policies, activities, and accomplishments is an important part of a public relations specialist's job.

Working Conditions: Some public relations specialists work a standard 35- to 40-hour week, but unpaid overtime is common. Occasionally, they must be at the job or on call around the clock, especially if there is an emergency or crisis. Public relations offices are busy places; work schedules can be irregular and frequently interrupted. Schedules often have to be rearranged so that workers can meet deadlines, deliver speeches, attend meetings and community activities, or travel.

Education, Training, Qualifications: There are no defined standards for entry into a public relations career. A degree from a two-year (four-year preferred) college combined with some experience gained through an internship or summer job is considered good preparation for public relations work. In fact, internships are becoming vital to obtaining employment. The ability to communicate effectively is essential. Many entry-level public relations specialists have a college major in public relations, journalism, advertising, or communication. Some firms seek graduates who have worked in electronic or print journalism. Other employers seek applicants with demonstrated communication skills and training or experience in field related to the firm's business – information technology, health science, engineering, sales, or finance, for example. Many colleges help students gain part-time internships in public relations that provide valuable training and experience. The U.S. Armed Forces also can be an excellent place to gain training and experience. Membership in local chapters of the Public Relations Student Society of America or the International Association of Business Communicators provides an opportunity for students to exchange views with public relations specialists and to make professional contacts that may help them find a job in the field. A portfolio of published articles, television or radio programs, slide presentations, and other work is an asset in finding a job. Writing for a school publication or television or radio station provides valuable experience and material for one's portfolio.

People who choose public relations as a career need an outgoing personality, self-confidence, an understanding of human psychology, and an enthusiasm for motivating people. They should be competitive, yet able to function as part of a team and open to new ideas.

Earnings: Median annual earnings for salaried public relations specialists were $41,710 in 2002. Median annual earnings in the industries employing the largest numbers of public relations specialists in 2002 were: advertising and related services, $48,070; local government, $42,000; business, professional, labor, political and similar organizations, $39,330; and colleges, universities, and professional schools, $36,820.

Key Contacts: For additional information on public relations careers, contact:

- **Public Relations Society of America, Inc.:** 33 Maiden Lane, 11th Floor, New York, NY 10038-5150. Website: www.prsa.org.

- **International Association of Business Communicators:** One Hallidie Plaza, Suite 600, San Francisco, CA 94102. Website: www. iabc.com.

Recreation and Fitness Workers

- ⮩ **Annual Earnings:** Varies from $18,100 to $54,500
- ⮩ **Education/Training:** High school diploma to college degree
- ⮩ **Outlook:** Good

Employment Outlook: Competition will be keen for career positions as recreation workers because the field attracts many applicants and because the number of career positions is limited compared with the number of lower level seasonal jobs. Opportunities for staff positions should be best for persons with formal training and experience gained in part-time or seasonal recreation jobs. Overall employment of recreation and fitness workers is expected to grow faster than the average for all occupations through 2012, as an increasing number of people spend more time and money on recreation, fitness, and leisure services and as more businesses recognize the benefits of recreation and fitness programs and other services such as wellness programs. The recreation field provides a large number of temporary, seasonal jobs.

Nature of Work: Recreational and fitness workers plan, organize, and direct recreational activities, such as aerobics, arts, and crafts, the performing arts, camping, and sports in local playgrounds and recreation areas, parks, community centers, health clubs, fitness centers, religious organizations, camps, theme parks, and tourist attractions. Increasingly, recreational and fitness workers are found in workplaces, where they organize and direct leisure activities and athletic programs for employees of all ages.

Recreation workers hold a variety of positions at different levels of responsibility. *Recreation leaders*, who are responsible for a recreation program's daily operation, primarily organize and direct participants. *Activity specialists* provide instruction and coach groups in specialties such as art, music, drama, swimming, or tennis. *Recreation supervisors* oversee recreation leaders and plan, organize, and manage recreational activities. *Directors of recreation and parks* develop and manage comprehensive recreation programs in parks, playgrounds, and other settings. *Recreational therapists*, who work in a related occupation, help individuals recover from or adjust to illness, disability, or specific social problems. *Camp counselors* lead and instruct children and teenagers in outdoor-oriented forms of recreation, such as swimming, hiking, horseback riding, and camping.

Fitness workers instruct or coach groups or individuals in various exercise activities. *Fitness trainers* help clients to assess their level of physical fitness and help them to set and reach fitness goals. *Personal trainers* work with clients on a one-on-one basis in either a gym or the client's home. *Aerobics instructors* conduct group exercise sessions. *Fitness directors* oversee the operations of a health club or fitness center.

Working Conditions: Recreation and fitness workers may work in a variety of settings – for example, a health club, cruise ship, woodland recreational park, or playground in the center of a large urban community. Most recreation workers spend much of their time outdoors and may work in a variety of weather conditions, whereas most fitness workers spend their time indoors at fitness centers and health clubs. Recreation and fitness directors and supervisors, however, typically spend most of their time in an office, planning programs and special events. Recreation and fitness workers at all levels risk suffering injuries during physical activities.

Many recreation and fitness workers work about 40 hours a week. People entering this field, especially camp counselors, should expect some night and weekend work and irregular hours. About 36 percent work part time and many recreation jobs are seasonal.

Education, Training, Qualifications: Educational requirements for recreation workers range from a high school diploma – or sometime less for many summer jobs – to graduate degrees for some administration positions in large public recreation systems. Specialized training or experience in a particular field, such as art, music, drama, or athletics, is an asset for many jobs. Some jobs also require certification. A bachelor's degree and experience are preferred for most recreation supervisor jobs and required for higher level administrative jobs. Programs leading to an associate or bachelor's degree in parks and recreation, leisure studies, or related fields are offered at several hundred colleges and universities. Generally, fitness trainers and aerobic instructors must obtain a certification in the fitness field to obtain employment. Certification may be offered in various areas of exercise such as personal training, weight training, and aerobics.

Earnings: While this is not a well paid occupational field, it does offer a great deal of attractive job-related activities, especially if you have a passion for recreation, fitness, and the outdoors. Indeed, many people in this field get paid, however meager, for what they really love to do. Many self-employed individuals in this field, especially those who own their own recreation and fitness businesses or serve as personal trainers and consultants, do very well financially.

Median annual earnings vary considerably in this field. Median hourly earnings of recreation workers who worked full time in 2002 were $8.59 ($18,100 per year). The middle 50 percent earned between $7.09 and $11.36, while the top 10 percent earned $15.72 or more. However, earnings of recreation directors and others in supervisory or managerial positions can be substantially higher. Median hourly earnings in the industries employing the largest numbers of recreation workers in 2002 were:

- Nursing care facilities $9.30
- Local government $8.98
- Individual and family services $8.71
- Civic and social organizations $7.73
- Other amusement and recreation industries $7.53

Median hourly earnings of fitness trainers and aerobics instructors in 2002 were $11.51. The middle percent earned between $8.06 and $18.18, while the top 10 percent earned $26.22 or more. Earnings of successful self-employed personal trainers can be much higher. Median hourly earnings in the industries employing the largest numbers of recreation workers in 2002 were:

- Other amusement and recreation industries $13.81
- Civic and social organizations $9.24
- Other schools and instruction $8.93

Key Contacts: For information on jobs in recreation, contact employers such as local government departments of parks and recreation, nursing and personal care facilities, the Boy or Girl Scouts, or local social or religious organizations.

For information on careers, certification, and academic programs in parks and recreation, contact:

- **National Recreation and Park Association:** Division of Professional Services, 22377 Belmont Ridge Road, Ashburn, VA 20148-4150. Website: www.nrpa.org.

For career information about camp counselors, contact:

- **American Camping Association:** 5000 State Road 67 North, Martinsville, IN 46151. Website: www.acacamps.org.

For information on careers and certification in the fitness field, contact:

- **American Council on Exercise:** 4851 Paramount Drive, San Diego, CA 92123. Website: www.acefitness.org.

- **National Strength and Conditioning Association:** 1885 Bob Johnson Drive, Colorado Springs, CO 80906. Website: www.nsca-lift.org.

- **American College of Sports Medicine:** P.O. Bo 1440, Indianapolis, IN 46206-1440. Website: www.acsm.org.

Television, Video, and Motion Picture Camera Operators and Editors

⇨ **Annual Earnings:** $32,720
⇨ **Education/Training:** Experience and training
⇨ **Outlook:** Good

Employment Outlook: Television, video, and motion picture camera operators and editors can expect keen competition for job openings because the work is attractive to many people. Employment of camera operators and editors is expected to grow about as fast as the average for all occupations in the decade ahead. Rapid expansion of the entertainment market, especially motion picture production and distribution, will spur growth of camera operators. In addition, computer and Internet services will provide new outlets for interactive productions. Growth will be tempered, however, by the increased off-shore production of motion pictures. Camera operators will be needed to film made-for-the-Internet broadcasts, such as live music videos, digital movies, sports features, and general information on entertainment programming.

Nature of Work: Television, video, and motion picture camera operations produce images that tell a story, inform or entertain an audience, or record an event. Film and video editors edit soundtracks, film, and video for the motion picture, cable, and broadcast television industries. Some camera operators do their own editing. Camera operators use television, video, or motion picture cameras to shoot a wide range of material, including television series, studio programs, news and sporting events, music videos, motion pictures, documentaries, and training sessions. Some camera operators film or videotape private ceremonies and special events. Studio camera operators work in a broadcast studio and usually videotape their subjects from a fixed position. News camera operations, also called electronic news gathering (ENG) operators, work as part of a reporting team, following newsworthy events as they unfold. Camera operators employed in the entertainment field use motion picture cameras to film movies, television programs, and commercials. Those who film motion pictures are also known as cinematographers.

Working Conditions: Working conditions for camera operators and editors vary considerably. Those employed in government, television and cable networks, and advertising agencies usually work a five-day, 40-hour week. By contrast, ENG operators often work long, irregular hours and must be available to work on short notice. Camera operators and editors working in motion picture production also may work long, irregular hours. Some camera operators – especially ENG operators covering accidents, natural disasters, civil unrest, or military conflicts – work in uncomfortable or even dangerous surroundings. Many camera operators must wait long hours in all kinds of weather for an event to take place and must stand or walk for long periods while carrying heavy equipment.

Education, Training, Qualifications: Employers usually seek applicants with a "good eye," imagination, and creativity, as well as a good technical understanding of how the camera operates. Television, video, and motion picture camera operators and editors usually acquire their skills through on-the-job training or formal postsecondary training at vocational schools, colleges, universities, or photographic institutes. Formal education may be required for some positions. Many universities, community and junior colleges, vocational-technical institutes, and private trade and technical schools offer courses in camera operation and videography.

Earnings: Median annual earnings for television, video, and motion picture camera operators were $32,720 in 2002. The middle 50 percent earned between $20,610 and $51,000. Median annual earnings were $46,540 in the motion picture and video industries and $25,830 in radio and television broadcasting. Median annual earnings for film and video editors were $38,270 in 2002. The middle 50 percent earned between $26,780 and $55,300. Median annual earnings were $41,440 in the motion picture and video industries, which employ the largest numbers of film and video editors.

Key Contacts: Information about career and employment opportunities for camera operators and film and video editors is available from local offices of state employment service agencies, local offices of the relevant trade unions, and local television and film production companies that employ these workers. Some camera operators belong to unions, including the International Alliance of Theatrical Stage Employees and the National Association of Broadcast Employees and Technicians.

10

Travel and Hospitality Jobs

F EW INDUSTRIES PROVIDE as many great job and career opportunities for people without a four-year degree than the travel and hospitality industry. Highly segmented, this industry encompasses everything from airlines, cruise lines, tour operators, and car rental agencies to hotels, resorts, and rail services. The travel and hospitality industry is especially noted for focusing on performance and promoting talent from within its ranks. Indeed, many general managers of major hotels began their careers at the very bottom – doorman, front desk clerk, or porter – and were promoted within to increasingly responsible positions.

Many entry-level positions within this industry only require a high school diploma and a demonstrated ability to learn and achieve goals. Similar to other industries, employers within the travel and hospitality industry increasingly require candidates to have higher levels of education and training for entry into and advancement within this industry. Many vocational education schools, community colleges, and universities offer specialized short- and long-term programs in travel and hospitality. For anyone without a four-year degree, the travel and hospitality industry offers some of the more rewarding short- and long-term job and career opportunities.

A Special Example

In this chapter we examine the travel and hospitality employment complex in much greater depth than other occupational fields simply because this industry offers a disproportionate number of excellent job and career opportunities for people without a four-year degree and for those who neither have the interests or resources to complete a two-year technical degree. Many of the jobs defining this exciting industry cross-cut other industries and only require basic skills, interest, motivation, drive, and a willingness to learn. If many of the jobs outlined in previous chapters are less than appealing to you, chances are you may find your dream job in one of the many segments that define the relatively open and inviting travel and hospitality industry. This also is an example of an industry undergoing tremendous economic stress and restructuring. It's often during such times that new opportunities arise for enterprising individuals who are willing to invest their futures in what may well be some exciting career opportunities in the future.

A Huge Rebounding Industry

According to the Travel Industry Association of America, in 2002 travel was a $535.5 billion industry within the United States – down from $570.5 billion in 2000. Employing nearly 8 million people, it's the country's second largest employer. In 28 states, travel is the first, second, or third largest industry, which generates a tremendous amount of employment and tax revenue (nearly $85 billion).

Despite once rosy growth projections, all is not well in today's travel industry as many once high-flying players scramble to survive in a new economy characterized by a roller coaster of stagnant, declining, and resurging travel. While normally a growth industry, increasing at nearly 3 percent annually during the 1990s, the travel industry took major economic hits in 2001 and 2002 with the double whammy of a global recession and the chilling events of 9/11. In 2003 the industry experienced a triple whammy as a war in Iraq further discouraged travel and put the travel industry into an even deeper recession. In 2002 domestic air revenue passenger miles (RPMs) declined by 2.5 percent. In the same year, American Airlines lost $3.5 billion, the largest loss in airline history; United Airlines lost $3.2 billion and declared Chapter 11 bankruptcy; Delta lost $1.3 billion; and other major airlines were not far behind. Business travel declined for the fourth straight year, down by 4.3 percent from 2001, while leisure travel increased by 2 percent. At the same time, the lodging sector remained relatively stagnant, with demand for rooms increasing less than 1 percent. Overall, employment declined in most sectors of the travel industry during 2002:

Air Travel	-9.3 percent
Hotel/Motel	-4.5 percent
Restaurants	-1.4 percent

This represented a loss of 140,610 jobs in the lodging industry and a decline of 85,890 jobs in the airline industry. However, as expected, the travel industry rebounded in 2004 with renewed growth as more and more people began traveling again. Annual growth of 3 to 4 percent was expected in the foreseeable future as long as the economy continued to grow and no major terrorist activities would shock the industry.

A Challenged Industry

During the past decade the travel and hospitality industry had been one of the largest and fastest growing industries in the world. As business and leisure travel grew in the booming 1990s, so did airlines, cruise lines, hotels, tour operators, and car rentals, and other travel and

The travel industry will undergo major changes in the decade ahead.

hospitality providers. The industry appeared to be on an inevitable growth trend with numerous job opportunities available throughout the industry. During this period the travel and hospitality industry also underwent major restructuring due to its dynamic growth, the role of the Internet, and increased competition among airlines, hotels, and tour operators. The industry was expected to grow even bigger in the decade ahead, out-performing most other industries.

The rosy assumption, based on nearly eight years of unprecedented economic growth, was that as the world's economies improved, businesses expanded, an affluent population aged, and more and more people traveled, the travel and hospitality industry would undergo major expansion in the years ahead. It would offer some of the most exciting job and career opportunities for people who love travel. If you were interested in the travel and hospitality industry, the 1990s were the time to get into what was expected to be an extremely rewarding long-term career.

How times have changed and clouded what was assumed to be a dynamic, optimistic, and expansive industry. The industry's vitality has always hedged on economic growth and security. A faltering global economy coupled by a U.S. bubble economy and security threats of international and domestic terrorism hit the travel and hospitality industry hard in the early 2000s. As business and leisure travel declined, so did various segments of a highly over-invested industry. Several airlines, cruise lines, tour operators, car rental companies, and hotels either went bankrupt, merged, or experienced major financial problems as they laid off thousands of employees. Trying to survive in the troubled world of travel became imperative for many people in this industry. By the year 2002, finding a job in this wonderful industry, especially among airlines, had became increasingly difficult because of the general economic downturn and the fact that this industry was rapidly shedding jobs. More and more individuals postponed business and leisure travel or made last-minute travel decisions in response to attractive travel specials. At the same time, by 2003 the travel industry was aggressively attempting to "revitalize the industry" as well as "reduce its high distribution costs" – code words for cutting personnel, eliminating middlemen, and downgrading services. Not surprisingly, such changes did not bode well for anyone attempting to launch a career as a commercial pilot, flight attendant, cruise director, or travel agent!

> *Despite a recent boom and bust cycle, millions of people still travel, and economies do change for the better.*

Nonetheless, millions of people still travel, and economies do change for the better. Indeed, this industry frequently experiences booms and busts in response to economic and security changes. In fact, worldwide tourism in 2002 actually grew by 3.2 percent despite global economic difficulties and threats of war and terrorism. According to the World Tourist Organization (WTO), international tourist arrivals increased from 693 million in 2001 to 715 million in 2003. While tourist arrivals in the United States were down and fewer Americans traveled abroad, tourism in Europe, Asia, and the South Pacific increased by nearly 5 percent, with Spain, Italy, Greece, the United Kingdom, and Australia doing very well. Accordingly, the travel industry remains very large and vibrant, although it is undergoing major restructuring in the United States, especially consolidation, because of difficult economic times and the continuing application of technology to travel planning. For example, some observers believe only two major U.S. air carriers will survive in the decade ahead. Several cruise lines may merge because of over-capacity. Online travel services are likely to further erode the traditional role of the commission-based travel agent.

Most important of all for job seekers, the travel and hospitality industry remains one of the most exciting and satisfying of any industry. During tough economic times, competition will be keen for many jobs which only a few years ago appeared plentiful. For dedicated and passionate travel professionals, many of whom have weathered previous economic cycles, this industry will continue to reward them in many ways. For some people, this may be the perfect time to break into an uncertain industry, especially if they have the right set of skills and motivations to contribute to an employer's bottom line or are entrepreneurial enough to launch their own travel business.

The Industry and Its Many Players

The travel industry is much more than the stereotypical travel agent arranging tickets, tours, and hotels for tour groups and anxious tourists. This is a highly segmented industry consisting of a network of mutually dependent players – airlines, hotels, resorts, cruise lines, restaurants, wholesalers, incentive groups, retail tour agents, car rental companies, catering firms, meeting planners, corporate travel divisions, educators, journalists, photographers, and travel writers. These as well as a host of related organizations, individuals, and jobs are focused on the business of moving and managing people from one location to another.

The travel industry is a challenging, exciting, and highly entrepreneurial industry. Its many players report a high degree of job satisfaction. Indeed, many claim to have found *"the best job in the world"* – and with all the perks to prove it! Public relations directors in major hotels, for example, often meet and entertain celebrities, work closely with the local business community, and participate in numerous community activities – a worklife many still can't believe they "fell into" in the travel industry.

While many of the businesses, such as major airlines and hotel chains, are huge corporations, most travel-related businesses appear big but are actually small and highly entrepreneurial. They appear big because they are connected to one another through efficient communication and marketing systems which place everyone within a mutually interdependent network of business transactions. It's the type of business where there is a high degree of competition as well as a high degree of mutual dependence and cooperation. Individuals working in this industry manage to advance their careers by moving from one player to another with relative ease.

Having the Right Stuff

If your major motivation for seeking a job is your desire to travel and see and experience new places, and if you seek challenges, like to do different things, and have a sense of entrepreneurship, you should seriously investigate the variety of job and career opportunities available in the travel industry. If you are especially interested in an international job, this may be the perfect industry for you. In contrast to many other international jobs that require a great deal of education, foreign language expertise, and international experience, the international travel business favors those who demonstrate entrepreneurship and job performance skills relevant to the particular industry. In other words, it's much easier to break into this field than into many other international fields which require high levels of education and experience. Many individuals with only a high school education and little initial experience are able to pursue successful careers in the travel industry.

Positives and Negatives

Like any other industry, the travel industry has its positives and negatives. Depending on which segment of the industry you enter, you will find few high paying jobs. In fact, individuals in these industries make about 20 to 30 percent less than people in other industries, including government. However, they do get special travel benefits and perks not available in other industries, and members of this industry report a high degree of job satisfaction. Many people in the industry do not travel as much as they originally thought they would, or they travel too much to the point where travel is no longer as exciting as it once was.

At the same time, given the highly segmented and interdependent nature of the industry, careers in travel may involve working for several segments within the industry. For example, you may start out working on a cruise line, then later work for a hotel or resort chain, and finally move into the incentive travel business or airlines. This mobility among segments within the industry leads to interesting and challenging career changes and work environments. It enables individuals to advance their careers with many different employers within and between segments of the industry.

A Highly Segmented and Integrated Industry

The travel industry is the ultimate example of a highly segmented yet integrated industry where entrepreneurship plays a key role in the continuing vitality and expansion of the industry as well as the career mobility of individuals within the industry. Within the United States, it's an industry organized to move over $550 billion in travel spending each year. It employs nearly 8 million people in over 500,000 businesses, from small mom and pop travel agencies to large corporate hotels and airlines. Huge franchised travel agencies, such as CarlsonWagonlit (www. carlsontravel.com) and American Express Travel Services (www.american

This is a truly global industry with a great deal of movement of employees among countries and segments of the industry.

express.com), incentive travel groups such as Carlson (www.carlsontravel experience.com) and Maritz (www.maritztravel.com), and the military- and government-dominated Navigant/SatoTravel (www.satotravel.com), offer thousands of job opportunities in the travel industry. When linked to travel industries in other countries – including airlines, hotels, tour companies, ground operators, and incentive groups – this is a truly global industry characterized by a great deal of movement of employees among countries and segments of the industry.

The major segments or sub-industries and players within the travel industry include operators, suppliers, promoters, and supporters:

- accommodations and lodging industry
- advertising
- advertising agencies
- airlines
- airport and aviation management groups
- bus lines
- car rentals
- computer support services
- convention and meeting planners
- corporate travel managers
- cruise lines
- culture and arts promotion groups
- government tourist promotion offices
- incentive travel companies
- public relations
- publishing and journalism
- rail services
- research and marketing groups
- resorts and spas
- restaurants
- sales and marketing
- theme parks
- tour guiding
- tour operators
- tourist sites and attractions
- travel agencies and operators
- travel clubs
- travel education and training

- travel insurance
- travel websites (e-travel)
- travel writers and photographers

Not surprisingly, the travel industry employs numerous types of workers from accountants, computer specialists, and lawyers to market researchers, artists, and doctors. Many people also are able to freelance in this industry as part- and full-time professionals serving as wholesalers, travel agents, writers, photographers, trainers, and consultants.

While many people in this industry do little travel, others may do a great deal of travel as part of their day-to-day work. Onboard cruise personnel, tour operators, guides, travel agents, travel writers, and photographers are frequently "on assignment" covering a variety of destinations. They are the well-heeled travelers of this industry. On the other hand, individuals working in hotels, resorts, spas, restaurants, and e-travel and those involved with such support services as public relations, advertising, education, research, and law may do very little travel. However, if they work abroad, they may be involved in exciting international work environments that enable them to engage in the type of travel they most desire.

Airline Industry

Take, for example, the airline industry. Here's one of the most interesting and rewarding industries in the travel business. Despite an 11-percent drop in employment during 2001 – from 732,000 to 653,000 jobs – everyone seems to love this high-flying feast-and-famine industry. For airline employees, jet fuel seems to get in their blood! For airport security personnel, this appears to be a growth industry as thousands of new positions have been created since 2002 to ensure greater airport and airline security.

A highly volatile industry, due to a combination of airline deregulation since 1978, occasional recessions, and major mergers and restructuring, the airline industry nonetheless offers excellent opportunities for individuals interested in travel. Today, over 130 carriers operate within the U.S. Three major carriers – United, American, and Delta – control over 60 percent of the airline market as well as monopolize air travel in and out of their major hubs (Chicago, Atlanta, Dallas/Ft. Worth).

Over 650,000 individuals work for the airline industry. U.S. airlines with the largest number of employees include:

Airlines	Employees (January 2002) (Full time and part time)
Alaska	10,515
American Airlines	91,076
American Eagle	9,038
American Trans Air	6,967
American West	12,181
Continental Airlines	39,461
Delta Airlines	74,103
DHL	10,634
Federal Express	141,028
Northwest Airlines	45,701
Southwest Airlines	32,674
United Airlines	84,113
USAir	37,095

Other national and regional airlines, such as Air Wisconsin, Aloha, Atlantic Southeast, Frontier, Hawaiian, Horizon, JetBlue, Midway Express, and Spirit employ between 2,000 and 4,000 each.

Like any big business, the airlines seek individuals with a variety of business and technical skills – accountants, salespeople, clerical workers, word processors, computer programmers and technicians, managers, marketers, engineers, mechanics, security personnel, public relations specialists – as well as individuals with skills more specific to the industry – pilots, flight attendants, and ticketing and reservation clerks.

Future Growth and Hiring

The U.S. airline industry transports nearly 600 million passengers a year. A highly competitive industry which often experiences cutthroat competition, periodic shake-outs, consolidation, and major financial losses, the airlines are expected to face several challenges in the next few years. Indeed, expect major U.S. airlines to further consolidate as two or more major airlines go out of business.

On the other hand, hiring does not necessarily follow general growth and decline patterns. Airline personnel, are among the highest paid individuals within the travel industry, and job satisfaction tends to be higher among airline personnel than employees in most other industries. An attractive employment arena for thousands of individuals, competition for airline jobs is high and attrition is low. Except for retirees, few people voluntarily leave their airline jobs for other employment opportunities. Competition for airline jobs is particularly intense during economic downturns which also become periods of consolidation.

Positions

Positions within the airline industry are generally divided into the following six areas:

1. **Flight Operations**: Includes a variety of jobs essential for flight operations, from pilots and flight attendants to baggage handlers and meteorologists. The major such positions include:

   - Captain
   - Co-Pilot
   - Second Officer/Flight Engineer
   - Flight Attendant
   - Operations Agent
   - Flight Dispatcher
   - Meteorologist

2. **Maintenance and Engineering**: Includes several major positions for ensuring the proper maintenance and mechanical operations of aircraft:

   - Maintenance Inspector
   - Airframe and Power Plant (Engineer A&P) Mechanic
   - Instrument Technician
   - Radio Technician
   - Engineer

3. **Administration, Sales, and Marketing**: Includes numerous positions central to the maintenance of day-to-day operations and the competitive position of airlines. Good entry-level opportunities, which tend to expand during periods of consolidation, include:

- Reservations Agent
- Ticket Agent
- Airport Operations Agent
- Passenger Service Agent
- Fleet Service Employee
- Sales Representative
- District Sales Manager
- District Operations Manager
- Freight Airport Operations Agent
- Freight Telephone Sales Representative
- Fleet Service Clerk

4. **Management/Special Positions**: Includes a variety of positions that may overlap with other positions and which may be particular to a specific airline. Among these are:

- Crew Scheduler
- Incentive Sales Representative
- Inspector
- Instructor
- Programmer/Analyst
- Purchasing Agent
- Supervisor
- Industrial Engineer
- Foreman
- Executive Secretary
- Passenger Service Manager
- Personnel Representative
- Web Developer

Depending on the airline, numerous specialty areas offer a variety of job opportunities:

- Tour Operations
- Aircraft Purchase and Sales
- Charters
- Freight/Cargo
- Insurance
- Properties and Facilities
- Labor Relations
- Community and Environmental Affairs
- Purchasing
- Internet

5. **Computer Reservation Systems:** The lifeblood of the airline industry is its reservation system. Several positions relate to the operations of the four major systems – Sabre (America), Apollo (United), Worldspan (Delta), and SystemOne:

- Computer Programmer
- Technician
- Sales Representative
- Marketing Representative

6. **Food, Beverage, and Catering Services:** While most airlines contract for their food and beverage services, American Airlines operates its own meal service (Sky Chef). They hire for a variety of positions for handling their in-flight kitchen operations, from chefs to salad makers.

Thousands of additional jobs, such as security personnel, baggage handlers, car rental personnel, and food service workers found at airports, further define the airline industry.

Benefits

Many airline positions, especially pilots and flight attendants, involve extensive travel. Other positions may involve little or no travel. Compensation with major airlines is generally good compared to jobs in other segments of the travel industry. In addition, airline personnel and their families receive excellent travel benefits – free or nearly free travel on a standby, space-available basis as well as major discounts on confirmed reserved space.

Breaking In

Breaking into the airline industry depends on your particular skills and perseverance as well as the state of the economy. Most jobs are highly competitive, with some positions generating 1,000 applicants for every vacancy. Many positions require specialized education and training. The best job opportunities that also offer good career advancement opportunities will be disproportionately found at the hubs of the three major airlines (Chicago, Atlanta, Dallas/Ft. Worth) that hire over 60 percent of airline personnel.

Don't forget the dozens of smaller national and regional airlines in the U.S. Many offer excellent job opportunities and are easier to break into than the major airlines. Indeed, Dallas-based Southwest Airlines (www.southwest.com) is considered by many informed observers of the airline industry to be the best place for airline professionals to work. It remains one of America's best managed organizations that also boasts extremely high employee morale and job satisfaction. Relatively new, rapidly expanding, and profitable Salt Lake City- and New York-based JetBlue Airways (www.jetblue.com) also offers numerous job opportunities.

Small airlines headquartered abroad, many in Third World countries, offer opportunities for enterprising and highly skilled job seekers. While the pay may not be great and the equipment may be antiquated – pilots in Papua New Guinea, for example, may earn less than $30,000 a year, fly questionably maintained aircraft, and operate aircraft without a co-pilot – such airlines do offer opportunities to gain experience in the industry. And experience increasingly counts in this highly competitive global industry.

Resources

Several major trade publications provide useful information on developments within the airline industry as well as job information:

- *Air Transport World*   www.atwonline.com
- *AviationNow*   www.aviationnow.com

- *Aviation Week's AVweb*   www.avweb.com
- *Commuter/Regional Airline News*   www.aviationtoday.com
- *Travel Agent Magazine*   www.travelagentcentral.com
- *Travel Trade*   www.traveltrade.com
- *Travel Weekly*   www.twcrossroads.com

The following gateway site provides contact information and links to hundreds of aviation magazines, newspapers, and newsletters around the world: www.aero.com/publications/magazine.htm.

Useful Websites

Several websites provide a wealth of information on career opportunities in the airline industry. Some specialize in flight attendants (www.airline career.com) and pilots (www.pilotswanted.com) while others include a variety of ground and air crew positions (www.aviationjobsonline.com):

- AirlineCareer.com   www.airlinecareer.com
- Airline Employee
  Placement Service   www.aeps.com
- Airline JobsSite   www.airlinejobsite.com
- Airport Job Hub   www.airportjobhub.com
- Airport Job Kiosk   www.airportjobkiosk.com
- Aviation Information
  Resources   www.jet-jobs.com
- Aviation Job Search   www.aviationjobsearch.com
- AviationJobsOnline   www.aviationjobsonline.com
- AviationNet   www.aviationnet.com
- Find a Pilot   www.findapilot.com
- FlightDeck Recruitment   www.flightdeckrecruitment.com
- Helicopter Employment   www.avemployment.com
- JetCareers   www.jetcareers.com
- Pilots Wanted   www.pilotswanted.com
- Traveljobz.net   www.traveljobz.net

Other segments of the travel and hospitality industry are similarly huge and complex. Most of them, especially those dealing with food and accommodations, offer numerous job and career opportunities for people without a four-year degree. For information on many of these jobs, see our companion volume, *Jobs for Travel Lovers: Opportunities at Home and Abroad* (Impact Publications, 2003) and Karen Rubin's *Inside Secrets to Finding a Career in Travel* (JIST Publishing, 2001).

Air Traffic Controllers

> ➪ **Annual Earnings:** $91,600
> ➪ **Education/Training:** Work experience to four-year degree
> ➪ **Outlook:** Good

Employment Outlook: Employment of air traffic controllers is expected to grow about as fast as the average in the decade ahead. Increasing air traffic will require more controllers to handle the additional work. New computerized systems will assist the controller by automatically making many of the routine decisions. This will allow controllers to handle more traffic, thus increasing their productivity. Federal budget constraints also may limit hiring of air traffic controllers.

Air traffic controllers held about 26,000 jobs in 2002. The vast majority were employed by the Federal Aviation Administration (FAA) and work at airports – in towers and flight service stations – and in air route traffic control centers. A few serve as instructors at the FAA Academy in Oklahoma City; conduct research at the FAA national experimental center near Atlantic City, NJ; work for the Department of Defense; or work for private air traffic companies providing service to non-FAA towers.

Nature of Work: Air traffic controllers coordinate the movement of air traffic to ensure that planes stay a safe distance apart. Their primary concern is safety, but controllers also must direct plane efficiently to minimize delays. Some regulate airport traffic; others regulate flights between airports. Both airport tower and en route controllers usually control several planes at a time. Often they have to make quick decisions about completely different activities.

Working Conditions: Controllers work a basic 40-hour week; however, they may work additional hours for which they receive overtime pay or equal time off. Because most control towers and centers operate 24 hours a day, seven days a week, controllers rotate night and weekend shifts. During busy times, controllers must work rapidly and efficiently. Total concentration is required to keep track of several planes at the same time and to make certain that all pilots receive correct instructions. The mental stress of being responsible for the safety of several aircraft and their passengers can be exhausting for some persons.

Education, Training, Qualifications: To become an air traffic controller, a person must enroll in an FAA-approved education program and pass a pre-employment test that measures his/her ability to learn the controller's duties in order to qualify for job openings in the air traffic control system. (Exceptions are air traffic controllers with prior experience and military veterans.) The pre-employment test is currently offered only to students enrolled in an FAA-approved education program. In addition, applicants must have three years of full-time work experience or four years of college, or an equivalent combination of both.

Upon successful completion of an FAA – approved program, individuals who receive school recommendation and who meet the basic qualification requirements, including age limit and achievement of a qualifying score on the FAA pre-employment test, become eligible for employment as an air traffic controller. Candidates must also pass a medical exam, drug screening, and security clearance before they can be hired.

Upon selection, employees attend the FAA Academy in Oklahoma City for 12 weeks of training, during which they learn the fundamentals of the airway system, FAA regulations, controller equipment, and aircraft performance characteristics, as well as more specialized tasks. After graduation, it takes several years of progressively more responsible work experience, interspersed with considerable classroom instruction and independent study, to become a fully licensed controller.

Earnings: This is one of the highest paid jobs for people without a four-year degree. Median annual earnings of air traffic controllers in 2002 were $91,600. The middle 50 percent earned between $65,480 and $112,550. Both the worker's job responsibilities and the complexity of the particular facility determine a controller's pay. For example, controllers who work at FAA's busiest air traffic control facilities earn higher pay.

Key Contacts: Career information on how to qualify and apply for a job as an air traffic controller is available through:

- **Federal Aviation Administration:** 800 Independence Avenue, SW, Washington, DC 20591. Website: www.faa.gov.

Aircraft and Avionics Equipment Mechanics and Service Technicians

⭢ **Annual Earnings:** Around $43,000
⭢ **Education/Training:** On-the-job training and certificate
⭢ **Outlook:** Excellent

Employment Outlook: Opportunities for aircraft and avionics equipment mechanics and service technician jobs should be excellent for persons who have completed aircraft mechanic training programs. Employment of aircraft mechanics is expected to increase about as fast as the average for all occupations in the decade ahead. As more and more people are expected to fly in the decade ahead, the number of aircraft requiring servicing will increase accordingly.

Aircraft and avionics equipment and service technicians held about 154,000 jobs in 2002; about one in six of these workers was an avionics technician. Nearly 40 percent of aircraft and avionics equipment mechanics and technicians worked for air transportation companies, and close to 20 percent worked for private maintenance and repair facilities. About 20 percent worked for the federal government, and about 13 percent worked for aerospace products and parts manufacturing firms. Most of the rest worked for companies that operate their own planes to transport executives and cargo.

Nature of work: To keep aircraft in peak operating condition, aircraft and avionics equipment mechanics and service technicians perform scheduled maintenance, make repairs, and complete inspections required by the Federal Aviation Administration (FAA). Some mechanics work on one of many different types of aircraft, such as jets, propeller-driven airplanes, or helicopters. Others specialize in one section of a particular type of aircraft, such as the engine, hydraulics, or electrical system.

Avionics systems are now an integral part of aircraft design and have vastly improved aircraft capability. Avionics technicians repair and maintain components used for aircraft navigation and radio communications, weather radar systems, and other instruments that control flight, engine, and other primary functions. Because of technological advances, an increasing amount of time is spent repairing electronic systems, such as computerized controls. Technicians may also be required to analyze and develop solutions to complex electronic problems.

Working Conditions: Mechanics usually work in hangars or in other indoor areas, although they can work outdoors – sometimes in unpleasant weather – when hangars are full or when repairs must be made quickly. Mechanics often work under time pressure to maintain flight schedules or, in general aviation, to keep from inconveniencing customers. At the same time, mechanics have a tremendous responsibility to maintain safety standards, and this can cause the job to be stressful. Frequently mechanics must lift or pull heavy objects weighing as much as 70 pounds. They occasionally must work in precarious positions on scaffolds or ladders. Aircraft mechanics usually work 40 hours a week on eight-hour shifts around the clock. Overtime work is frequent.

Education, Training, Qualifications: The majority of mechanics who work on civilian aircraft are certified by the FAA as "airframe mechanic" or "power plant mechanic," or "avionics repair specialist." The FAA requires at least 18 months of work experience for an airframe, power plant or avionics repairer's certificate. Completion of a program at an FAA-certified mechanic school can substitute for the work experience requirement. Applicants for all certificates also must pass written and oral tests and demonstrate that they can do the work authorized by the certificate. Although a few people become mechanics through on-the-job training, most learn their job in one of about 200 trade schools certified by the FAA. Some aircraft mechanics in the military acquire enough general experience to satisfy the work experience requirements for the FAA certificate. In general, however, jobs in the military services are too specialized to provide the broad experience required by the FAA. Courses in math and science are helpful, as they demonstrate many of the principles involved in the operation of aircraft. Development of writing skills is useful because mechanics are often required to submit reports.

Earnings: Median hourly earnings of aircraft mechanics and service technicians were about $20.71 in 2002 ($43,100 per year). For avionics technicians, median earnings were about $42,100 per year). Mechanics who work on jets for the major airlines generally earn more than those working on other aircraft. Airline mechanics and their families receive reduced-fare transportation on their own and most other airlines. Almost four in 10 aircraft and avionics equipment mechanics and service technicians are members of unions or covered by union agreements.

Key Contacts: Information about jobs with a particular airline can be obtained by contacting the personnel manager of the company. For general information about aircraft and avionics equipment mechanics and service technicians, contact:

- Professional Aviation Maintenance Association: 717 Princess Street, Alexandria, VA 22314. Website: www.pama.org.

Airline Pilots and Flight Engineers

⇨ **Annual Earnings:** $47,970 to $109,580
⇨ **Education/Training:** High school diploma to college degree
⇨ **Outlook:** Good

Employment Outlook: Overall, the employment of aircraft pilots is projected to increase about as fast as average for all occupations in the coming decade. In the long run, demand for air travel is expected to track increases in the population and growth of the economy. In the short run, however, employment of pilots is generally sensitive to cyclical swings in the economy. During recessions, when a decline in the demand for air travel forces airlines to curtail the number of flights, airlines may temporarily furlough some pilots. The number of flight engineers is projected to decline in the decade ahead as new planes needing only two pilots replace older planes that required flight engineers. Pilots also will experience some productivity improvements as airlines switch to larger planes and adopt the low-fare carrier model that emphasizes faster turnaround times for flights, keeping more pilots in the air rather than waiting on the ground.

Civilian aircraft pilots and flight engineers held about 100,000 jobs in 2002. About 79,000 worked as airline pilots, copilots, and flight engineers. The remainder were commercial pilots who worked as flight instructors at local airports or for large businesses that fly company cargo and executives in their own planes or helicopters. Some commercial pilots flew small planes for air-taxi companies, usually to or from lightly traveled airports not served by major airlines. Others worked for a variety of businesses, performing tasks such as dusting crops, inspecting pipelines, or conducting sightseeing trips. Federal, state, and local governments also employed pilots. A few pilots were self-employed.

Nature of Work: Pilots are highly trained professionals who fly airplanes and helicopters to carry out a wide variety of tasks. Most are airline pilots, copilots, and flight engineers who transport passengers and cargo, but one out of five pilots is a commercial pilot involved in more unusual tasks, such as dusting crops, spreading seed for reforestation, testing aircraft, flying passengers and cargo to areas not served by regular airlines, directing firefighters' efforts, tracking criminals, monitoring traffic, and rescuing and evacuating injured persons.

Except on small aircraft, two pilots usually make up the cockpit crew. Some large aircraft have a third pilot – the flight engineer – who assists the other pilots by monitoring and operating many of the instruments and systems, making minor in-flight repairs, and watching for other aircraft. New technology can perform many flight tasks, and virtually all new aircraft now fly with only two pilots who rely more heavily on computerized controls.

Before departure pilots check their aircraft, make sure baggage has been loaded correctly, confer with dispatchers and aviation weather forecasters, and choose a route, altitude, and speed that will provide the fastest, safest, smoothest flight. Takeoff and landing are the most difficult parts of the flight. Unless the weather is bad, the actual flight is relatively easy. In contrast, helicopters are used for short trips at fairly low altitude, so pilots must be constantly on the lookout for trees, bridges, power lines, transmission towers, and other dangerous obstacles.

Pilots for charter operators or businesses may perform more non-flying duties such as loading the aircraft. Some pilots are instructors. A few specially trained pilots are examiners or "check pilots" who periodically fly with pilot's license applicants to make sure they are proficient.

Working Conditions: By law, airline pilots cannot fly more than 100 hours a month or more than 1,000 hours a year. Most airline pilots fly an average of 75 hours and work an additional 75 hours a month performing non-flying duties. Most pilots have a variable work schedule, working several days, then several days off. Most spend a considerable amount of time away from home because the majority of flights involve overnight layovers. When pilots are away from home, the airlines provide hotel accommodations, transportation between the airport and the hotel, and an allowance for meals and other allowable expenses. Airlines operate flights at all hours of the day and night, so work schedules often are irregular. Flight assignments are based on seniority.

Commercial pilots also may have irregular schedules, flying 30 hours one month and 90 hours the next. Because these pilots frequently have many non-flying responsibilities, they have much less free time than do airline pilots. Except for business pilots, most do not remain away from home overnight. However, they may work odd hours.

Airline pilots, especially those on international routes, often suffer jet lag – fatigue caused by many hours of flying through different time zones. The work of test pilots, who check the flight performance of new and experimental aircraft, may be dangerous. Pilots who dust crops may be exposed to hazardous chemicals and seldom have the benefit of a regular landing strip. Helicopter pilots involved in rescue and police work may be subject to personal injury. The mental stress of being responsible for a safe flight, regardless of weather, can be tiring.

Education, Training, Qualifications: All pilots who are paid to transport passengers or cargo must have a commercial pilot's license with an instrument rating issued by the Federal Aviation Administration (FAA). Helicopter pilots must hold a commercial pilot's certificate with a helicopter rating. To qualify for these licenses, applicants must be at least 18 years old and have at least 250 hours of flight experience. The experience required can be reduced through participation in certain flight school curricula approved by the FAA. Applicants must also pass a strict physical examination to make sure they are in good health and have 20/20 vision with or without glasses, good hearing, and no physical handicaps that could impair their performance. They must pass a written test and demonstrate their flying ability to FAA or designated examiners.

Airline pilots must fulfill additional requirements. Applicants for an airline transport license must be at least 23 years old and have a minimum of 1,500 hours of flying experience, including night and instrument flying, and must pass FAA written and flight examinations. Usually they also have one or more advanced ratings, such as multi-engine aircraft or aircraft-type ratings, depending upon the requirements of their particular job.

The U.S. Armed Forces have always been an important source of trained pilots for civilian jobs. Persons without Armed Forces training may become pilots by attending flight schools or taking lessons from individual FAA-certified flight instructors. The FAA has certified about 600 civilian flying schools, including some colleges and universities that offer degree credit for pilot training. The number of trained pilots leaving the military is not expected to grow very much as the need for pilots in civil aviation continues to grow. As a result, FAA-certified schools will train a larger share of pilots than in the past. Although some small airlines will hire high school graduates, most airlines require at least two years of college. Most entrants into this field have a college degree.

Earnings: Earnings of aircraft pilots and flight engineers vary greatly depending whether they work as airline or commercial pilots. Earnings of airline pilots are among the highest in the nation, and depend on factors such as the type, size, and maximum speed of the plane and the number of hours flown. For example, pilots who fly jet aircraft usually earn higher salaries than do pilots who fly turbo-props. Airline pilots and flight engineers may earn extra pay for night and international flights. The median earnings of airline pilots in 2002 were $109,580, and more than 25 percent earned more than $145,000. The median earnings of commercial pilots were $47,970 for the same period, with the highest 10 percent earning more than $101,460.

Airline pilots receive an expense allowance or "per diem" for every hour they are away from home. Pilots and their immediate families are usually entitled to free or reduced fare transportation on their own and other airlines. More than half of all aircraft pilots are members of unions.

Key Contacts: Information about job openings, salaries for a particular airline, and qualifications required may be obtained by contacting the personnel manager of the airline. For information on airline pilots, contact:

- **Aerospace Education Foundation:** 1501 Lee Highway, Arlington, VA 22209-1198. Website: www.aef.org.

- **Air Line Pilots Association:** 535 Herndon Parkway, Herndon, VA 20170. Website: www.alpa.org.

- **Air Transport Association of America, Inc.:** 1301 Pennsylvania Avenue, NW, Suite 1100, Washington, DC 20004. Website: www.air-transport.org.

- **Regional Airline Association:** 2025 M Street, NW, Washington, DC 20036. Website: www.raa.org.

For information on helicopter pilots contact:

- **Helicopter Association International:** 1635 Prince St., Alexandria, VA 22314. Website: www.ROTOR.com.

For information about job opportunities in companies other than airlines, consult the classified section of aviation trade magazines and apply to companies that operate aircraft at local airports.

Chefs, Cooks, and Food Preparation Workers

⇨ **Annual Earnings:** Varies greatly from $18,000 to over $50,000
⇨ **Education/Training:** High school diploma plus training
⇨ **Outlook:** Excellent

Employment Outlook: Overall employment of chefs, cooks, and food preparation workers is expected to increase about as fast as the average for all occupations in the decade ahead. Employment growth will be spurred by increases in population, household income, and leisure time that will allow people to dine out and take vacations more often. In addition, growth in the number of two-income households will lead more families to opt for the convenience of dining out. Competition for jobs in the top kitchens of higher end restaurants should be keen. Minimal education and training requirements, combined with a large number of part-time positions, make employment as chefs, cooks, and food preparation workers attractive to people seeking first-time or short-term employment, a source of additional income, or a flexible schedule.

Nature of Work: Chefs, cooks, and other food preparation workers prepare a wide range of foods – from soups, snacks, and salads to entrees, side dishes, and desserts – for restaurants, institutions, bakeries, and fast-food outlets. Chefs are the most highly skilled, trained, and experienced kitchen workers. Executive chefs coordinate the work of the kitchen staff and often direct certain kinds of food preparation. They decide the size of servings, sometimes plan menus, and buy food supplies. Larger restaurants and food service establishments tend to have varied menus and larger kitchen staffs. They often include several chefs and cooks, sometimes called assistant or line cooks, along with other less skilled kitchen workers, such as food preparation workers. Each chef or cook works an assigned station that is equipped with the types of stoves, grills, pans, and ingredients needed for the foods prepared at each station. Job titles often reflect the principal ingredient prepared or the type of cooking preformed – vegetable cook, fry cook, or grill cook.

Chefs, cooks, and food preparation workers held nearly 3 million jobs in 2002. The distribution of jobs among the various types of chefs, cooks, and food preparation workers was as follows:

- Food preparation workers   850,000
- Cooks, restaurant   727,000
- Cooks, fast food   588,000
- Cooks, institution and cafeteria   436,000
- Cooks, short order   227,000
- Chefs and head cooks   132,000
- Cooks, private household   8,000

Working Conditions: Many restaurant and institutional kitchens have modern equipment, convenient work areas, and air-conditioning; but others, particularly in older and smaller eating places, are frequently not as well equipped. Workers generally must withstand the pressure and strain of working in close quarters during busy periods, stand for hours at a time, lift heavy pots and kettles, and work near hot ovens and grills. Work hours in restaurants may include late evening, holiday, and weekend work, while hours in cafeterias in factories, schools, or other institutions may be more regular. The wide range in dining hours and the need for fully staffed kitchens during all open hours create work opportunities for individuals seeking supplemental income, flexible work hours, or variable schedules.

Education, Training, Qualifications: Most kitchen workers start as fast-food or short-order cooks, or in one of the other less skilled kitchen positions that require little education or training and allow them to acquire their skills on the job. An increasing number of chefs and cooks obtain their training through high school or post-high school vocational programs and two- or four-year colleges. Chefs and cooks may also be trained in apprenticeship programs offered by professional culinary institutes, industry associations, and trade unions. Some large hotels and restaurants operate their own training programs for cooks and chefs. Executive chefs and head cooks who work in fine restaurants require many years of training and experience and an intense desire to cook. The American Culinary Federation accredits over 100 formal training programs and sponsors apprenticeship programs around the country.

Earnings: Wages of chefs, cooks, and other kitchen workers vary depending on where they work. Elegant restaurants and hotels pay the highest wages. Many executive chefs earn over $50,000 a year. Top chefs can earn twice that much. In 2002, median hourly earnings for chefs and head cooks were $13.43. The middle 50 percent earned between $9.86 and $19.03. The highest 10 percent earned more than $25.86 per hour ($55,900 pre year). Median hourly earnings of other cooks and food preparation workers in 2002 were:

- Restaurant cooks $9.16
- Institution and cafeteria cooks $8.72
- Food preparation workers $7.85
- Short-order cooks $7.82
- Fast-food cooks $6.90

Some employers provide employees with uniforms and free meals.

Key Contacts: For information on career opportunities and educational programs for chefs, cooks, and other kitchen workers, contact local employers, local offices of the state employment service, or:

- **American Culinary Federation:** 180 Center Place Way, St. Augustine, FL 32095. Website: www.acfchefs.org.

- **International Council on Hotel, Restaurant, and Institutional Education:** 2613 North Parham Road, 2nd Floor, Richmond, VA 23294. Website: www.chrie.org.

- **National Restaurant Association:** 1200 17th Street, NW, Washington, DC 20036-3097. Website: www.restaurant.org.

Cruise Line Jobs

⇨ **Annual Earnings:** Varies
⇨ **Education/Training:** High school diploma to college
⇨ **Outlook:** Excellent

Employment Outlook: Job opportunities with cruise lines should increase at a faster rate than most jobs for the decade ahead as more and more cruise ships come on line to accommodate the increased demand for cruise vacations. Indeed, the cruise industry has experienced phenomenal growth during the past decade as interest in cruise vacations has increased and as more and more mega-cruise ships have come on line. Each year cruise ships carry nearly 8 million North American passengers. The number of passengers is likely to double over the coming decade as more and more people choose cruise ships as their favorite mode of vacation-resort travel. In response to this projected growth in passengers, nearly 50 new cruise ships have come on line during the past five years. Such growth translates into more and more jobs in this much sought-after industry.

Cruise ship jobs are highly competitive. Operating like large resorts whose main purpose is to pamper their guests during short three- to 14-day cruises, most cruise ships maintain a high staff-per-passenger ratio. They hire for every type of department and position you would find in five-star resorts – housekeeping, kitchen, entertainment, health, fitness, tours, gaming, guest relations, engineering, maintenance, hair salon, and gift shop. They hire accountants, cooks, waiters, engineers, casino operators, pursers, photographers, massage therapists, cosmetologists, doctors, nurses, entertainers, youth counselors, water sports instructors, fitness instructors, and lecturers. However, they disproportionately hire crew members from Southern Europe and Asia who traditionally occupy these lower-paying jobs.

Nature of Work: There are many myths about cruise line jobs. The biggest myths are that these jobs are all fun and games, they pay well, and there are plenty of opportunities available onboard for Americans. The realities are that most cruise line jobs involve hard work and do not pay well, and few Americans find jobs onboard. Cruise ship jobs involve long hours, a great deal of stress, a willingness to work with a diverse multinational team, an ability to please all types of passengers, and the willingness to give exceptional and exacting service. Above all, you must be people-oriented, tolerant, flexible, and handle stress well. You must have the disposition of a servant – the customer is always right, even though he or she may be a jerk!

If you have a family, an onboard cruise ship job is likely to involve long separations. For many Americans, it's the type of job best enjoyed by young single individuals regard these cruise ship jobs as short-term travel positions or entry-level positions for moving within the larger travel and hospitality industry. Many Americans will spend three to five years working with cruise lines – accumulating valuable travel and resort experience – before "settling down" to more stable family-oriented jobs on shore.

Few Americans work onboard, and those that do tend to be found in a very limited number of "American" positions – entertainment, gift shop, youth counselor, physical fitness, and sports. You won't find many Americans piloting ships, managing restaurants, serving tables, cooking food, or making beds. These positions tend to be dominated by other nationals. Most American involvement with the cruise ship industry tends to be on shore – in marketing, sales, and computer reservation systems.

The significance of such employment within a multinational context has different meanings for different nationals. For many nationals, cruise ship jobs are more than just short-term travel jobs; they are great job opportunities – well paid, secure, and prestigious compared to the limited job opportunities back home. While many foreign nationals – especially those from such Third World countries as the Philippines and Indonesia who occupy numerous low-paying positions in housekeeping and kitchen – make cruise ship jobs a long-term career, few Americans pursue such jobs as a career. Greeks and Italians tend to be in charge of food and beverage services and general ship operations. Given the limited job options back home, cruise ship jobs for such nationals are considered excellent paying, secure, and prestigious jobs. They can save money to support their families back home.

Americans tend to be disproportionately found in the entertainment, physical fitness, public relations, youth counseling, spa, shop, casino, and marketing and sales end of cruise ship jobs. Despite all the glamour, cruise ship pay and lifestyles simply are not sufficiently attractive for many Americans to continue long-term in this industry. Americans also are not noted for their talent in dispensing exceptional, exacting, and high level service that is the hallmark of many cruise lines. Many Americans typically pursue cruise ship jobs in the hopes of moving on to other jobs within the travel and hospitality industry, especially with hotels, resorts, restaurants, casinos, and night clubs. A cruise ship job is often a short stop along the way to other more rewarding jobs and careers.

Breaking into the cruise industry is relatively easy given the high turnover rate of personnel and the availability of numerous entry-level positions. Functioning as a combination floating city, resort, and hotel, most cruise ships operate with a staff of 300 to 900 who provide a wide range of services. As a result, cruise lines are constantly hiring for all types of positions. The most common shipboard opportunities are found in:

- **Front desk/purser's desk:** Positions include chief purser, assistant purser, guest services staff members.

- **Boutiques/shops:** sales staff and cashiers.

- **Restaurants and bars:** Chef, sous chef pastry cook, baker, wine steward, buffet staff, food and beverage staff, bartender, Maitre d', wait staff, busboy, butcher, ice carver, dishwasher.

- **Casino:** Cashier, dealer, slot technician.

- **Salon and spa:** Massage therapist, cosmetologist, hair stylist, nail technician, masseur/masseuse.

- **Show lounges:** Dancer, singer, comedian, magician, lecturer, sound technician, band member, disk jockey, and other types of entertainers.

- **Activities:** Youth counselor, activities coordinator, instructor (yoga, chess, bridge, diving, golf, tennis, dance, water sports), shore excursion, sports director, swimming pool/deck attendant.

- **Operations:** Computer specialist, electrician, machinist, and painter.

- **Photography:** Photographer.

- **Medical:** Physician, dentist, and nurse.

The cruise industry is a great entry point into the travel industry. Most positions require little or no experience, though a few positions require many years of experience. If you target your job search, make the right contacts, and are persistent, you should be able to land a job with a cruise line.

As you conduct a job search, you should be aware that many onboard positions are not controlled by the cruise lines. Gift shops, beauty salons, casinos, sports and recreation, and entertainment are often concessions operated by contractors or concessionaires. For example, dancers, musicians, singers, massage therapists, cosmetologists, and medical doctors are often hired through firms that control these onboard concessions. If a position you desire relates to these concessions, you will need to make employment contacts with the appropriate concessionaire rather than the cruise line.

Most cruise lines require an online application or a mailed, faxed, or e-mailed resume and cover letter. Another approach is to send a copy of your resume, along with an accompanying cover letter, directly to the personnel office of a cruise line. Specify on the envelope whether you are applying for a "shipside" or a "shoreside" position, identify which department you wish to work for, and/or call ahead to get the name of the department or person you should address your correspondence to.

Cruise lines recruit individuals for both shoreside and shipboard positions. The four largest cruise lines, which employ the largest staffs, include the following:

- **Carnival Cruise Lines**   www.carnival.com
- **Princess Cruises**   www.princesscruises.com
- **Royal Caribbean International** www.royalcaribbean.com
- **Star Cruises/Norwegian**   www2.starcruises.com
  Cruise Lines/Orient Lines   www.ncl.com
                                     www.orientlines.com

Other major cruise lines you may want to direct your job search toward include:

- **American Cruise Lines**   www.americancruiselines.com
- **Celebrity Cruises**   www.celebrity-cruises.com
- **Clipper Cruise Line**   www.clippercruise.com
- **Costa Cruises**   www.costacruise.com
- **Crystal Cruises**   www.crystalcruises.com
- **Cunard**   www.cunard.com
- **Delta Queen Steamboat Co.**   www.deltaqueen.com
- **Disney Cruise Line**   www.disneycruise.com
- **Freighter World Cruises**   www.freighterworld.com
- **Galapagos Tours and Cruises**   www.galapagos-inc.com
- **Holland America Line**   www.hollandamerica.com
- **Lindblad Expeditions**   www.specialexpeditions.com
- **Radisson Seven Seas Cruises**   www.rssc.com
- **ResidenSea**   www.residensea.com
- **Royal Olympia Cruises**   www.roc.gr
- **Seabourn Cruise Line**   www.seabourn.com
- **Sea Cloud Cruises**   www.seacloud.com
- **Silversea Cruises**   www.silversea.com
- **Society Expeditions**   www.societyexpeditions.com
- **Tall Ship Adventures**   www.tallshipadventures.on.ca
- **United States Lines**   www.unitedstateslines.com
- **Viking River Cruises**   www.vikingrivercruises.com
- **Windjammer Barefoot Cruises**   www.windjammer.com
- **Windstar Cruises**   www.windstarcruises.com

Be sure to familiarize yourself with each cruise line's operations. For example, the Disney Cruise Lines and Carnival Cruises are very family- and youth-oriented, requiring many youth counselors. Crystal and Seabourn Cruises are very upscale, offering many five-star amenities and the services of spa personnel and academic lecturers. Norwegian Cruise Lines is noted for its sports programs and theme cruises. If you survey the companies' websites, you'll get a good idea of various opportunities available with such companies. Best of all, you can apply for jobs online 24 hours a day!

Key Contacts: One of the best resources for surveying job opportunities in the cruise industry is Mary Fallon Miller's *How to Get a Job With a Cruise Line,* 5th Edition (Ticket to Adventure, 2001). The book is filled with useful tips on how to land a cruise job. It includes a comprehensive survey of the major cruise lines and concessionaires, descriptions of positions, information on training opportunities and special programs, insiders' stories, tips on writing resumes and completing applications, and names, addresses, and phone numbers for contacting potential employers. Several websites also offer books and application packages for cruise ship jobs which include job search tips and addresses of major cruise employers and employment firms:

- Cruise Jobs   www.cruisejobs.com
- Cruise Line Jobs   www.cruiselinejobs.com
- Cruise Ship Entertainment   www.cruiseshipentertainment.com
- Cruise Ship Jobs   www.shipjobs.com
- CruiseJobFinder   www.cruisejobfinder.com

To keep abreast of developments in the cruise industry, as well as to learn more about particular cruise lines, we recommend surveying such trade magazines as *Cruise Desk, Cruise Trade, Cruise and Vacation Views, Leisure Travel News, Tour and Travel News, The Travel Counselor, Travel Trade,* and *Travel Weekly.* Several online publications also cover the cruise industry:

- Cruise News   www.cruise-news.com
- Cruise News Daily   www.cruisenewsdaily.com
- Cruise Week News   www.cruise-week.com
- CruiseMates   www.cruisemates.com

Several associations focus on cruise lines. You may want to contact these associations for information on cruise lines as well as develop useful contacts for networking within the industry:

- Cruise Lines International
  Association   www.cruising.org
- International Council of
  Cruise Lines   www.iccl.org
- Niche Cruise Marketing
  Alliance   www.nichecruise.com
- AlaskaCruises.com   www.alaskacruises.org

Several websites provide job search assistance. Some of the sites charge job seekers for marketing their resumes to cruise lines and concessionaires. Others are free to job seekers:

- Cruise Employment Databank   www.nwcruisejobs.com
- Cruise-Jobs   www.cruise-jobs.com
- CruiseJobLink   www.cruisejoblink.com
- Hospitality Careers Online   www.hcareers.com
- JobMonkey   www.jobmonkey.com/cruise
- My Cruise Ship Job   www.mycruiseshipjob.com
- New World Cruise Ship
  Employment Agency   www.cruiseshipjob.com

Flight Attendants

↪ **Annual Earnings:** $43,140
↪ **Education/Training:** High school diploma plus training
↪ **Outlook:** Good

Employment Outlook: Opportunities for flight attendants should improve considerably in the decade ahead as the airline industry continues to recover from a major downturn attendant with the effects of the 9/11 terrorist attacks on the United States. Employment of flight attendants is expected to grow about as fast as the average for all occupations in the decade ahead. Population growth and an improving economy are expected to boost the number of airline passengers.

Flights attendants held about 104,000 jobs in 2002. Commercial airlines employed the vast majority of flight attendants, most of whom lived in their employer's home base city. A small number of flight attendants worked large companies that operated corporate aircraft for business purposes.

Nature of Work: Major airlines are required by law to provide flight attendants for the safety of the traveling public. Although the primary job of flight attendants is to ensure that safety regulations are followed, they also try to make flights comfortable and enjoyable for passengers. As passengers board the plane, flight attendants greet them, check their tickets, and tell them where to store coats and carry-on items. Flight attendants instruct all passengers in the use of emergency equipment and check that seat belts are fastened, trays upright, and personal items properly stowed. During the flight, flight attendants reassure passengers, assist any who need help or become ill, and heat and distribute precooked meals or snacks. Prior to landing, flight attendants collect headsets, and take inventory of alcoholic beverages and moneys collected.

Working Conditions: Because airlines operate around-the-clock, year-round, flight attendants may work nights, holidays, and weekends. On-duty time is usually limited to 12 hours per day, with a daily maximum of 14 hours. Attendants usually fly 65 to 85 hours a month and, in addition, generally spend 50 hours a month on the ground preparing flights, writing reports, and waiting for planes to arrive. They may be away from their home base at least one-third of the time. During this time, the airlines provide hotel accommodations and an allowance for meals. Flight attendants must be flexible, reliable, and willing to relocate. Flight attendants are susceptible to injury because of the job demands in a moving aircraft. Flight attendants are kept busy – especially on short flights – and must stand for long periods. No matter how tiring the job, they must remain pleasant and efficient.

Education, Training, Qualifications: Although nearly 50 percent of flight attendants have a college degree and over 70 percent have some college education, entry into this occupation only requires a high school diploma. Those with several years of college and experience dealing with people are preferred. Applicants who attend schools and colleges that offer flight attendant training may have an advantage over other applicants. Highly desirable areas of study include psychology and education – people-oriented disciplines. Applicants must be at least 18 to 21 years old. There are height requirements for the purpose of reaching overhead bins, and most airlines want weight proportionate to height. Vision must be correctable to 20/30 or better with glasses or contact lenses (uncorrected no worse than 20/200).

Once hired, all candidates undergo training ranging from three to eight weeks, depending on the size and type of carrier. Training takes place at the airline's flight training center. New trainees are not considered employees of the airline until they successfully complete the training program. Some airlines charge individuals for training. Toward the end of their training, students go on practice flights. Flight attendants are required to go through periodic retraining and pass an FAA safety examination in order to continue flying. Because assignments are based on seniority, usually only the most experienced attendants get their choice of assignments. Advancement takes longer than in the past, because flight attendants are remaining in this career longer than they used to.

Earnings: Median annual earnings of flight attendants were $43,140 in 2002. The middle 50 percent earned between $31,660 and $66,260. New hires usually begin at the same pay scale regardless of experience, and all flight attendants receive the same future pay increases. Flight attendants receive extra compensation for night and international flights and for increased hours. Some airlines offer incentive pay for working holidays or taking positions that require additional responsibility or paperwork. Most airlines guarantee a minimum of 65 to 85 hours per month, with the option to work additional hours. Flight attendants also receive a "per diem" allowance for meals and expenses while on duty away from home. In addition, flight attendants and their immediate families are entitled to free fares on their own airline and reduced fares on most other airlines. The majority of flight attendants hold union membership.

Key Contacts: Information about job opportunities and qualifications required for work at a particular airline may be obtained by contacting the airline's human resources office. Check out the websites of airlines for employment information, such as:

- American Airlines   www.aa.com
- Continental Airlines   www.continental.com
- Delta Air Lines   www.delta.com
- JetBlue Airlines   www.jetblue.com
- Northwest Airlines   www.nwa.com
- Southwest Airlines   www.iflyswa.com
- United Airlines   www.ual.com

These organizations provide job search and placement assistance for flight attendants:

- AirlineCareer.com   www.airlinecareer.com
- Airline Employee
  Placement Service   www.aeps.com
- Aujobs.com   www.aujobs.com

Also contact:

- **Association of Flight Attendants:** 1275 K Street, NW, 5th Floor, Washington, DC 20005. Website: www.afanet.org.

Food and Beverage Service Workers

- ➪ **Annual Earnings:** Varies with hourly wages and tips
- ➪ **Education/Training:** None required
- ➪ **Outlook:** Excellent

Employment Outlook: Employment is expected to grow faster than average due to the anticipated increase in the population, personal income, and leisure time. Replacement needs because of high turnover will result in plentiful job openings.

Nature of Work: Waiters and waitresses take customers' orders, serve food and beverages, prepare itemized checks, and sometimes accept payments. In some establishments waiters and waitresses may perform additional duties such as escorting guests to tables, setting and clearing tables, or cashiering.

Bartenders fill drink orders taken by waiters from customers seated in the restaurant as well as take orders from customers seated at the bar. Most bartenders must know dozens of drink recipes and be able to mix drinks accurately, quickly, and without waste. Bartenders collect payment, operate the cash register, clean up after customers have left, and may also serve food to customers seated at the bar.

Hosts and hostesses welcome guests, direct patrons to where they may leave coats, and indicate where they may wait until their table is ready. Hosts and hostesses assign guests to tables, escort them to their seats, and provide menus.

Dining room attendants and bartender helpers assist waiters, waitresses, and bartenders by keeping the serving area stocked with supplies, cleaning tables, and removing dirty dishes to the kitchen.

Fast-food workers take orders, get the ordered items, serve them to the customer, and accept payment. They may cook and package French fries, make coffee, and fill beverage cups.

Working Conditions: Food and beverage workers are on their feet most of the time and often have to carry heavy trays of food, dishes, and glassware. During busy dining periods, they are under pressure to serve customers quickly. Many food and beverage workers are expected to work evenings, weekends, and holidays; some work split shifts. Although some food and beverage workers work 40 hours or more per week, the majority are employed part-time.

Education, Training, Qualifications: There are no specific educational requirements for food and beverage service jobs. Although many employers prefer to hire high school graduates for waiter, waitress, bartender, host, and hostess positions, completion of high school is generally not required for fast-food workers, or dining room attendants and bartender helpers. For many persons, these jobs serve as a source of immediate income rather than a career. Most food and beverage workers pick up their skills on the job by observing and working with more experienced workers.

Earnings: Food and beverage service workers derive their earnings from a combination of hourly wages and customer tips. In 2002, median hourly earnings (including tips) of waiters and waitresses were $6.80. The middle 50 percent earned between $6.13 and $8.00. Waiters at some of the very top restaurants are known to make over $50,000 a year. For most waiters and waitresses, higher earnings are primarily the result of receiving more in tips rather than higher wages. Tips generally average 10-20 percent of the guests' checks, so waiters and waitresses working in busy, expensive restaurants earn the most.

In 2002, full-time bartenders had median hourly earnings (including tips) of $7.21. The middle 50 percent earned between $6.33 and $9.02. Like waiters and waitresses, bartenders employed in public bars may receive more than half of their earnings as tips. Service bartenders often are paid higher hourly wages to offset their lower tip earnings.

Median hourly earnings (including tips) other food and beverage workers in 2002 were:

- Dining room and cafeteria attendants $6.99
- Hosts and hostesses $7.36
- Combined food preparation and serving workers $6.97
- Counter attendants in cafeterias, food
  concessions, and coffee shops $7.32
- Dishwashers $7.15
- Nonrestaurant food servers $7.52

Many beginning or inexperienced workers start earning the federal minimum wage of $5.15 an hour. However, a few states set minimum wages higher than the federal minimum.

Key Contacts: For information on food and beverage service jobs contact:

- **International Council on Hotel, Restaurant, and Institutional Education:** 2613 North Parham Road, 2nd Floor, Richmond, VA 23294. Website: www.chrie.org.

- **National Restaurant Association:** 1200 17th Street, NW, Washington, DC 20036-3097. Website: www.restaurant.org.

Hotel Managers and Assistants

⇨ **Annual Earnings:** Varies from $30,000 to $80,000
⇨ **Education/Training:** Training and college work
⇨ **Outlook:** Excellent

Employment Outlook: The growing volume of business and vacation travel, as well as expected increases in foreign tourism, will increase demand for hotels and motels, spurring above-average employment growth in the decade ahead.

Nature of Work: Hotel managers are responsible for the efficient and profitable operation of their establishments. In a small hotel, motel, or inn with a limited staff, a single manager may direct all aspects of operations. However, large hotels may employ hundreds of workers, and the manager may be aided by a number of assistant managers assigned among departments responsible for various aspects of operations. Within guidelines established by the owners of the hotel or executives of the hotel chain, the general manager sets room rates, allocates funds to departments, approves expenditures, and establishes standards for service to guests, decor, housekeeping, food quality, and banquet operations.

Working Conditions: Since hotels are open around the clock, night and weekend work is common. Many hotel managers work considerably more than 40 hours per week. Managers who live in the hotel usually have regular work schedules, but they may be called for work at any time. Dealing with the pressures of coordinating a wide range of functions as well irate or fussy patrons can be stressful.

Education, Training, Qualifications: Postsecondary training in hotel or restaurant management is preferred for most hotel management positions, although a college liberal arts degree may be sufficient when coupled with related hotel experience. In the past, many managers were promoted from the ranks of front desk clerks and other positions within the hotel. Increasingly, postsecondary education is preferred. However, experience working in a hotel – even part time while in school – is an asset to persons seeking to enter hotel management careers. A bachelor's degree in hotel and restaurant administration provides particularly strong preparation for a career in hotel management. Graduates of hotel or restaurant management programs usually start as trainee assistant managers, or at least advance to such positions more quickly. Large hotel and motel chains may offer better opportunities for advancement than small, independently owned establishments, but relocation every several years often is necessary for advancement.

Earnings: Salaries of hotel managers varied greatly according to their responsibilities and the size of the hotel in which they worked. In 2002, annual salaries of assistant hotel managers averaged $42,000. Food and beverage managers averaged $45,000 a year. Front office managers averaged $31,000 a year. Salaries of general managers averaged nearly $55,000, but this represented a range of $40,000 to $85,000, depending on the size of the establishment. Managers also may earn bonuses (up to 25 percent) in some hotels, and they and their families may be furnished with lodging, meals, parking, laundry, and other services.

Key Contacts: For information on careers in hotel management contact:

- **The American Hotel and Lodging Association:** Information Center, 1201 New York Avenue, NW, Suite 600, Washington, DC 20005-3931. Website: www.ahla.com.

- **International Council on Hotel, Restaurant, and Institutional Education:** 2613 North Parham Road, 2nd Floor, Richmond, VA 23294. Website: www.chrie.org.

- **The Educational Institute of the American Hotel and Motel Association:** 800 N. Magnolia Avenue, Suite 1800, Orlando, FL 32803. Website: www.ei-ahla.org.

Hotel, Motel, and Resort Desk Clerks

- ➪ **Annual Earnings:** $20,000
- ➪ **Education/Training:** High school diploma or equivalent
- ➪ **Outlook:** Excellent

Employment Outlook: Employment is expected to grow faster than average for most occupations in the decade ahead as the number of hotels, motels, and other lodging establishments increases in response to increased business travel and tourism. Opportunities for part-time work should be plentiful. Employment of desk clerks is sensitive to cyclical swings in the economy. During recessions, vacation and business travel declines, and hotels and motels need fewer clerks.

Nature of Work: Hotel and motel desk clerks may register guests, assign rooms, and answer questions about available services, checkout times, the local community, and other matters. Because most smaller hotels and motels have minimal staffs, the clerk also may function as a bookkeeper, advance reservation agent, cashier, and/or telephone operator.

Working Conditions: Hotel and motel desk clerks are on their feet most of the time. During holidays and other busy periods, these clerks may find the work hectic due to the large number of guests or travelers who must be served. When service does not flow smoothly – because of mishandled reservations, for example – these clerks act as a buffer between the establishment and its customers.

Education, Training, Qualifications: A high school diploma or its equivalent usually is required. Hotel and motel desk clerk job orientation is usually brief and includes an explanation of the job duties and information about the establishment, such as room location and available services. They start work on the job under the guidance of a supervisor or experienced clerk. They may need additional training in data processing or office machine operations to use computerized reservation, room assignment, and billing systems.

Earnings: In 2002, the average annual earnings of full-time hotel and motel clerks were around $20,000. Earnings depend on the location, size, and type of establishment in which they work. Large luxury hotels and those located in metropolitan and resort areas generally pay clerks more than less expensive ones and those located in less populated areas. In general, hotels pay higher salaries than motels or other types of lodging establishments.

Key Contacts: Information on careers in the lodging industry may be obtained from:

- **The Educational Institute of the American Hotel and Lodging Association:** 800 N. Magnolia Avenue, Suite 1800, Orlando, FL 32803. Website: www.ei-ahla.org.

Restaurant and Food Service Managers

➪ **Annual Earnings:** $35,700
➪ **Education/Training:** Training and college
➪ **Outlook:** Excellent

Employment Outlook: Growth in the number of eating and drinking establishments will result in faster than average growth in employment in the decade ahead. Job opportunities will be especially good for those with an associate or bachelor's degree in restaurant and institutional food service management.

Projected employment growth varies by industry. Most new jobs will arise in full-service restaurants and limited-service earning places as the number of these establishments increases along with the population. Manager jobs in special food services, an industry that includes food service contractors, will increase as hotels, schools, health care facilities, and other businesses contract out their food services to firms in this industry. Food service manager jobs still are expected to increase in hotels, schools, and health care facilities, but growth will be slowed as contracting out becomes more common.

Nature of Work: Efficient and profitable operation of restaurants and institutional food service facilities requires that managers and assistant managers select and appropriately price interesting menu items, efficiently use food and other supplies, achieve consistent quality in food preparation and service, recruit and train adequate numbers of workers and supervise their work, and attend to the administrative aspects of the business. In larger establishments, much of the administrative work is delegated to a bookkeeper, but in others the manager must keep accurate records of the hours and wages of employees, prepare the payroll, and do paperwork to comply with licensing laws and reporting requirements of tax, wage and hour, unemployment compensation, and Social Security laws. They must also ensure that accounts with suppliers are paid on a regular basis. Today many managers are able to ease the burden of recordkeeping through the use of computers.

In most full-service restaurants and institutional food service facilities, the management team consists of a general manager, one or more assistant managers, and an executive chef. The executive chef is responsible for all food preparation activities, including running kitchen operations, planning menus, and maintaining quality standards for food service. One of the most important tasks of food service managers is assisting executive chefs as they select successful menu items. Many restaurants rarely change their menus while others make frequent alterations. Managers or executive chefs estimate food needs, place orders with distributors, and schedule the delivery of fresh food and supplies. Managers interview, hire, train, and, when necessary, fire employees. They also tally the cash and charge receipts received and balance them against the record of sales. They are responsible for depositing the day's receipts at the bank or securing them in a safe place. Finally, managers are responsible for locking up the establishment, checking that ovens, grills, and lights are off, and switching on alarm systems.

Working Conditions: Since evenings and weekends are popular dining periods, night and weekend work is common. Many restaurant and food service mangers work 50 hours or more per week. However, some managers of institutional food service facilities work more conventional hours because factory and office cafeterias are often open only on weekdays for breakfast and lunch.

When problems occur it is the responsibility of the manager to resolve them with minimal disruption to customers. The job can be hectic during peak dining hours, and dealing with irritable customers or uncooperative employees can be particularly stressful.

Education, Training, Qualifications: Many restaurant and food service manager positions are filled by promoting experienced food and beverage preparation and service workers. Waiters, waitresses, chefs, and fast-food workers who have demonstrated their potential for handling increased responsibility sometimes advance to assistant manager or management trainee jobs when openings occur. However, most food service management companies and restaurant chains recruit management trainees from among graduates of two- and four-year college programs. They prefer to hire persons with degrees in restaurant and institutional food service management. A bachelor's degree in restaurant and food service management provides especially strong preparation for a career in this occupation.

Earnings: Earnings vary greatly according to the type and size of the establishment. In 2002, the median annual earnings of salaried food service managers were $35,790. The middle 50 percent earned between $27,910 and $47,120. Median annual earnings in the industries employing the largest numbers of food service managers in 2002 were as follows:

- Special food services $40,720
- Traveler accommodation $39,210
- Full-service restaurants $37,280
- Nursing care facilities $33,910

- Limited-service eating places $33,590
- Elementary secondary schools $31,210

In addition to receiving typical benefits, most salaried food service managers are provided free meals and the opportunity for additional training, depending on their length of service.

Key Contacts: For additional information on education, training, and a career as a food service manager, contact:

- **International Council on Hotel, Restaurant, and Institutional Education:** 2613 North Parham Road, 2nd Floor, Richmond, VA 23294. Website: www.chrie.org.

- **National Restaurant Association Educational Foundation:** 175 West Jackson Blvd., Suite 1500, Chicago, IL 60604-2814. Website: www. nraef.org.

Additional information about job opportunities in food service management may be obtained from local employers and from local offices of state employment service agencies.

Tour Operators and Guides

- ➪ **Annual Earnings:** Varies
- ➪ **Education/Training:** On-the-job training
- ➪ **Outlook:** Good

Employment Outlook: The job outlook for tour operators and guides should be good in the coming decade as more and more people travel and use such services. The specialty tour business should continue to expand in the decade ahead as more and more people choose to go beyond the standard destinations and sightseeing that has largely defined tour operations during the past 30 years. At the same time, many travel agencies, faced with a declining general travel market, have developed new niche markets centered on specialty travel. Accordingly, job opportunities will continue to expand for individuals with expertise in specialty travel and for entrepreneurs interested in starting their own specialty travel agency

Nature of Work: One of the most exciting ends of the travel industry are the numerous companies that organize and conduct tours. They produce travel products which they market to travel agencies, corporations, and individuals. Highly specialized, entrepreneurial, and competitive, these companies are responsible for putting together packaged tours as well as providing both outbound and inbound tour services. Jobs involve everything from organizing packages, marketing tours, and selling services to making reservations, coordinating inbound ground services, and actually conducting tours. People who like to travel love these jobs!

During the past 15 years the number of specialty tour operators has increased dramatically. Most are small two- to seven-person operations which specialize in destinations (Europe, the Caribbean, Asia, Africa, Latin America); activities (ballooning, mountain climbing, white water rafting, safaris, bicycling, scuba diving); educational experiences (museums, archeological ruins, culture, university courses); lifestyle choices (environment, habitats, nudism, cooking, shopping, crafts); and markets (women, youth, retirees, teachers, singles, religious groups, people with disabilities, grandparents, gays, ethnic groups, alumni, veterans). Others are large well established firms, such as American Express, Travcoa, Abercrombie & Kent, and Globus, which offer hundreds of different tour options to special destinations. The average firm is run by four full-time and two part-time employees and sells 80 different tours to 2,500 clients a year. In the larger scheme of things, these are small travel operations. For a good overview of this industry, subscribe to the biannual *Specialty Travel Index*, which includes 500+ tour operators that offer more than 1,000 specialty tours:

> **Specialty Travel Index**
> 305 San Anselmo Ave., Suite 309
> San Anselmo, CA 94960
> Website: www.spectrav.com

Tour managers – also known as tour guides or tour escorts – experience the greatest amount of on-the-job travel. The work is very demanding. Tour managers must be well organized, responsible, and great diplomats who handle a host of daily demands. Given the seasonal nature of this business, most tour managers are freelancers who are hired by tour operators for specific itineraries. Many individuals prefer this lifestyle because it enables them to travel as well as have several months off each year to pursue other interests.

Working Conditions: Tour operators and guides work in a variety of settings, depending on the nature of the position and tour business. Some primarily work in well equipped offices while others primarily operate in field locations where they lead tour groups on several types of tours. Adventure guides work in the outdoors and frequently encounter challenging and stressful work situations.

Education, Training, Qualifications: Many individuals in this field have a high school diploma or a few years of college. Many also have four-year degrees. The major qualification for tour operators and guides is experience. Many individuals in this industry receive on-the-job training.

Earnings: The major benefits for tour operators are the ability to travel free or at low cost to exciting destinations, participate in stimulating programs, and work with interesting people. Salaries of tour operators and tour guides are relatively low. However, many talented tour guides do very well on tips from satisfied clients, making $55,000 a year or more – with tips comprising two-thirds of their earnings. Given the highly competitive nature of the industry and the pressure to offer good value to clients, profit margins for tour operators tend to be very narrow.

Most individuals working in this end of the travel business, including presidents and managers of tour firms, earn under $50,000 a year; many earn under $35,000 a year. This is the type of industry many people enter because they primarily enjoy the non-monetary benefits of the business.

Key Contacts: For a good online directory to specialty travel firms and activities, be sure to explore Google's directory to nearly 25,000 such firms:

http://directory.google.com/Top/Recreation/Travel/Specialty_Travel/

If you are interested in pursuing jobs with tour operators, contact these organizations:

- **American Sightseeing International:** 2727 Steeles Ave. W., #301, Toronto, Ontario M3J 3G9. Website: www.americansightseeing.org.

- **American Society of Travel Agents:** 1101 King Street, Suite 200, Alexandria, VA 22314. Website: www.astanet.com.

- **National Tour Association:** 546 East Main Street, Lexington, KY 40508. Website: www.ntaonline.com.

- **Travel Industry Association of America:** 1100 New York Avenue, NW, Suite 450, Washington, DC 20005. Website: www.tia.org.

- **U.S. Tour Operators Association:** 275 Madison Avenue, Suite 2014, New York, NY 10016. Website: www.ustoa.com.

11

Business, Sales, and Related Jobs

IF YOU ARE SELF-MOTIVATED and goal-oriented, enjoy meeting strangers, and are good at persuading others to buy a product or service, a job or career in one of many sales fields may be right for you. While a four-year degree is often a plus for individuals who deal with highly technical and scientific products and services, such as pharmaceuticals, computers, weapons systems, and financial services, many sales fields, such as automotive, real estate, and insurance, are open to anyone who has demonstrated skills to learn a product, network for clients, and present and close deals. Regardless of their educational backgrounds, talented salespeople working in commission-based fields with high-ticket items can realize substantial annual earnings.

You don't need a four-year degree to be a good and productive salesperson. Effective selling skills often center on attitude, personality, communication, prospecting, perseverance, organization, and follow-through. Good salespeople can often transfer their skills from one occupational field to another because of the generic nature of their skills. An individual who starts out selling automobiles may later move into insurance and real estate.

Advertising Sales Agents

- ➪ **Annual Earnings:** $44,960
- ➪ **Education/Training:** Moderate-term on-the-job training
- ➪ **Outlook:** Good

Employment Outlook: In 2002, there were 157,000 persons working as advertising sales agents soliciting advertisements for inclusion in publications such as newspapers and magazines, television/radio advertising time, and custom-made signs. Employment for advertising sales agents in the decade ahead is expected to grow as fast as average, assuming the economy will grow at a relatively steady state.

Nature of Work: Calls on prospects, advises clients of various types of programming for electronic media, layouts and design for publications, signs and displays. Sells advertising space, time, or signage; presents contract for client to sign, and may be involved in actual production of advertising.

Working Conditions: Working conditions vary. Although some work is office based, a great deal of time is spent meeting with clients and potential clients – usually at their offices.

Education, Training, Qualifications: Good sales and marketing skills for showing, promoting, and selling products and services. This includes marketing strategy, product demonstration, sales techniques, and sales control systems. Many advertising sales agents have completed some college, such as a two-year associate degree.

Earnings: Median annual earnings of advertising sales agents were $44,960 in 2002. Many sales agents work on a combination of a base salary plus commissions on sales volume or receive only a commission on their sales revenue.

Key Contacts: For information on careers in advertising, contact:

- **Advertising Educational Foundation:** 220 East 42nd Street, Suite 3300, New York, NY 10017. Website: www.aef.com/start.asp.

- **American Association of Advertising Agencies:** 405 Lexington Avenue, 18th Floor, New York, NY 10174. Website: www.aaaa.org.

- **Association of National Advertisers**: 708 Third Avenue, New York, NY 10017. Website: www.ana.net.

- **American Advertising Federation**: 1101 Vermont Avenue, NW, Suite 500, Washington, DC 20005. Website: www.aaf.org.

Claims Examiners:
Property and Casualty Insurance

⇨ **Annual Earnings:** $33,120
⇨ **Education/Training:** Long-term on-the-job training
⇨ **Outlook:** Good – about average

Employment Outlook: Employment of claims adjusters is expected to grow about as fast as the average for all occupations during the coming decade. While new technology is reducing the amount of time it takes for adjusters to complete a claim, as long as more insurance policies are being sold to accommodate a growing population, there will be a need for adjusters. Further, as the elderly population increases, there will be a greater need for health care, resulting in more claims.

Nature of Work: Examiners work primarily for property and casualty insurance companies for whom they review a wide variety of settled claims for property damage, liability, or bodily injury. The review is to determine that payments and settlements have been made in accordance with company practices and procedures. They report over-payments or under-payments, and other irregularities and confer with legal counsel on claims that require litigation.

Working Conditions: Work settings and conditions vary. Most claims examiners employed by life and health insurance companies work a five-day, 40-hour week in a typical office environment. Beginning examiners work on small claims under the supervision of an experienced worker.

Education, Training, Qualifications: Although many claims examiners do not have a four-year degree, most companies prefer to hire persons with at least a two-year degree. No specific major is recommended. Because they often work closely with claimants, witnesses, and other insurance professionals, examiners must be able to communicate effectively. Knowledge of computer applications is important. Some companies require applicants to pass a series of written aptitude tests designed to measure communication, analytical, and general mathematical skills. Continuing education (CE) in claims is important because changing federal and state laws and court decisions frequently affect how claims are handled or who is covered by insurance policies. Licensing requirements vary by state.

Earnings: Median annual earnings of claims adjusters were $43,020 in 2002. The middle 50 percent earned between $33,120 and $56,170.

Key Contacts: Career and licensing information is available through:

- **Insurance Institute of America:** 720 Providence Road, P.O. Box 3016, Malvern, PA 19355-0716. Website: www.aicpcu.org.

- **The American College:** 270 South Bryn Mawr Avenue, Bryn Mawr, PA 19010-2196. Website: www.amercoll.edu.

- **International Claim Association:** 1255 23rd Street, NW, Suite 200, Washington, DC 20037. Website: www.claim.org.

Insurance Adjusters and Investigators

⇨ **Annual Earnings:** $43,020
⇨ **Education/Training:** Long-term on-the-job training
⇨ **Outlook:** Good – about average

Employment Outlook: Employment of claims adjusters and investigators is expected to grow about as fast as the average for all occupations in the decade ahead. Many insurance carriers are downsizing their claims staff in an effort to contain costs. Larger companies are relying more on customer service representatives in call centers to handle the recording of the necessary details of the claim, allowing adjusters to spend more of their time investigating claims. New technology also is reducing the amount of time it takes for an adjuster to complete a claim, thereby increasing the number of claims that one adjuster can handle. Despite recent gains in productivity resulting from technological advances, these jobs are not easily automated. Adjusters still are needed to contact policyholders, inspect damaged property, and consult with experts. However, as long as more insurance policies are being sold to accommodate a growing population, there will be a need for adjusters and investigators.

Nature of Work: Adjusters and investigators work primarily for insurance companies to investigate and assess damage to property. Interviews/corresponds with claimants and witnesses, consult police and hospital records, and inspect property damage. Analyzes information and reports findings and recommendations. Adjusters investigate claims, negotiate settlements, and authorize payments; investigators deal with claims when there is a question of liability and where fraud or criminal activity is suspected.

Working Conditions: Working conditions vary greatly. Many claims adjusters work outside the office, inspecting damaged buildings or automobiles. Adjusters are able to arrange their schedules to accommodate evening/weekend appointments with clients. This results in adjusters working irregular schedules or more than 40 hours a week – especially when there are a lot of claims. Insurance investigators often work irregular hours because of the need to conduct surveillance and contact people who are not available during normal working hours. Some days may be spent in the office doing database searches and writing reports. Other times they may be out of the office performing surveillance activities or interviewing witnesses. Some work can involve confrontation and be stressful and dangerous.

Education, Training, Qualifications: Training and entry requirements vary widely. While many employers prefer a college degrees, many insurance adjusters and investigators do not have four-year degree. No specific major is recommended, but business courses, for example, might be helpful to an adjuster specializing in claims involving financial loss due to strikes, equipment breakdowns, or damage to merchandise. Communication skills are important, as is knowledge of computer applications. A valid driver's license and a good driving record are required for workers for whom travel is an important aspect of their job. Some companies require applicants to pass written aptitude tests designed to measure communication, analytical, and general mathematical skills. Licensing requirements vary by state. Continuing education (CE) in claims is important because new federal and state laws and court decisions affect how claims are handled or who is covered by insurance policies. Many vocational colleges offer two-year programs in auto-body repair covering how to estimate and repair vehicles.

Earnings: Median annual earnings of claims adjusters and investigators were $43,020 in 2002. The middle 50 percent earned between $33,120 and $56,170. Many claims adjusters, especially those who work for insurance companies, receive additional bonuses and benefits as part of their job.

Key Contacts: Career and licensing information is available through:

- **Insurance Institute of America:** 720 Providence Road, P.O. Box 3016, Malvern, PA 19355-0716. Website: www.aicpcu.org.

- **The American College:** 270 South Bryn Mawr Avenue, Bryn Mawr, PA 19010-2196. Website: www.amercoll.edu.

- **International Claim Association:** 1255 23rd Street, NW, Suite 200, Washington, DC 20037. Website: www.claim.org.

Insurance Sales Agents

- ➪ **Annual Earnings:** $40,750
- ➪ **Education/Training:** High school diploma to college degree
- ➪ **Outlook:** Good

Employment Outlook: Although slower-than-average employment growth is expected among insurance agents in the decade ahead, opportunities for agents will be favorable for persons with the right qualifications and skills. Multilingual agents should be in high demand because they can serve a wider range of customers.

Nature of Work: Insurance sales agents hep individuals, families, and businesses select insurance policies that provide the best protection for their lives, health, and property. Commonly referred to as "producers" in the insurance industry, these salespeople sell one or more types of insurance, such as property and casualty, life, health, disability, and long-term care. An increasing number of insurance sales agents are offering comprehensive financial planning services to their clients.

Working Conditions: Most insurance sales agents are based in small offices, from which they contact clients and provide information on the policies they sell. However, much of their time may be spent outside their offices traveling locally to meet with clients, close sales, or investigate claims. Agents usually determine their own hours of work and often schedule evening and weekend appointments for the convenience of clients. Although most agents work a 40-hour week, some work 60 hours a week or longer.

Education, Training, Qualifications: While most insurance companies and independent agencies prefer to hire college graduates – especially those who have majored in business or economics, high school graduates are occasionally hired if they have proven sales ability or have been successful in other types of work. In fact, many entrants to insurance sales agent jobs transfer from other occupations. Insurance sales agents must obtain a license in the states where they plan to do business. In most states, licenses are issued only to applicants who complete specified prelicensing courses and who pass state examinations covering insurance fundamentals and state insurance laws.

Earnings: The median annual earnings of wage and salary insurance sales agents were $40,750 in 2002. The middle 50 percent earned between $28,860 and $64,450. Many independent agents are paid by commission only, whereas sales workers who are employees of an agency or an insurance carrier may be paid in one of three ways: salary only, salary plus commission, or salary plus bonus.

Key Contacts: Occupational information about insurance agents is available from the home office of many life and casualty insurance companies. For information about insurance sales careers and training, contact:

- **Independent Insurance Agents of America:** 127 S. Peyton Street, Alexandria, VA 22314. Website: www.iiaa.org.

- **National Association of Health Underwriters:** 2000 N. 14th Street, Suite 450, Arlington, VA 22201. Website: www.nahu.org.

- **Insurance Information Institute:** 110 William Street, New York, NY 10038. Website: www.iii.org.

Real Estate Brokers and Sales Agents

⇨ **Annual Earnings:** $30,930 to $50,330
⇨ **Education/Training:** Experience and training
⇨ **Outlook:** Good

Employment Outlook: Although real estate has been one of the booming sectors of the U.S. economy in the first few years of the 21st century, employment of real estate brokers and sales agents is expected to grow more slowly than the average for all occupations in the coming decade. Increasing use of information technology will continue to raise the productivity of agents and brokers, limiting the potential for job growth to a certain extent. Real estate agents and brokers will continue to experience moderate employment growth due to the increasing housing needs of a growing population, as well as the perception that real estate is a good investment.

Nature of Work: Real estate agents usually are independent sales workers who provide their services to a licensed real estate broker on a contract basis. In return, the broker pays the agent a portion of the commission earned form the agent's sale of the property. Brokers are independent businesspeople who sell real estate owned by others; they also may rent or manage properties for a fee. In addition to selling, agents and brokers spend a significant amount of time obtaining listings - agreements by owners to place properties for sale with the firm. Most real estate brokers and sales agents sell residential property. A small number, usually employed in large or specialized firms, sell commercial, industrial, agricultural, or other types of real estate.

Working Conditions: Advances in telecommunications and the ability to retrieve data about properties over the Internet allow many real estate brokers and sales agents to work out of their homes instead of real estate offices. Even with this convenience, much of the time of these workers is pent away form their desks – showing properties to customers, analyzing properties for sales, meeting with prospective clients, or researching the state of the market. Agents and brokers often work more than a standard 40-hour week. They usually work evenings and weekends and are always on call to suit the needs of clients. Business is usually shower during the winter season. Although the hours are long and frequently irregular, most agents and brokers have the freedom to determine their own schedule.

Education, Training, Qualifications: Reals estate brokers and sales agents much be licensed. Prospect agents must be high school graduates, at least 18 years old, and pass a written test. Most states require candidates for the general sales license to complete between 30 and 90 hours of classroom instruction. Those seeking a broker's license need between 60 and 90 hours of formal training and a specific amount of experience selling real estate, usually one to three years.

Earnings: Median annual earnings of salaried real estate agents, including commissions, were $30,930 in 2002. The middle 50 percent earned between $21,010 and $52,860 a year. Median annual earnings of salaried real estate brokers, including commission, were $50,330 in 2002. The middle 50 percent earned between $29,240 and $90,170 a year.

Key Contacts: Information about opportunities in real estate is available on the website of the following professional association:

- **National Association of Realtors:** Website: www.realtor.org.

Retail Salespersons

▷ **Annual Earnings:** Varies greatly, from minimum wage on up
▷ **Education/Training:** High school diploma or equivalent
▷ **Outlook:** Good

Employment Outlook: Employment of retail salespersons are expected to be good because of the need to replace the large number of workers who transfer to other occupations or leave the labor force each year. Employment is expected to grow about as fast as the average for all occupation in the decade ahead, reflecting rising retail sales stemming form a growing population. Opportunities for part-time work should be abundant, and demand will be strong for temporary workers during peak selling periods, such as the end-of-year holiday season. The availability of part-time and temporary work attracts many people seeking to supplement their income.

Nature of Work: These are not great paying jobs – indeed, many are minimum wage positions – but they are often significant stepping stones to other types of sales jobs and careers. Whether selling shoes, computer equipment, or automobiles, retail salespersons assist customers in finding what they are looking for and try to interest them in buying the merchandise. They describe a product's features, demonstrate its use, or show various models and colors. For some sales jobs, particularly those involving expensive and complex items, retail salespersons need special knowledge or skills.

Working Conditions: Most salespersons in retail trade work in clean, comfortable, well-lighted stores. However, they often stand for long periods and may need supervisory approval to leave the sales floor. The Monday-through-Friday, 9-to-5 workweek is the exception rather than the rule in retail sales. Most salespersons work evenings and weekends, particularly during sales and other peak retail periods. Retail sales persons held about 2.1 million wage and salary jobs in 2002.

Education, Training, Qualifications: There usually are no formal education requirements for this type of work, although a high school diploma or equivalent is preferred. Employers look for people who enjoy working with others and who have the tact and patience to deal with difficult customers. In most small stores, an experienced employee or the proprietor instructs newly hired sales personnel in making out sales checks and operating cash registers. In large stores, training programs are more formal and are usually conducted over several days.

Earnings: The starting wage for many retail sales operations in the federal minimum wage, which was $5.15 an hour in 2002. Median hourly earnings of retail salesperson, including commission, were $8.51 in 2002. The middle 50 percent earned between $7.08 and $11.30 an hour. Median hourly earnings in the industries employing the largest numbers of retail salespersons in 2002 were as follows:

- Automobile dealers $18.25
- Building material and supplies dealers $10.41
- Department stores $8.12
- Other general merchandise stores $7.84
- Clothing stores $7.77

Compensation systems vary by type of establishment and merchandise sold. Salespersons receive hourly wages, commissions, or a combination of wages and commissions.

Key Contacts: Information on careers in retail sales may be obtained from the personnel offices of local stores or form state merchants' associations. General information about retailing is available from:

- **National Retail Federation:** 325 7th Street, NW, Suite 1100, Washington, DC 20004.

Information about retail sales employment opportunities is available from:

- **Retail, Wholesale, and Department Store Union:** 30 East 29th Street, 4th Floor, New York, NY 10016. Website: www.rwdsu.org.

Information about training for a career in automobile sales is available form:

- **National Automobile Dealers Association:** Public Relations Department, 8400 Westpark Drive, McLean, VA 22102-3591. Website: www.nada.org.

Sales Representatives, Wholesale and Manufacturing

⇨ **Annual Earnings:** $55,740
⇨ **Education/Training:** Some college helpful
⇨ **Outlook:** Excellent

Employment Outlook: Employment is expected to grow about as fast as average due to continued growth in the variety and number of goods sold and from openings resulting from the need to replace workers who transfer to other occupations or leave the labor force. Job prospects for wholesale sales representatives will be better than those for manufacturing sales representatives because manufacturers are expected to continue contracting out sales duties to independent agents rather than using in-house or direct selling personnel.

Nature of Work: Regardless of the type of product they sell, sales representatives' primary duties are to interest wholesale and retail buyers and purchasing agents in their merchandise, and to address any of the client's questions or concerns. Sales representatives also advise clients on methods to reduce costs, use their products, and increase sales. Sales representatives spend much of their time traveling to and visiting with prospective buyers and current clients. Obtaining new accounts is an important part of the job. Sales representatives follow leads from other clients, track advertisements in trade journals, and participate in trade shows and conferences. Sales representatives have several duties beyond selling products. They also analyze sales statistics; prepare reports; and handle administrative duties, such as filing their expense report, scheduling appointments, and making travel plans.

Manufacturers' and wholesale sales representatives held about 1.9 million jobs in 2002. About half of all salaried representatives worked in wholesale trade. Others were employed in manufacturing and mining.

Working Conditions: Some sales representatives have large territories and travel considerably. A sales region may cover several states, so they may be away from home for several days or weeks at a time. Others work near their "home base" and travel mostly by automobile. Due to the nature of their work and the amount of travel, sales representatives may work more than 40 hours per week. Sales representatives often are on their feet for long periods and may carry heavy sample products, which necessitates some physical stamina. Dealing with different types of people can be stimulating but demanding. Sales representatives often face competition from representatives of other companies. Companies usually set goals or quotas that representatives are expected to meet. Because their earnings depend on commissions, manufacturers' agents are also under pressure to maintain and expand their clientele.

Education, Training, Qualifications: The background needed for sales jobs varies by product line and market. Many employers hire individuals with previous sales experience who do not have a college degree, but often prefer those with some college education. For some consumer products, factors such as sales ability, personality, and familiarity with brands are more important than educational background. On the other hand, firms selling complex, technical products may require a technical degree in addition to some sales experience. Many sales representatives attend seminars in sales techniques or take courses in marketing, economics, communication, or even a foreign language to provide the extra edge needed to make sales. Many companies have formal training programs for beginning sales representatives lasting up to two years. In some programs, trainees rotate among jobs in plants and offices to learn all phases of production, installation, and distribution of the product. New workers may get training by accompanying experienced workers on their sales calls.

Those who want to become sales representatives should be goal oriented and persuasive, and work well both independently and as part of a team. A pleasant personality and appearance, the ability to communicate well with people, and problem-solving skills are highly valued. Furthermore, completing a sale can take several months and thus requires patience and perseverance.

Earnings: Compensation methods vary significantly by the type of firm and product sold. Most employers use a combination of salary and commission or salary plus bonus. Commissions usually are based on the amount of sales, whereas bonuses may depend on individual performance, on the performance of all sales workers in the group or district, or on the company's performance.

Key Contacts: Information on careers for manufacturers' representatives and agents is available from:

- **Manufacturers' Agents National Association:** P.O. Box 3467, Laguna Hills, CA 92654-3467. Website: www.manaonline.org.

- **Manufacturers' Representatives Educational Research Foundation:** P.O. Box 247, Geneva, IL 60134. Website: www.mrerf.org.

Travel Agents

⤷ **Annual Earnings:** $26,630
⤷ **Education/Training:** High school diploma and training
⤷ **Outlook:** Fair to excellent

Employment Outlook: Employment of travel agents is expected to decline in the decade ahead. Most openings will occur as experienced agents transfer to other occupations or leave the labor force. Because of the projected decline and the fact that a number of people are attracted by the travel benefits associated with this occupation, keep competition for jobs is expected. An increasing reliance on the Internet to book travel, as well as industry consolidation, will continue to reduce the need for travel agents. Moderating the employment decline, however, are projections for increased spending on tourism and travel over the next decade. With rising household incomes, smaller families, and an increasing number of older people who are more likely to travel, more people are expected to travel on vacation – and to do so more frequently – than in the past. Business travel also should bounce back from recession and terrorism related lows as business activity expands.

While some forecasters have predicted the steady decline of travel agents due to the impact of the Internet, others see the resurgence of travel agents because of the restructuring of the traditional travel agent role. Indeed, more and more travel agencies have embraced the Internet by integrating it into their operations. But most important of all, more and more travel agents have become specialists who market cruises and specialty tours to their clients. While many travelers use the Internet to book airlines and hotel rooms and research designations, many of these same travelers are expected to use travel agents for arranging cruises and special tour packages. The future looks very bright for entrepreneurial travel agents who use the Internet to promote their services as well as offer unique travel programs to their clients.

Nature of Work: Depending on the needs of the client, travel agents give advice on destinations, make arrangements for transportation, hotel accommodations, car rentals, tours, and recreation, or plan the right vacation package or business/pleasure trip combination. They may advise on weather conditions, restaurants, tourist attractions and recreation. For international travel, agents also provide information on customs regulations, required papers and currency exchange rates. Travel agents may visit hotels, resorts and restaurants to rate, firsthand, their comfort and quality.

Travel agents consult a variety of published and computer-based sources for information on departure and arrival times, fares, and hotel ratings and accommodations. Travel agents also promote their services, using telemarketing, direct mail, and the Internet. They make presentations to social and special-interest groups, arrange advertising displays, and suggest company-sponsored trips to business managers. Depending on the size of the travel agency, an agent may specialize by type of travel, such as leisure or business, or a regional or country destination, such as Europe, Africa, North America, India, Australia, or Brazil. Many are increasingly focusing on adventure travel as well as the rapidly growing lifestyle travel market that includes gay and lesbian travel, accessible travel, and luxury travel.

Working Conditions: Travel agents spend most of their time behind a desk conferring with clients, completing paperwork, contacting airlines and hotels for travel arrangements, and promoting group tours. They may work under a great deal of pressure during vacation seasons. Many agents, especially those who are self-employed, frequently work long hours. With advanced computer systems and telecommunication networks, some travel agents are able to work at home.

Travel agents held about 118,000 jobs in 2002 and are found in every part of the country. More than eight out of ten agents worked for travel agencies. Nearly one in ten was self-employed.

Education, Training, Qualifications: Formal or specialized training is becoming increasingly important for travel agents since few agencies are willing to train people on the job. Many vocational schools offer 3- to 12-week full-time training programs, as well as evening and Saturday programs. Travel courses are also offered in public adult education programs and in community and four-year colleges. A few colleges offer a bachelor's and a master's degree in travel and tourism. Although few college courses relate directly to the travel industry, courses in computer science, geography, foreign language and history are most useful. The American Society of Travel Agents (ASTA) and the Institute of Certified Travel Agents offer a travel correspondence course. Some people start as reservation clerks or receptionists in travel agencies. All employers require computer skills of workers whose jobs involved the operation of airline and centralized reservation systems. Experienced travel agents can take advanced self-study or group-study courses from the Travel Institute that lead to the Certified Travel Counselor (CTC) designation.

Earnings: Experience, sales ability, and the size and location of the agency determine the salary of a travel agent. Median annual earnings of travel agents were $26,630 in 2002. The middle 50 percent earned between $20,800 and $33,580. Earnings of travel agents who own their agencies depend mainly on commissions from airlines and other carriers, cruise lines, tour operators, and lodging establishments. However, commissions for booking airline tickets have dramatically declined during the past few years as airlines decided to eliminate the traditional agency commission structure. While travel agents still book airline tickets for clients, they now charge $15 to $25 booking fees for such services. As a result, airline ticketing is no longer a major source of income for travel agents. When they travel, agents usually get substantially reduced rates for transportation and accommodations.

Key Contacts: For further information on training opportunities contact:

- **American Society of Travel Agents:** 1101 King Street, Alexandria, VA 22314. Website: www.astanet.com.

For information on training and certification qualifications, contact:

- **The Travel Institute:** 148 Linden Street, Suite 305, Wellesley, MA 02482. Website: www.thetravelinstitute.com.

12

Transportation, Maintenance, Service, and Office Jobs

I N THIS FINAL CHAPTER we outline a few jobs that are of special interest to individuals without a four-year degree. Most of these jobs are on the U.S. Department of Labor's list of the 20 jobs with high median earnings and a significant number of job openings in the decade ahead (see our chart on page 15). They also are some of the safest jobs – relatively recession-proof and impossible to offshore. Entry into one of these jobs should lead to a relatively comfortable and secure employment future.

Similar to many other jobs outlined in previous chapters, the ones summarized here require more and more education and training that take place outside traditional educational institutions. As many jobs become more technical in nature, they require highly motivated individuals who are willing and able to learn new skills and take on increased responsibilities. They must think like entrepreneurs – their boss is their client who seeks quality services. If their client becomes unhappy with their work, their job should disappear. Just make sure you understand that long-term job security is all about being an effective entrepreneur!

251

Automotive Service Technicians and Mechanics

▷ **Annual Earnings:** $30,600
▷ **Education/Training:** High school and training
▷ **Outlook:** Good

Employment Outlook: Automotive service technicians and mechanics held about 818,000 jobs in 2002. Employment of automotive service technicians and mechanics is expected to increase about as fast as average in the decade ahead. Population growth will boost demand for motor vehicles, which will require regular maintenance and service. Growth of the labor force and in the number of families in which both spouses need vehicles to commute to work will contribute to increased vehicle sales and employment in this industry. Growth of personal income will also contribute to families owning multiple vehicles. Employment growth will continue to be concentrated in automobile dealerships and independent automotive repair shops. Many new jobs also will be created in small retail operations that offer after-warranty repairs, such as oil changes, brake repair, air-conditioner service, and other minor repairs. Most persons who enter the occupation can expect steady work, because changes in general economic conditions and developments in other industries have little effect on the automotive repair business.

Nature of Work: The ability to diagnose the source of a problem quickly and accurately requires good reasoning ability and a thorough knowledge of automobiles. The work of automotive service technicians and mechanics has evolved from mechanical repair to a high-tech job. Today, integrated electronic systems and complex computers run vehicles and measure their performance while on the road. Technicians must have the ability to work with electronic diagnostic equipment and computer-based technical reference materials.

Automotive service technicians and mechanics use their high-tech skills to inspect, maintain, and repair automobiles and light trucks that have gasoline engines. The increasing sophistication of automotive technology, including new hybrid vehicles, now requires workers who can use computerized shop equipment and work with electronic components while maintaining their skills with traditional hand tools. Service technicians use a variety of tools in their work – power tools such as pneumatic wrenches to remove bolts quickly; machine tools like lathes and grinding machines to rebuild brakes; welding and flame-cutting equipment to remove and repair exhaust systems; and jacks and hoists to lift cars and engines. They also use common hand tools, such as screwdrivers, pliers, and wrenches, to work on small parts and in hard-to-reach places. Automotive service technicians in large shops have increasingly become specialized.

Working Conditions: About half of automotive service technicians work a standard 40-hour week, but almost 30 percent work more than 40 hours a week. Many of those working extended hours are self-employed technicians. To satisfy customer service needs, some service shops offer evening and weekend service. Generally, service technicians work indoors in well-ventilated and -lighted repair shops. However, some shops are drafty and noisy. Although they fix some problems with simple computerized adjustments, technicians frequently work with dirty and greasy parts, and in physically awkward positions. They often lift heavy parts and tools. Minor cuts, burns, and bruises are common, but technicians usually avoid serious accidents when the shop is kept clean and orderly and safety practices are observed.

Education, Training, Qualifications: Automotive technology is rapidly increasing in sophistication, and most training authorities strongly recommend that persons seeking automotive service technician and mechanic jobs complete a formal training program in high school or in a postsecondary vocational school. However, some service technicians still learn the trade solely by assisting and learning from experienced workers.

Many high schools, community colleges, and public and private vocational and technical schools offer automotive service technician training programs. The traditional postsecondary programs usually provide a thorough career preparation that expands upon the student's high school repair experience. Postsecondary automotive technician training programs vary greatly in format, but normally provide intensive career preparation through a combination of classroom instruction and hands-on practice. Some trade and technical school programs provide concentrated training for six months to a year, depending on how many hours the student attends each week. Community college programs normally spread the training over two years; supplement the automotive training with instruction in English, basic mathematics, computers, and other subjects; and award an associate degree or certificate. Some students earn repair certificates and opt to leave the program to begin their career before graduation. Recently, some programs have added to their curricula training on employability skills such as customer service and stress management. Employers find that these skills help technicians handle the additional responsibilities of dealing with the customers and parts vendors.

Most employers regard the successful completion of a vocational training program in automotive service technology as the best preparation for trainee positions. Experience working on motor vehicles in the Armed Forces or as a hobby also is valuable. Because of the complexity of new vehicles, a growing number of employers require the completion of high school and additional post-secondary training.

Earnings: Median hourly earnings of automotive service technicians and mechanics, including those on commission, were $14.71 in 2002. The highest 10 percent earned more than $25.21. Median annual earnings in the industries employing the largest number of service technicians in 2002 were: local government, $18.04; automobile dealers, $17.66; gasoline stations, $13.04; automotive repair and maintenance, $12.77; and automotive parts, accessories, and tire stores, $12.60. Many experienced technicians employed by automobile dealers and independent repair shops receive a commission related to the labor cost charged to the customer. Employers frequently guarantee commissioned mechanics and technicians a minimum weekly salary. Some automotive service technicians are members of labor unions.

Key Contacts: For more details about work opportunities, contact local automobile dealers and repair shops or local offices of the state employment service. The state employment service may also have information about training programs. A list of certified automotive service technician training programs can be obtained from:

- **National Automotive Technicians Education Foundation:** 101 Blue Seal Drive, Suite 101, Leesburg, VA 20175. Website: www. natef.org.

For a directory of accredited private trade and technical schools that offer programs in automotive service technician training, contact:

- **Accrediting Commission of Career Schools and Colleges of Technology:** 2101 Wilson Blvd., Suite 302, Arlington, VA 22201. Website: www.accsct.org.

For a list of public automotive service technician training programs, contact:

- **SkillsUSA-VICA:** P.O. Box 3000, Leesburg, VA 20177-0300. Website: www.skillsusa.org.

Information on automobile manufacturer-sponsored programs in automotive service technology can be obtained from:

- **Automotive Youth Educational Systems (AYES):** 50 W. Big Beaver, Suite 145, Troy, MI 48084. Website: www.ayes.org.

Information on how to become a certified automotive service technician is available from:

- **National Institute for Automotive Service Excellence (ASE):** 101 Blue Seal Drive SE, Suite 101, Leesburg, VA 20175. Website: www. asecert.org.

For general information about a career as an automotive service technician, contact:

- **National Automobile Dealers Association:** 8400 Westpark Drive, McLean, VA 22102. Website: www.nada.org.

- **Automotive Retailing Today:** 8400 Westpark Drive, MS#2, McLean, VA 22102. Website: www.autoretailing.org.

Cargo and Freight Agents

- ⇨ **Annual Earnings:** $31,400
- ⇨ **Education/Training:** High school diploma
- ⇨ **Outlook:** Good

Employment Outlook: Employment of cargo and freight agents is expected to grow about as fast as the average for all occupations in the decade ahead in response to the continuing growth of cargo traffic and next-day shipping services.

Nature of Work: Cargo and freight agents arrange for and track incoming and outgoing cargo and freight shipments in airline, train, or trucking terminals or on shipping docks. They expedite the movement of shipments by determining the route that shipments are to take and by preparing all necessary shipping documents.

Working Conditions: Cargo and freight agents work in a variety of settings. Some work in warehouses, stockrooms, or shipping and receiving rooms while others may spend time in cold storage rooms or outside on loading platforms, where they are exposed to the weather.

Education, Training, Qualifications: A high school diploma is usually sufficient for entry in these positions.

Earnings: The median hourly earnings in 2002 for cargo and freight agents were $15.10 ($31,400 per year).

Key Contacts: Information on job opportunities for cargo and freight agents is available from local employers and local offices of the state employment service.

Customer Service Representatives

> ⇨ **Annual Earnings:** $26,240
> ⇨ **Education/Training:** High school diploma
> ⇨ **Outlook:** Excellent

Employment Outlook: Employment of customer service representatives is expected to grow faster than the average for all occupations in the decade ahead, with more job openings than job seekers. Bilingual job seekers will find numerous opportunities since their language skills are in much demand.

Nature of Work:.Customer service representatives serve as a direct point of contact for customers. They are responsible for ensuring that their company's customers receive an adequate level of service or help with their questions and concerns. They answer questions, provide information, and help resolve problems. In some organizations, customer service representatives spend their entire day on the telephone. Customer service representatives held about 1.9 million jobs in 2002. More than one in four worked in finance and insurance.

Working Conditions: Although customer service representatives can work in a variety of settings, most work in areas that are clean and well lit. Many work in call or customer contact centers. In this type of environment, workers generally have their own workstation or cubicle space and are equipped with a telephone, headset, and computer. Some work evenings, nights, weekends, and holidays, depending on the nature of a company's operations.

Education, Training, Qualifications: A high school diploma or the equivalent is the most common educational requirement for customer service representatives. Most individuals are given some training immediately after being hired. Many of these jobs are entry level.

Earnings: In 2002, median annual earnings for wage and salary customer service representatives were $26,240. The middle 50 percent earned between $20,960 and $33,540. Median annual earnings in the industries employing the largest numbers of these workers in 2002 were:

- Wired telecommunications carriers $38,980
- Insurance carriers $28,560
- Agencies, brokerages, and other
  insurance-related activities $28,270
- Management of companies and enterprises $27,990
- Nondepository credit intermediation $25,600
- Employment services $22,510
- Electronic shopping and mail-order houses $21,530
- Business support services $21,130
- Grocery stores $17,230

Key Contacts: State employment service offices can provide information about employment opportunities for customer service representatives.

Executive Secretaries and Administrative Assistants

- ⇨ **Annual Earnings:** $33,410
- ⇨ **Education/Training:** High school and training
- ⇨ **Outlook:** Good

Employment Outlook: Executive secretaries and administrative assistants held about 4.1 million jobs in 2002, ranking among the largest occupations in the U.S. economy. Overall employment of executive secretaries and administrative assistants is expected to grow more slowly than the average for all occupations in the coming decade. In addition to those resulting from growth, numerous job openings will result from the need to replace workers who transfer to other occupations or leave this very large occupation for other reasons each year. Opportunities should be best for applicants with extensive knowledge of software applications.

Projected employment of secretaries will vary by occupational specialty. Employment growth in health care and social assistance and legal services industries should lead to average growth for medical and legal secretaries. Rapidly growing industries – such as administrative and support services, health care and social assistance, educational services (private), and professional scientific and technical services – will continue to generate most new job opportunities. A decline in employment is expected for all other executive secretaries except legal or medical. They account for almost half of all secretaries and administrative assistants.

Nature of Work: As the reliance on technology continues to expand in offices, the role of the office professional has greatly evolved. Office automation and organizational restructuring have led executive secretaries and administrative assistants to assume a wider range of new responsibilities once reserved for managerial and professional staff. Many secretaries and administrative assistants now provide training and orientation for new staff, conduct research on the Internet, and operate and troubleshoot new office technologies. In the midst of these changes, however, their core responsibilities have remained much the same – performing and coordinating an office's administrative activities, and storing, retrieving, and integrating information for dissemination to staff and clients.

Specific job duties vary with experience and titles. Executive secretaries and administrative assistants perform fewer clerical tasks than do other secretaries. In addition to arranging calls and scheduling meetings, they may handle more complex responsibilities such as conducting research, preparing statistical reports, training employees, and supervising other clerical staff. Some secretaries and administrative assistants, such as legal and medical secretaries, perform highly specialized work requiring knowledge of technical terminology and procedures. For instance, legal secretaries prepare correspondence and legal papers such as summonses, complaints, motions, responses, and subpoenas under the supervision of an attorney or paralegal. They also may review legal journals and assist in other ways with legal research, as by verifying quotes and citations in legal briefs. Medical secretaries transcribe dictation, prepare correspondence, and assist physicians or medical scientists with reports, speeches, articles, and conference proceedings. Most medical secretaries need to be familiar with insurance rules, billing practices, and hospital or laboratory procedures. Other technical secretaries who assist engineers or scientists may prepare correspondence, maintain the technical library, and gather and edit materials for scientific papers.

Working Conditions: Executive secretaries and administrative assistants usually work in schools, hospitals, corporate settings, or legal and medical offices. Their jobs often involve sitting for long periods. If they spend a lot of time typing, particularly at a video display terminal, they may encounter problems of eyestrain, stress, and repetitive motion, such as carpal tunnel syndrome. Office work can lend itself to alternative or flexible working arrangements, such as part-time work or telecommuting – especially if the job requires extensive computer use. The majority of executive secretaries and legal assistants are full-time employees who work a standard 40-hour week.

Education, Training, Qualifications: High school graduates who have basic office skills may qualify for entry-level secretarial positions. However, employers increasingly require extensive knowledge of software applications, such as word processing, spreadsheets, and database management. Secretaries and administrative assistants should be proficient in keyboarding and good at spelling, punctuation, grammar, and oral communication. Because secretaries and administrative assistants must be tactful in their dealings with people, employers also look for good interpersonal skills.

Secretaries and administrative assistants acquire skills in various ways. Training ranges from high school vocational education programs that teach office skills and keyboarding to one- and two-year programs in office administration offered by business schools, vocational-technical institutes, and community colleges. However, many skills tend to be acquired through on-the-job instruction. Specialized training programs are available for students planning to become medical or legal secretaries or administrative technology specialists. Associate degrees, bachelor's degrees, and professional certifications are becoming increasingly important as business becomes more global. As secretaries and administrative assistants gain experience, they can earn several different designations. Prominent designations include the Certified Professional Secretary (CPS) or the Certified Administrative Professional (CAP) designations, which can be earned by meeting certain experience and/or educational requirements and passing an examination. With additional training, many legal secretaries become paralegals.

Earnings: Median annual earnings of executive secretaries and administrative assistants were $33,410 in 2002. The highest 10 percent earned more than $50,420. Median annual earnings in the industries employing the largest numbers of executive secretaries and administrative assistants were: management of companies and enterprises, $36,770; local government, $34,600; colleges, universities, and professional schools, $32,210; state government, $31,220; and employment services, $29,700. Median annual earnings of legal secretaries were $35,020 in 2002. Medical secretaries earned a median annual salary of $25,430 in 2002. Median annual earnings of secretaries, except legal, medical, and executive, were about $25,290 in 2002.

Key Contacts: State employment offices provide information about job openings for secretaries and administrative assistants. For information on the Certified Professional Secretary or Certified Administrative Professional designations, contact:

- **International Association of Administrative Professionals**: 10502 NW Ambassador Dr., P.O. Box 20404, Kansas City, MO 64195-0404. Website: www.iaap-hq.org.

Information on the Accredited Legal Secretary (ALS), Professional Legal Secretary (PLS), and Paralegal certifications is available from:

- **NALS, Inc.:** 314 East 3rd Street, Suite 210, Tulsa, OK 74120. Website: www.nals.org.

Financial Clerks

- ▷ **Annual Earnings:** Varies, from $20,400 to $29.600
- ▷ **Education/Training:** High school and training
- ▷ **Outlook:** Fair to good

Employment Outlook: Overall employment of financial clerks is expected to experience slower-than-average growth in the decade ahead despite the continued growth in business transactions. Office automation will adversely affect the demand for financial clerks. However, some financial clerks will fare better than others, especially bill collectors, who are in much demand.

Nature of Work: Financial clerks keep track of money, recording all amounts coming into or leaving an organizations. They occupy a variety of positions from which they perform various financial recordkeeping duties, from bill collectors and bookkeepers to auditing and payroll clerks. Despite the growing use of automation, interaction with the public and with co-workers remains a basic part of the job for many financial clerks.

Working Conditions: With the exception of gaming cage workers, financial clerks typically are employed in an office environment. Bill collectors who work for third-party collection agencies may spend most of their days on the phone in a call-center environment. A growing number of financial clerks – particularly medial billers – work at home, and many work part time.

Education, Training, Qualifications: Most financial clerks are required to have at least a high school diploma. Some college education, especially in accounting, is increasingly required by employers. For occupations such as bookkeepers, accounting clerks, and procurement clerks, an associate degree in business or accounting often is required.

Earnings: Salaries of financial clerks vary considerably. Median hourly earnings of full-time financial clerks in 2002 were:

- Procurement clerks $14.23
- Payroll and timekeeping clerks $13.94
- Bookkeeping, accounting, and auditing clerks $13.16
- Bill and account collectors $12.88
- Billing and posting clerks and machine operators $12.55
- Gaming cage workers $10.47
- Tellers $9.81

Key Contacts: Information on employment opportunities is available from local offices of the state employment service or through professional associations, such as:

- **Association of Credit and Collection Professionals:** P.O. Box 39106, Minneapolis, MN 55439. Website: www.acainternational.org.

- **American Institute of Professional Bookkeepers:** 6001 Montrose Road, Suite 500, Rockville, MD 20852. Website: www.aipb.org.

Maintenance and Repair Workers

⇨ **Annual Earnings:** $29,400
⇨ **Education/Training:** High school and training
⇨ **Outlook:** Excellent

Employment Outlook: General maintenance and repair workers held 1.3 million jobs in 2002. They were employed in almost every industry. About one in five worked in manufacturing industries, almost evenly distributed through all sectors. About 17 percent worked for different government bodies. Others worked for wholesale and retail firms and for real-estate firms that operate office and apartment buildings. Employment of general maintenance and repair workers is expected to grow about as fast as average for all occupations in the decade ahead. However, job openings should be plentiful. Maintenance and repair is a large occupation with significant turnover, and many job openings should result from the need to replace workers who transfer to other occupations or stop working for other reasons.

Employment is related to the number of buildings – for example, office and apartment buildings, stores, schools, hospitals, hotels, and factories – and the amount of equipment needing repair. However, as machinery becomes more advanced and requires less maintenance, the need for general maintenance and repair workers diminishes.

Nature of Work: Most craft workers specialize in one kind of work, such as plumbing or carpentry. General maintenance and repair workers, however, have skills in many different crafts. They repair and maintain machines, mechanical equipment, and buildings, and work on plumbing, electrical, and air-conditioning and heating systems. They build partitions, make plaster or drywall repairs, and fix or paint roofs, windows, doors, floors, woodwork, and other parts of building structures. They also maintain and repair specialized equipment and machinery found in cafeterias, laundries, hospitals, stores, offices, and factories. Typical duties include troubleshooting and fixing faulty electrical switches, repairing air-conditioning motors, and unclogging drains. New buildings sometimes have computer-controlled systems, requiring workers to acquire basic computer skills.

General maintenance and repair workers inspect and diagnose problems and determine the best way to correct them, frequently checking blueprints, repair manuals, and parts catalogs. They replace or fix work or broken parts, where necessary, or make adjustments to correct malfunctioning equipment and machines. General maintenance and repair workers also perform preventive maintenance and ensure that machines continue to run smoothly, building systems operate efficiently, and the physical condition of buildings does not deteriorate. Employees in small establishments, where they are often the only maintenance worker, make all repairs, except for very large or difficult jobs. In larger establishments, their duties may be limited to the general maintenance of everything in a workshop or a particular area.

Working Conditions: General maintenance and repair workers often carry out several different tasks in a single day, at any number of locations. They may work inside a single building or in several different buildings. They may have to stand for long periods, lift heavy objects, and work in uncomfortably hot or cold environments, in awkward and cramped positions, or on ladders. They are subject to electrical shock, burns, falls, cuts, and bruises. Most general maintenance workers work a 40-hour week. Some work evening, night, or weekend shifts or are on call for emergency repairs. Those employed in small establishments often operate with only limited supervision. Those working in larger establishments frequently are under the direct supervision of an experienced worker.

Education, Training, Qualifications: Many general maintenance and repair workers learn their skills informally on the job. They start as helpers, watching and learning from skilled maintenance workers. Some learn their skills by working as helpers to other repair or construction workers, including carpenters, electricians, or machinery repairers. Necessary skills also can be learned in high school shop classes and postsecondary trade or vocational schools. It generally takes from one to four years of on-the-job training or school, or a combination of both, to become fully qualified – depending on the skill level.

Graduation from high school is preferred for entry into this occupation. High school courses in mechanical drawing, electricity, woodworking, blueprint reading, science, mathematics, and computers are useful. Mechanical aptitude, the ability to use shop mathematics, and manual dexterity are important. Good health is necessary because the job involves a great of walking, standing, reaching, and heavy lifting. Many positions require the ability to work without direct supervision. Many general maintenance and repair workers in large organizations advance to maintenance supervisor or become a craftworker such as an electrician, a heating and air-conditioning mechanic, or a plumber. Within small organizations, promotion opportunities are limited.

Earnings: Median hourly earnings of general maintenance and repair workers were $14.12 in 2002. The highest 10 percent earned more than $22.78. Median hourly earnings in the industries employing the largest numbers of general maintenance and repair workers in 2002 were: local government, $14.83; elementary and secondary schools, $14.01; activities related to real estate, $11.79; lessors of real estate, $11.54; and traveler accommodations, $10.58. Some general maintenance and repair workers are members of unions.

Key Contacts: Information about job opportunities may be obtained from local employers and local offices of the State Employment Service.

Truck Drivers

⇨ **Annual Earnings:** $33,210
⇨ **Education/Training:** Training and license
⇨ **Outlook:** Good

Employment Outlook: Employment is expected to grow about as fast as average for all occupations in the decade ahead. Job opportunities in this large occupation should be plentiful because of the growing demand for truck transportation services and the need to replace drivers who leave the occupation. The increased use of rail, air, and ship transportation requires truck drivers to pick up and deliver shipments. Demand for long-distance drivers will remain strong because these drivers transport perishable and time-sensitive goods more efficiently than do alternative modes of transportation.

Nature of Work: The work of truck drivers varies. Long-distance drivers may make short "turnaround" hauls where they deliver a load to a nearby city, pick up another loaded trailer, and drive back to their home base in one day. Other runs take an entire day or longer, and drivers remain away from home overnight. Local truck drivers may pick up a loaded truck in the morning and spend the rest of the day making deliveries or may make several trips between their dispatch point and customers to make deliveries.

Working Conditions: Truck driving has become less physically demanding because most trucks now have more comfortable seats, better ventilation, and improved cab designs. However, driving for many hours at a stretch, unloading cargo, and making deliveries can be tiring. Driving in bad weather, heavy traffic, or mountains can be nerve-racking. Some self-employed long-distance truck drivers who own as well as operate their trucks spend over 240 days a year away from home. Local truck drivers frequently work 48 hours or more a week. Many who handle food for chain grocery stores, produce markets, or bakeries drive at night or early in the morning. Many load and unload their own trucks, which requires considerable lifting, carrying, and walking.

Education, Training, Qualifications: Qualifications are established by state and federal regulations. All truck drivers must have a driver's license issued by the state in which they live, and most employers strongly prefer a good driving record. All drivers of trucks designed to carry at least 26,000 pounds are required to obtain a special commercial driver's license. Many firms require that drivers be at least 25 years old, be able to lift heavy objects, and have driven trucks for three to five years. Many prefer to hire high school graduates and require annual physical examinations. Since drivers often deal directly with the company's customers, they must get along well with people.

Earnings: As a rule, local truck drivers are paid by the hour and receive extra pay for working overtime – usually after 40 hours. Long-distance drivers are generally paid by the mile and their rate per mile can vary greatly. In 2002, truck drivers had average straight-time hourly earnings of $15.97. The middle 50 percent earned between $12.51 and $20.01 an hour.

Median hourly earnings in the industries employing the largest numbers of heavy truck and tractor-trailer drivers in 2002 were as follows:

- General freight trucking $17.56
- Grocery and related product wholesalers $16.90
- Specialized freight trucking $15.79
- Other specialty trade contractors $14.25
- Cement and concrete product manufacturing $14.14

Median hourly earnings of light or delivery services truck drivers were $11.48 in 2002. The middle 50 percent earned between $8.75 and $15.58 an hour. Median hourly earnings in the industries employing the largest numbers of light or delivery service truck drivers in 2002 were as follows:

- Couriers $17.48
- General freight trucking $14.92
- Grocery and related product wholesalers $12.26
- Building material and supplies dealers $10.83
- Automotive parts, accessories, and tire stores $7.82

Median hourly earnings of driver/sales workers, including commission, were $9.92 in 2002. The middle 50 percent earned between $6.98 and $14.70 an hour. Median hourly earnings in the industries employing the largest numbers of driver/sales workers in 2002 were as follows:

- Specialty food stores $14.98
- Drycleaning and laundry services $14.74
- Grocery and related product wholesalers $12.66
- Limited-service eating places $6.78
- Full-service restaurants $6.47

Most long-distance drivers operate tractor-trailers, and their earnings vary from as little as $24,000 annually to over $50,000. Most self-employed truck drivers are primarily engaged in long-distance hauling, and earnings of $26,000 to $32,000 a year are common after deducting living expenses and the costs associated with operating their trucks.

Key Contacts: Information on career opportunities in truck driving may be obtained from:

- **American Trucking Associations, Inc.:** 2200 Mill Road, Alexandria, VA 22314. Website: www.trucking.org.

- **International Brotherhood of Teamsters:** 25 Louisiana Avenue, NW, Washington, DC 20001. Website: www.teamster.org.

A list of certified tractor-trailer driver training courses may be obtained from:

- **Professional Truck Driver Institute:** 2200 Mill Road, Alexandria, VA 22314. Website: www.ptdi.org.

Index to Jobs

The Authors

FOR MORE THAN TWO DECADES Ron and Caryl Krannich, Ph.Ds, have pursued a passion – assisting hundreds of thousands of individuals, from students, the unemployed, and ex-offenders to military personnel, international job seekers, and CEOs, in making critical job and career transitions. Focusing on key job search skills, career changes, and employment fields, their impressive body of work has helped shape career thinking and behavior both in the United States and abroad. Their sound advice has changed numerous lives, including their own!

Ron and Caryl are two of America's leading career and travel writers who have authored, co-authored, or ghost-written more than 70 books. A former Peace Corps Volunteer and Fulbright Scholar, Ron received his Ph.D. in Political Science from Northern Illinois University. Caryl received her Ph.D. in Speech Communication from Penn State University. Together they operate Development Concepts Incorporated, a training, consulting, and publishing firm in Virginia.

The Krannichs are both former university professors, high school teachers, management trainers, and consultants. As trainers and consultants, they have completed numerous projects on management, career

268

development, local government, population planning, and rural development in the United States and abroad. Their career books focus on key job search skills, military and civilian career transitions, government and international careers, travel jobs, and nonprofit organizations and include such classics as *High Impact Resumes and Letters*, *Interview for Success*, and *Change Your Job, Change Your Life*. Their books represent one of today's most comprehensive collections of career writing. With nearly 3 million copies in print, their publications are widely available in bookstores, libraries, and career centers. No strangers to the Internet world, they have written *America's Top Internet Job Sites* and *The Directory of Websites for International Jobs* and published several Internet recruitment and job search books. They also have developed career-related websites: www.impactpublications.com, www.winningthejob.com, www.contentforcareers.com, and www.veteransworld.com. Many of their career tips have appeared on such major websites as www.monster.com, www.careerbuilder.com, www.employmentguide.com, and www.campus careercenter.com.

Ron and Caryl live a double life with travel being their best kept *"do what you love"* career secret. Authors of over 20 travel-shopping guidebooks on various destinations around the world, they continue to pursue their international and travel interests through their innovative *Treasures and Pleasures of...Best of the Best* travel-shopping series and related websites: www.ishoparoundtheworld.com, www.contentfortravel.com, and www. travel-smarter.com. When not found at their home and business in Virginia, they are probably somewhere in Europe, Asia, Africa, the Middle East, the South Pacific, the Caribbean, or the Americas following their other passion – researching and writing about quality antiques, arts, crafts, jewelry, hotels, and restaurants as well as adhering to the career advice they give to others: *"Pursue a passion that enables you to do what you really love to do."*

As both career and travel experts, the Krannichs' work is frequently featured in major newspapers, magazines, and newsletters as well as on radio, television, and the Internet. Available for interviews, consultation, and presentations, they can be contacted as follows:

Ron and Caryl Krannich
krannich@impactpublications.com

Career Resources

THE FOLLOWING CAREER RESOURCES are available directly from Impact Publications. Full descriptions of each title as well as ten downloadable catalogs, videos, and software can be found on our website: www.impactpublications.com. Complete the following form or list the titles, include shipping (see formula at the end), enclose payment, and send your order to:

IMPACT PUBLICATIONS
9104 Manassas Drive, Suite N
Manassas Park, VA 20111-5211 USA
1-800-361-1055 (orders only)
Tel. 703-361-7300 or Fax 703-335-9486
Email address: info@impactpublications.com
Quick & easy online ordering: www.impactpublications.com

Orders from individuals must be prepaid by check, money order, or major credit card. We accept telephone, fax, and email orders.

Qty.	TITLES	Price	TOTAL

Featured Title

	America's Top 100 Jobs for People Without a Four-Year Degree	$19.95	_____

Companion Titles By Authors

	America's Top Internet Job Sites	$19.95	_____
	America's Top Jobs for People Re-Entering the Workforce	$19.95	_____
	Change Your Job, Change Your Life	$21.95	_____
	Discover the Best Jobs for You	$15.95	_____

270

_____ Dynamite Salary Negotiations $15.95 _____
_____ I Want to Do Something Else, But I'm Not
Sure What It Is $15.95 _____
_____ Interview for Success $15.95 _____
_____ The Job Hunting Guide $14.95 _____
_____ Job Hunting Tips for People With
Not-So-Hot Backgrounds $17.95 _____
_____ Job Interview Tips for People With
Not-So-Hot Backgrounds $14.95 _____
_____ Nail the Job Interview $13.95 _____
_____ No One Will Hire Me! $13.95 _____
_____ Savvy Interviewing: The Nonverbal Advantage $12.95 _____
_____ The Savvy Networker $13.95 _____

Resumes for People Without a Four-Year Degree

_____ Best Resumes for People Without a Four-Year Degree $19.95 _____
_____ Blue Collar Resumes $11.99 _____
_____ Expert Resumes for Computer and Web Jobs $16.95 _____
_____ Expert Resumes for Manufacturing Careers $16.95 _____
_____ Gallery of Best Resumes for People Without
a Four-Year Degree $16.95 _____
_____ Military Resumes and Cover Letters $21.95 _____
_____ Real Resumes for Administrative Support,
Office, and Secretarial Jobs $16.95 _____
_____ Real Resumes for Auto Industry Jobs $16.95 _____
_____ Real Resumes for Aviation and Travel Jobs $16.95 _____
_____ Real Resumes for Computer Jobs $16.95 _____
_____ Real Resumes for Construction Jobs $16.95 _____
_____ Real Resumes for Financial Jobs $16.95 _____
_____ Real Resumes for Firefighting Jobs $16.95 _____
_____ Real Resumes for Jobs in Nonprofit Organizations $16.95 _____
_____ Real Resumes for Legal and Paralegal Jobs $16.95 _____
_____ Real Resumes for Manufacturing $16.95 _____
_____ Real Resumes for Media, Newspapers, Broadcasting,
and Public Affairs Jobs $16.95 _____
_____ Real Resumes for Medical Industry Jobs $16.95 _____
_____ Real Resumes for Nursing Jobs $16.95 _____
_____ Real Resumes for Police, Law Enforcement
and Security Job $16.95 _____
_____ Real Resumes for Restaurant Food Service
and Hotel Jobs $16.95 _____
_____ Real Resumes for Retailing, Modeling, Fashion,
and Beauty Jobs $16.95 _____
_____ Real Resumes for Sales Jobs $16.95 _____
_____ Real Resumes for Social Work and Counseling Jobs $16.95 _____
_____ Real Resumes for Sports Industry Jobs $16.95 _____
_____ Resumes for Advertising Careers $10.95 _____
_____ Resumes for Banking and Financial Careers $10.95 _____
_____ Resumes for Business Management Careers $10.95 _____
_____ Resumes for Communication Careers $10.95 _____

_____	Resumes for Environmental Careers	$10.95	_____
_____	Resumes for Government Careers	$10.95	_____
_____	Resumes for Health and Medical Careers	$10.95	_____
_____	Resumes for Health Care Professionals	$14.95	_____
_____	Resumes for High School Graduates	$10.95	_____
_____	Resumes for High Tech Careers	$10.95	_____
_____	Resumes for Re-Entering the Job Market	$10.95	_____
_____	Resumes for Sales and Marketing Careers	$10.95	_____
_____	Resumes for Social Service Careers	$10.95	_____

Career Exploration and Job Strategies

_____	5 Patterns of Extraordinary Careers	$17.95	_____
_____	25 Jobs That Have It All	$12.95	_____
_____	50 Cutting Edge Jobs	$15.95	_____
_____	95 Mistakes Job Seekers Make	$13.95	_____
_____	100 Great Jobs and How to Get Them	$17.95	_____
_____	101 Ways to Recession-Proof Your Career	$14.95	_____
_____	300 Best Jobs Without a Four-Year Degree	$16.95	_____
_____	Best Jobs for the 21st Century	$19.95	_____
_____	Career Change	$14.95	_____
_____	Career Intelligence	$15.95	_____
_____	Change Your Job, Change Your Life (9th Edition)	$21.95	_____
_____	Cool Careers for Dummies	$19.99	_____
_____	Directory of Executive Recruiters	$49.95	_____
_____	Five Secrets to Finding a Job	$12.95	_____
_____	High-Tech Careers for Low-Tech People	$14.95	_____
_____	How to Get a Job and Keep It	$16.95	_____
_____	How to Succeed Without a Career Path	$13.95	_____
_____	Job Hunting Guide: College to Career	$14.95	_____
_____	Job Search Handbook for People With Disabilities	$17.95	_____
_____	Knock 'Em Dead	$14.95	_____
_____	Me, Myself, and I, Inc.	$17.95	_____
_____	Monster Careers	$18.00	_____
_____	Occupational Outlook Handbook (biannual)	$16.90	_____
_____	O*NET Dictionary of Occupational Titles	$39.95	_____
_____	Quit Your Job and Grow Some Hair	$15.95	_____
_____	Rites of Passage at $100,000 to $1 Million+	$29.95	_____
_____	Secrets of the Hidden Job Market	$15.95	_____
_____	What Color Is Your Parachute? (annual)	$17.95	_____
_____	Working Identify	$26.95	_____

Internet Job Search

_____	100 Top Internet Job Sites	$12.95	_____
_____	America's Top Internet Job Sites	$19.95	_____
_____	CareerXroads	$26.95	_____
_____	Career Exploration On the Internet	$24.95	_____
_____	Cyberspace Job Search Kit	$18.95	_____
_____	Directory of Websites for International Jobs	$19.95	_____
_____	Guide to Internet Job Searching	$14.95	_____

Attitude and Motivation

_____	100 Ways to Motivate Yourself	$18.99	_____
_____	Attitude Is Everything	$14.95	_____
_____	Change Your Attitude	$15.99	_____
_____	Reinventing Yourself	$18.99	_____

Inspiration and Empowerment

_____	101 Secrets of Highly Effective Speakers	$15.95	_____
_____	Do What You Love for the Rest of Your Life	$24.95	_____
_____	Dream It Do It	$16.95	_____
_____	Life Strategies	$13.95	_____
_____	Practical Dreamer's Handbook	$13.95	_____
_____	Self Matters	$14.00	_____
_____	Seven Habits of Highly Effective People	$15.00	_____
_____	Who Moved My Cheese?	$19.95	_____

Testing and Assessment

_____	Career Tests	$12.95	_____
_____	Discover the Best Jobs for You	$15.95	_____
_____	Discover What You're Best At	$14.00	_____
_____	Do What You Are	$18.95	_____
_____	Finding Your Perfect Work	$16.95	_____
_____	I Could Do Anything If Only I Knew What It Was	$14.95	_____
_____	I Want to Do Something Else, But I'm Not Sure What It Is	$15.95	_____
_____	Now, Discover Your Strengths	$27.00	_____
_____	What Should I Do With My Life?	$14.95	_____
_____	What Type Am I?	$14.95	_____
_____	What's Your Type of Career?	$17.95	_____

Resumes and Letters

_____	101 Great Tips for a Dynamite Resume	$13.95	_____
_____	201 Dynamite Job Search Letters	$19.95	_____
_____	Best KeyWords for Resumes, Cover Letters, & Interviews	$17.95	_____
_____	Best Resumes and CVs for International Jobs	$24.95	_____
_____	Best Resumes for $100,000+ Jobs	$24.95	_____
_____	Best Resumes for People Without a Four-Year Degree	$19.95	_____
_____	Best Cover Letters for $100,000+ Jobs	$24.95	_____
_____	Cover Letters for Dummies	$16.99	_____
_____	Cover Letters That Knock 'Em Dead	$12.95	_____
_____	Cyberspace Resume Kit	$18.95	_____
_____	e-Resumes	$14.95	_____
_____	Gallery of Best Cover Letters	$18.95	_____
_____	Gallery of Best Resumes	$18.95	_____
_____	Haldane's Best Cover Letters for Professionals	$15.95	_____
_____	Haldane's Best Resumes for Professionals	$15.95	_____

_____ High Impact Resumes and Letters $19.95 _____
_____ Resume Shortcuts $14.95 _____
_____ Resumes for Dummies $16.99 _____
_____ Resumes in Cyberspace $14.95 _____
_____ The Savvy Resume Writer $12.95 _____

Networking

_____ Dynamite Telesearch $12.95 _____
_____ A Foot in the Door $14.95 _____
_____ How to Work a Room $14.00 _____
_____ Masters of Networking $16.95 _____
_____ Power Networking $14.95 _____
_____ The Savvy Networker $13.95 _____

Dress, Image, and Etiquette

_____ Dressing Smart for Men $16.95 _____
_____ Dressing Smart for the New Millennium $15.95 _____
_____ Dressing Smart for Women $16.95 _____
_____ Power Etiquette $14.95 _____

Interviews

_____ 101 Dynamite Questions to Ask
      At Your Job Interview $13.95 _____
_____ Haldane's Best Answers to Tough
      Interview Questions $15.95 _____
_____ Interview for Success $15.95 _____
_____ Job Interview Tips for People With
      Not-So-Hot Backgrounds $14.95 _____
_____ Job Interviews for Dummies $16.99 _____
_____ KeyWords to Nail Your Job Interview $17.95 _____
_____ Nail the Job Interview! $13.95 _____
_____ The Savvy Interviewer $10.95 _____

Salary Negotiations

_____ Dynamite Salary Negotiations $15.95 _____
_____ Get a Raise in 7 Days $14.95 _____
_____ Haldane's Best Salary Tips for Professionals $15.95 _____

Military in Transition

_____ Jobs and the Military Spouse $17.95 _____
_____ Military Resumes and Cover Letters $21.95 _____

Ex-Offenders in Transition

_____ 9 to 5 Beats Ten to Life $15.00 _____
_____ 99 Days and a Get Up $9.95 _____

_____ Ex-Offender's Job Search Companion $9.95 _____
_____ Man, I Need a Job $7.95 _____
_____ Putting the Bars Behind You (6 books) $64.70 _____

Government and Nonprofit Jobs

_____ Complete Guide to Public Employment $19.95 _____
_____ Federal Applications That Get Results $23.95 _____
_____ Federal Personnel Guide $12.00 _____
_____ FBI Careers $18.95 _____
_____ Find a Federal Job Fast! $15.95 _____
_____ Ten Steps to a Federal Job $39.95 _____

International and Travel Jobs

_____ Back Door Guide to Short-Term Job Adventures $21.95 _____
_____ Careers in International Affairs $24.95 _____
_____ Directory of Websites for International Jobs $19.95 _____
_____ Inside Secrets to Finding a Career in Travel $14.95 _____
_____ International Jobs $19.00 _____
_____ International Job Finder $19.95 _____
_____ Jobs for Travel Lovers $19.95 _____
_____ Teaching English Abroad $15.95 _____
_____ Work Your Way Around the World $17.95 _____

VIDEOS

Video Series

_____ 50 Best Jobs for the 21st Century $545.00 _____
_____ 60- Minute Self-Renewal Video Series $1999.95 _____
_____ Careers for the 21st Century Library $1,695.00 _____
_____ Job Finding for People With Disabilities $199.95 _____
_____ Job Search Skills Video Series $799.00 _____
_____ Job Success Without a College Degree Video Series $560.00 _____
_____ Managing Your Personal Finances Video Series $499.00 _____
_____ One Stop Career Center Video Series $599.00 _____
_____ Portfolio Resumes Series $150.00 _____
_____ Quick Job Search Video Series $545.00 _____
_____ Road to Re Employment Video Series $219.95 _____
_____ Welfare-to-Work Video Series $545.00 _____
_____ Work Maturity Skills Video Series $799.00 _____
_____ Workforce Development Video Kit $1,399.00 _____

Interview, Networking, and Salary Videos

_____ Build a Network for Work and Life $129.00 _____
_____ Common Mistakes People Make in Interviews $79.95 _____
_____ Exceptional Interviewing Tips $79.00 _____
_____ Extraordinary Answers to Interview Questions $79.95 _____
_____ Extreme Interview $69.00 _____

_____ Make a First Good Impression $129.00 _____
_____ Mastering the Interview $98.00 _____
_____ Seizing the Job Interview $79.00 _____
_____ Quick Interview Video $149.00 _____
_____ Quick Salary Negotiations Video $149.00 _____
_____ Why Should I Hire You? $129.00 _____

Dress and Image Videos

_____ Head to Toe $98.00 _____
_____ Looking Sharp: Dressing for Success $99.00 _____
_____ Looking Sharp: Grooming for Success $99.00 _____
_____ Tips and Techniques to Improve Your Total Image $98.00 _____

Resumes, Applications, and Cover Letter Videos

_____ The Complete Job Application $129.00 _____
_____ Effective Resumes $79.95 _____
_____ Ideal Resume $79.95 _____
_____ Quick Cover Letter Video $149.00 _____
_____ Quick Resume Video $149.00 _____
_____ Resumes, Cover Letters, and Portfolios $98.00 _____
_____ Ten Commandments of Resumes $79.95 _____
_____ Your Resume $99.00 _____

Assessment and Goal Setting Videos

_____ Career Path Interest Inventory $149.00 _____
_____ Career S.E.L.F. Assessment $89.00 _____
_____ Skills Identification $129.00 _____
_____ You DO Have Experience $149.00 _____

Attitude, Motivation, and Empowerment Videos

_____ Down But Not Out $129.00 _____
_____ Gumby Attitude $69.00 _____
_____ Know Yourself $109.95 _____
_____ Looking for Work With Attitude Plus $129.00 _____
_____ Positive Feet $99.00 _____
_____ Take This Job and Love It $79.95 _____

Career Exploration Videos

_____ Career Exploration and Planning $98.00 _____
_____ Great Jobs Without a College Degree $98.00 _____

Job Search Strategies Videos

_____ Tough Times Job Strategies $89.95 _____
_____ Very Quick Job Search Video $149.00 _____

SOFTWARE

____	Interview Skills for the Future	$199.00	_____
____	Job Browser Pro 1.3	$359.00	_____
____	Job Search Skills for the 21st Century	$199.00	_____
____	Multimedia Career Center	$385.00	_____
____	Multimedia Career Pathway	$199.00	_____
____	Multimedia Occupational GOE Assessment Prog.	$449.00	_____
____	Multimedia Personal Development Series	$450.00	_____
____	OOH Career Center	$349.95	_____
____	School-to-Work Career Center	$385.95	_____

SUBTOTAL   _____

Virginia residents add 5% sales tax   _____

POSTAGE/HANDLING ($5 for first
product and 8% of SUBTOTAL) $5.00

8% of SUBTOTAL ----------------------------------- ----- _____

TOTAL ENCLOSED ---------------------- _____

SHIP TO:

NAME _____

ADDRESS: _____

_____

_____

PAYMENT METHOD:

❑   I enclose check/money order for $ _____ made payable to
     IMPACT PUBLICATIONS.

❑   Please charge $ _____ to my credit card:

     ❑ Visa   ❑ MasterCard   ❑ American Express   ❑ Discover

     Card # _____ Expiration date: ____/____

     Signature _____

Keep in Touch . . .
On the Web!

www.impactpublications.com
www.ishoparoundtheworld.com
www.travel-smarter.com
www.contentfortravel.com
www.winningthejob.com
www.veteransworld.com
www.contentforcareers.com